NO LIMITS

Books by Dr. John C. Maxwell Can Teach You How to Be a REAL Success

Relationships

25 Ways to Win with People

Becoming a Person of Influence

Encouragement Changes Everything

Ethics 101

Everyone Communicates, Few Connect

The Power of Partnership

Relationships 101

Winning with People

Equipping

The 15 Invaluable Laws of Growth

The 17 Essential Qualities of a Team Player

The 17 Indisputable Laws of Teamwork

Developing the Leaders Around You

How Successful People Grow

Equipping 101

JumpStart Your Growth

JumpStart Your Priorities

Learning from the Giants

Make Today Count

Mentoring 101

My Dream Map

Partners in Prayer

Put Your Dream to the Test

Running with the Giants

Talent Is Never Enough

Today Matters

Wisdom from Women in the Bible

Your Road Map for Success

Attitude

Attitude 101

The Difference Maker

Failing Forward

Intentional Living

The Greatest Story Ever Told (journal)

How Successful People Think

JumpStart Your Thinking

Sometimes You Win—Sometimes You Learn

Sometimes You Win—Sometimes You Learn for Teens

Success 101

Thinking for a Change

The Winning Attitude

Leadership

The 10th Anniversary Edition of The 21 Irrefutable Laws of Leadership

The 21 Indispensable Qualities of a Leader

The 21 Most Powerful Minutes in a Leader's Day

The 360 Degree Leader

Developing the Leader Within You

JumpStart Your Leadership

Good Leaders Ask Great Questions

The 5 Levels of Leadership

Go For Gold

How Successful People Lead

Leadership 101

Leadership Gold

Leadership Promises for Every Day

What Successful People Know About Leadership

NO LIMITS

BLOW THE CAP OFF YOUR CAPACITY

JOHN C. MAXWELL

CENTER
STREET

NEW YORK   BOSTON   NASHVILLE

The author is represented by Yates & Yates, LLP, Literary Agency, Orange, California.

Center Street
Hachette Book Group
1290 Avenue of the Americas, New York, NY 10104
centerstreet.com
twitter.com/centerstreet

First Edition: March 2017

Center Street is a division of Hachette Book Group, Inc. The Center Street name and logo are trademarks of Hachette Book Group, Inc.

The publisher is not responsible for websites (or their content) that are not owned by the publisher.

The Hachette Speakers Bureau provides a wide range of authors for speaking events. To find out more, go to www.HachetteSpeakersBureau.com or call (866) 376-6591.

Library of Congress Cataloging-in-Publication Data has been applied for.

ISBNs: 978-1-4555-4828-6 (hardcover); 978-1-4789-2300-8 (signed edition); 978-1-4555-4824-8 (ebook); 978-1-4555-4829-3 (international edition); 978-1-4555-4175-1 (large print)

Printed in the United States of America

LSC-C

10 9 8 7 6 5 4 3 2 1

To Kevin Myers

I've observed you for more than thirty years, and I've been part of your life for twenty. Your hunger to grow, lead, and make a difference has set the tone for your life, and I've watched you blow the cap off your capacity time after time.

As much as anyone I know, you have proven that people can overcome the limits put on them by themselves and others. And your greatest impact is still ahead of you.

Contents

PART III—CHOICES:
DO THE THINGS THAT MAXIMIZE YOUR CAPACITY

Acknowledgments

Thank you to:

Charlie Wetzel, my writer

Stephanie Wetzel, my initial manuscript editor

Linda Eggers, my executive assistant

NO LIMITS

PART I

Awareness: Remove the Caps from Your Capacity

Know thyself.

—SOCRATES

I think self-knowledge is the rarest trait in a human being.

—ELIZABETH EDWARDS

I'm passionate about this book because I'm passionate about you! For fifty years I've worked to improve my life and to help improve the lives of others. Nothing brings me greater joy than helping others grow and get better. I've written this book specifically to lift you up and to help you increase your capacity.

How did I come to write this book? The idea came to me while I was enjoying one of my favorite things: great conversation over a meal with friends. While we were talking, one friend began to express the importance of potential and how people could reach it.

It led to a great discussion that lasted two hours. As we got ready to get up from the table, somebody said, "I've never read a book about capacity and how to reach it." Nobody else had either.

That conversation really stimulated me. And it stayed with me for two years. After revisiting the topic of capacity in my mind repeatedly, I began asking questions, listening to others, and learning about it. Eventually that led me to create the Capacity Challenge:

The Capacity Challenge
If you grow in your *awareness*, develop your *abilities*, and make the right *choices*, you can reach your capacity.

In other words,

AWARENESS + ABILITY + CHOICES = CAPACITY

That is the challenge I'm presenting to you in this book. If you're willing to accept it and follow the process I outline, your life will change!

The Capacity Challenge begins with *awareness*. Becoming aware was the first big step I took in blowing the cap off my capacity. And it happened early in my career. The model for pastors in those days was that of a shepherd who cared for the sheep. It was about maintaining and caring for the flock. It included doing a lot of counseling. So that was the model I thought I was supposed to follow.

But then I read a book titled *America's Fastest Growing Churches* by Elmer Towns. It was about reaching more people and leading a church with excellence. I couldn't put that book down. The stories were so inspiring.

After reading it, I wanted to visit every church in the book and meet their pastors. But how could I do this? These pastors didn't know me. And why would they take time to meet with me?

Then I got an idea. I would contact them and offer to pay them $100 for thirty minutes of their time. That was in 1971, when I made only $4,200 in an entire year. But I was desperate to find out what made these pastors become so successful. I was overjoyed when two of the ten pastors said yes to my request.

As soon as I knew I would get to meet with these leaders, I began writing down the questions I would ask them. I came up with a lot. Five pages full! Anticipation filled me as I sat down with these leaders and asked them questions as fast as I could. Obviously I didn't get through all the questions I had written down, but I did have a breakthrough in my personal and professional lives. My greatest discovery was that these pastors spent no time on counseling people. Instead, they spent all of their time *equipping* people.

At first, I didn't get it. I had to get them to explain it to me. Counseling helps people work through their weaknesses. Equipping helps people work on their strengths. The lights were starting to turn on!

> Counseling helps people work through their weaknesses. Equipping helps people work on their strengths.

Then they explained that people will more readily reach their potential when they work on their strengths rather than working on their weaknesses. That was when it hit me. These leaders were not shepherds, content to just look after a flock. They were ranchers. They had vision. They had the spirit of the pioneers who created something on the frontier. They were building and developing people, inviting people to become part of something greater than themselves. And together they were growing their churches, reaching more people, and making a difference.

That was the first day I realized how essential *awareness* is to reaching capacity. The only way I could help the people I was leading to do much better in their lives was to help them focus on their strengths more than their weaknesses. And—drumroll, please—the only way *I* could reach my capacity as a person and a leader was to practice and develop *my* strengths. It changed the way I did everything, and I soon discovered that I was a much better equipper than I was a counselor.

Before my awareness discovery, I saw myself as a shepherd taking care of the needs of my people. After that, I started to see myself and my role differently. I became a rancher leading and growing the people of my congregation.

For years I shared this story at conferences. Often during a Q & A someone will ask, "What was the most important thing you received from those two leaders you interviewed?" My answer is "awareness." I have often wondered, *How long would I have counseled people instead of equipping them if I had not met those two leaders?* I don't know the answer. But I do know this: we all need the help of someone else to become aware of how to become better at reaching our capacity.

I want to be someone who helps you become more self-aware. That's what this first section of the book is about. You've probably heard the saying "If I always do what I've always done, I'll always get what I've always gotten." I want to help you do something new— and get somewhere new. As we embark on this journey, I want to give you two thoughts:

1. Change doesn't always have to be drastic to be effective. Counseling people and equipping people have similarities. They both require caring for another person and spending time with them giving guidance and advice. All I had to do was change my focus from their weaknesses to their strengths. As you read through this book, and especially while reading this first part on awareness, be on the lookout for where you need to change your focus to become more aware of your potential.

2. Change is necessary for you to reach your capacity. As you read through the other two parts, you will find a greater emphasis on change. In part two on ability, you will be asked to work on some things that may not be natural strengths. You will find that difficult. Growth in skill areas, if they are not natural, is often slow and small. That's okay. Every little bit of positive change helps. It increases your capacity. However, when you get to part three, which is about choices, you will find it to be easier. In matters of choice, your changes can be achieved much more quickly. All of these changes, whether difficult or easy, are needed if you desire to increase your capacity and reach your potential.

Get ready to dive in. It's going to be an exciting journey. Developing awareness is going to allow you to recognize the changes that will help you blow the cap off your capacity. My hope is that by the time you're finished with the book, your capacity will be much greater than you ever imagined and you will be well on your way to living a no-limits life. Let's take this journey together.

1

Do You Know What's Limiting You?

All of my life I've been intrigued by capacity, though when I was young I would not have known to call it that. My favorite childhood story was *The Little Engine That Could*. When I was little, my mother read it to me often. When I could read on my own, I pulled it from the shelf again and again. I'd act it out for my family. I loved that the little engine believed in herself and was successful in getting over the hill because of that belief. Her capacity increased because she pushed herself to her limits.

I remember an illustration my dad used when speaking. An old-timer saw a boy fishing and went over to see how he was doing. The boy had already caught two small fish, but as the old man was walking over, the boy landed a huge bass.

"That's a beauty," the old man said as the boy unhooked the fish. But then the boy tossed the fish back into the water.

"What are you doing?" the old man cried out. "That was a whopper."

"Yeah," replied the boy, "but my frying pan is only nine inches wide." That one always made me laugh, and it made me aware of how a person's thinking can limit him.

I also vividly remember one of my teachers telling the story of three young boys whose route to school went alongside a high wall. Every day as the boys walked to school, they wondered what was on the other side of the wall. Finally one day, their curiosity grew so strong that one of the boys said, "Let's find out," and threw his cap over the wall. "Now I *have* to climb the wall to see what's on the other side," he declared.

The other two boys gawked at him in disbelief. But then as they watched him begin to climb, they threw their caps over the wall and joined him. They didn't want to be left behind. They wanted to experience the discovery themselves, not just hear about it secondhand.

I still remember thinking, *I would have thrown my cap over the wall, too.* I wanted to go new places, make new discoveries, push myself to do more than I thought I could do. I still do. Sometimes achieving those desires requires bold commitment. Many times since the day I first heard that story, I've mentally thrown my cap over the wall to commit myself to growth discoveries.

Today, I'm asking you to throw your cap over the wall.

Awareness Assets

My goal in writing this book is to help you be the little engine who could. I want to inspire you to blow off the caps that hold you down and limit your potential. I want to help you get outside of the nine-inch–frying pan mentality and expand your thinking and your ability. I want you to throw your cap over the wall. I want you to accept the capacity challenge and change your life. Are you willing to do that? If so, the process begins with awareness, with learning...

1. Your Capacity Isn't Set

If you're like most people, I bet you'd like more out of life than you are currently experiencing. Maybe you're not succeeding in all the ways you desire to in life. Perhaps you're less than fully satisfied with your progress. Are you getting done all that you want to do? Or do you want to see more, do more, be more? If you're like me, you want to achieve more. Even at nearly age seventy, I'm not satisfied. I want to keep growing and making a difference.

What's getting in your way? What's limiting you? Do you know? If you don't know what's limiting you, how will you remove it?

> If you don't know what's limiting you, how will you remove it?

You've probably heard the saying "If you want something done, give it to a busy person." It may sound counterintuitive, yet it's true. People who can get a lot done seem to be able to take on even more and remain productive. Why is that? Do some people simply have high capacity while others don't?

Have you given much thought to your capacity? Most people think theirs is set. You hear one person identified as "high capacity" and another as "low capacity," and you just accept it. What's your capacity? Have you defined it as high, low, or average? Do you think it's set? Maybe you haven't put a label on it, but you've probably settled into a level of achievement that you believe is what's possible for you.

That's a problem.

Too many people hear the word *capacity* and assume it's a limitation. They assume their capacity is set—especially if they're beyond a certain age. People give up on the idea that their capacity or their potential can grow. All they do is try to manage whatever they think they've got.

A lot of people think this way. Activist Roberto Verzola observed that economists are notorious for this kind of mind-set of limitations. Worse yet, they try to convince others to adopt it too. Verzola says,

The most fundamental assumption in economics is scarcity. This, in effect, assumes away abundance. Thus, most mainstream economists are not prepared to deal with abundance. They have few concepts that explain it. They have no equations that describe it. Confronted with it, they fall back on inadequate theories based on scarcity.[1]

In other words, they define the world in terms of its limitations. They also define people in terms of their limitations. That's too confining. Instead, we need to define our world and ourselves in terms of our possibilities.

While I believe 100 percent that people can grow, change their capacity, and increase their potential, I also acknowledge that all of us have caps on our capacity. Some caps are fixed. But most are not. We can't allow these unfixed caps to keep our lives from expanding. We can't let caps define our potential. We need to see beyond the caps and see our true capacity before we can blow off our caps and expand our capacity.

Charles Schulz, creator of the *Peanuts* comic strip, wrote, "Life is like a ten-speed bike. Most of us have gears we never use." What he's saying is that most of us have capacity that is untapped. We have capacity that we're not even aware of. But we can change that.

> **"Life is like a ten-speed bike. Most of us have gears we never use."**
> —*Charles Schulz*

2. You Can Become Aware of the Possibilities That Can Make You Better

This is where I want us to spend the majority of our time in this chapter. I want us to focus on awareness. All lasting growth requires awareness. Unfortunately, if you lack awareness, then you don't know that you are unaware. It's a blind spot. You don't know what you don't know, and you can't see that you are unable to see. That's a catch-22.

My journey to self-awareness was simple, but it did take time. It began with others helping me become aware. It took someone who *did* know to help me see it. This experience created a hunger in me to further develop my self-awareness. I began to wonder what else I was missing. What else didn't I know? I started wondering if there was something else out there for me.

This chapter communicates the process I developed. I don't assume that I've arrived. I still keep asking myself, *What am I missing?* But hopefully what I share with you will help you to become more self-aware, because that is essential to your reaching your capacity.

Self-awareness is a powerful skill. It enables you to see yourself clearly. It informs your decisions and helps you to weigh opportunities. It allows you to test your limits. It empowers you to understand other people. It makes partnership with others stronger. It allows you to maximize your strengths and minimize your weaknesses. It opens the door to greater capacity.

Here are some things to think about as you work to become more aware of your possibilities:

Attention: Looking for What I Need to Know

In my book *Winning with People*, I wrote about the Lens Principle, which says who we are determines how we see others. In that book, my focus was on how our perspective colors our view of the world, other people, and life. But it's also true that who we are determines how we see ourselves. We naturally tend to see things as we have always seen them. If we want to increase our capacity, we must see differently. We need to be willing to look at ourselves

> Who we are determines how we see others.

and our world in new ways. We need to pay attention and look for what we need to know.

Awareness: Discovering What I Need to Know

What stops people from reaching their capacity often isn't lack of desire. It's usually lack of awareness. Unfortunately, people don't become self-aware accidentally. On top of that, there are factors that also work against us and prevent us from developing great self-awareness, such as

- Excuses
- Success fantasies that are ungrounded in reality
- Talking without listening to others
- Unresolved negative emotions
- Habitual self-distraction
- Absence of personal reflection
- Unwillingness to pay the price to gain experience

Most people who have developed self-awareness have had to battle one or more of these factors to get where they are. They've had to work very hard. It takes a desire to make self-awareness discoveries. It takes discipline to look at yourself and reflect on your experiences. It takes maturity to ask others to help you with your blind spots.

Becoming self-aware also requires help from other people who can see you more clearly than you can see yourself. In the past when

I've worked with someone who wasn't self-aware, I've followed a process to help them discover what they need to know about themselves:

- **Relationship:** I start by building the relationship and letting them know they are important to me and that I want to help them. This gives them security and me credibility.

- **Exposure:** Once I've done the relational groundwork, I try to help them understand how important self-awareness is. They need to realize that if they do not make self-awareness a priority, they're going to be stuck in life and will be unable to move forward. But if they can learn to see themselves more clearly and begin to determine their capacity, they have a path forward toward increased capacity and reaching their potential. Then I can begin revealing their strengths and weaknesses to them with as much encouragement as I can offer.

- **Experiences:** Most people need to be shown a way forward to develop greater self-awareness. I've found that the best way is to put them in situations where they must acknowledge their weaknesses, utilize their strengths, learn from other leaders, and reflect on their experiences. If I'm their leader, I take responsibility for facilitating that.

- **Questions:** Asking people questions helps you to assess whether they are catching on and becoming more self-aware.

- **Review:** The most critical step in the awareness development process is a review of the results. Developing self-awareness is a process that takes time and repetition. Each time a mentor or leader sits down with a person and gives honest feedback, if that feedback is well received, the person takes another important step in the process.

- **Repeat:** The last thing I need to point out is that this isn't a onetime process. To help people who are unaware, I must teach them repeatedly.

Using this pattern, you can help an unaware person begin to develop self-awareness. But what if *you* are that unaware person? You need to find someone—a trusted friend, colleague, mentor, or family member—who can help you, direct you, and provide you with repeated honest feedback.

Discernment: Focusing on What I Need to Do

As you discover things about yourself, you must try to discern where to focus your attention. You can't do everything. As the old proverb says, "Chase two rabbits and you will catch neither."

As you make discoveries, where should you focus your attention? On your strengths. Maybe you already know this. When we focus on our weaknesses, the best we can do is work our way up to average. Nobody pays for that. No successful person hires someone to do a merely adequate job. Successful people desire excellence. Excellence comes from focusing on your strengths. Whatever you do well, try to do better. That's your greatest pathway forward to increased capacity. Later we'll look at the core capacities that all people possess and how you can develop yours.

Intention: Acting on What I Need to Do

In my book *Intentional Living*, I discuss the major difference between good intentions and intentional living. The former may make a person feel good, but it doesn't actually do anything positive for him or others. The key is action. We get results only when we take what we've learned and put it into action.

When I was in my twenties I became aware that I would have to become highly intentional about my personal growth if I was going to be able to make a difference in the world. So I sat down and wrote out something that I called "The Mundane Man." Here's how it went:

Sad is that day for any man when he is absolutely satisfied with the life that he is living, thoughts that he is thinking, deeds that he is doing, until there ceases to be forever knocking on the door of his soul, a desire to do something greater for God and his fellow-man.

I wrote that because I never wanted to become a mundane person. I believe none of us wants that, yet I think all of us could be in danger of becoming mundane. There is a natural downward pull that threatens to stop people from accepting the capacity challenge. We have to fight that inertia.

You need to become aware that you are currently living below your potential if you're going to do anything to improve. Even if you've been a highly productive and successful person, you can improve. You can increase your capacity. You have more in you that you have never tapped. And there is a path forward to greater potential if you are willing to take it.

3. You Can Remove the Caps from Your Capacity

The next step forward to increasing your capacity involves removing the caps that are holding you back. Have you ever heard or read about how elephants used to be trained? They could be made to stay in one place with only a small rope restricting them. That's incredible, considering that an adult male Asian elephant is ten feet tall at the shoulder and weighs about four tons. What was the secret?

When an elephant was very young and weighed only several hundred pounds, it was restricted by having a chain clasped to its leg and connected to a tree or deep stake. When the animal tried to move away and learned that it could not break the chain, it limited itself. It believed that whatever restriction was put on it—even a rope it could have easily broken—was more powerful than it was.

People are like those elephants. We often believe that some of the restrictions we may have experienced earlier in life are permanent. Or we've been told we have limitations that we actually don't possess, and these things are keeping us from taking the journey in life that we long for. These are the chains we need to break.

Awareness changes everything. As soon as we become aware that some of our "limitations" are artificial limitations, we can begin to overcome many of them. We can blow off these caps, which opens the way for growth. I'll talk more about this later.

In the book *If It Ain't Broke . . . Break It!* Robert Kriegel and Louis Patler write, "We don't have a clue as to what people's limits are. All the tests, stopwatches, and finish lines in the world can't measure human potential. When someone is pursuing their dream, they'll go far beyond what seem to be their limitations. The potential that exists within us is limitless and largely untapped."[2] That process begins with developing awareness of the caps that are restricting you.

4. You Can Develop the Capacities You Already Possess

Everyone has capacities that are based on their natural talents. Some of them require very specific abilities, such as those found in symphony musicians, professional athletes, and great artists. Others are more general in nature and rely on multiple skill sets. In this book, I identify and examine seven of these capacities:

Energy Capacity—Your Ability to Push On Physically
Emotional Capacity—Your Ability to Manage Your Emotions

Thinking Capacity—Your Ability to Think Effectively
People Capacity—Your Ability to Build Relationships
Creative Capacity—Your Ability to See Options and Find Answers
Production Capacity—Your Ability to Accomplish Results
Leadership Capacity—Your Ability to Lift and Lead Others

I'll teach you how to maximize the level of talent you have so that you can increase your capacity in each of these areas.

5. You Can Make Choices That Maximize Your Possibilities

You also have other capacities that rely more on your choices. While it's true that talent is still a factor, it is less important in these areas. I want to help you identify the choices you can make to increase your capacity:

Responsibility Capacity—Your Choice to Take Charge of Your Life
Character Capacity—Your Choices Based on Good Values
Abundance Capacity—Your Choice to Believe There Is More than Enough
Discipline Capacity—Your Choice to Focus Now and Follow Through
Intentionality Capacity—Your Choice to Deliberately Pursue Significance
Attitude Capacity—Your Choice to Be Positive Regardless of Circumstances
Risk Capacity—Your Choice to Get Out of Your Comfort Zone
Spiritual Capacity—Your Choice to Strengthen Your Faith
Growth Capacity—Your Choice to Focus on How Far You Can Go
Partnership Capacity—Your Choice to Collaborate with Others

> Momentum is not the result of one push. It is the result of many continual pushes over time.

I'll teach you how to increase your capacity in these areas, too. And when you pair the development of your capacities with the maximization of your choices, you start to develop personal momentum toward your potential. Momentum is not the result of one push. It is the result of many continual pushes over time.

How Far Can You Go?

Recently I came across a story told by Jesse Itzler that illustrates the limitations many of us allow to be put on ourselves. Itzler is someone who started his career in the music business as a rapper, became an entrepreneur, cofounded Marquis Jet, and later became one of the owners of the Atlanta Hawks. A very accomplished person, Itzler also enjoys participating in endurance races.

Itzler describes running a grueling endurance race as a member of a relay team and spotting another man running the race as a solo participant. He later found out that the man was a Navy SEAL. Itzler ended up asking the man to spend time with him and his family so they could learn from his experience and wisdom. Itzler also wanted the SEAL to train him. The SEAL agreed to do it—as long as Itzler promised to do *everything* he asked and didn't use his real name.

In his book *Living with a SEAL*, Itzler describes how on the appointed day, SEAL (as he was identified in the book) showed up at Itzler's Manhattan apartment at the exact minute he was expected. He was dressed in nothing but shorts, a T-shirt, and running shoes. It was the dead of winter. SEAL was unfazed.

For thirty-one days, SEAL pushed Jesse physically and mentally. They trained two, three, or four times a day. Sometimes they got up before dawn and ran in Central Park. Other times SEAL would spontaneously ask Jesse to do a grueling hour-long workout in his office in the middle of the workday. They'd run miles through snow and ice in the middle of the night. They'd do hundreds of push-ups and pull-ups. They'd go to a nearby frozen lake, break a hole in the ice, plunge into the freezing

> "If you want to be pushed to your limits, you have to train to your limits."
>
> —SEAL

water, and then sprint back to shelter before hypothermia would set in. "If you want to be pushed to your limits," SEAL explained, "you have to train to your limits."[3]

Over the course of the month they were together, Itzler was able to learn only a few pieces of information about his mentor. Much of SEAL's story remained a mystery. Jesse learned that SEAL would simply choose not to eat many times: "I just like to go to sleep hungry...so I wake up hungry. Life is all about staying out of your comfort zone."[4] Or he would sleep outside in subzero weather in nothing but pants and a light shirt: "If you don't challenge yourself, you don't know yourself."[5] But maybe the greatest lesson Jesse learned came from something SEAL told him about another race he once ran. Itzler writes,

I found out SEAL once entered a race where you could either run for twenty-four hours or forty-eight hours. Shocker: SEAL signed up for the forty-eight-hour one. At around the twenty-three-hour mark, he'd run approximately 130 miles, but he'd also torn his quad [quadriceps muscle]. He asked the race officials if they could just clock him out at twenty-four hours. When he was told they couldn't do that, he said, "ROGER THAT," asked for a roll of tape, and wrapped his quad. He walked (limped) on a torn quad for the last twenty-four hours to finish the race and complete the entire forty-eight hours.

SEAL's assessment was compelling: "When you think you're done, you're only at forty percent of what your body is capable of doing. That's just the limit that we put on ourselves."[6]

As Jesse's time with his Special Forces trainer came to an end, Jesse reflected on what he had learned and how it had changed him:

> The first day SEAL came to move in, he told me I needed to control my mind. I thought it was just a saying or a throwaway comment, but I think there might be more truth to it than I originally thought. Our minds sometimes tell us little lies about ourselves, and we believe them. We think we can't do this or that. It's not true. . . . I take a look at SEAL. . . . He just wants to get better tomorrow. That's what I want now, too.[7]

That was a good goal for Jesse. That's a good goal for me. And it's also a good goal for you. Maybe as you start this journey you should tell yourself that you're at only 40 percent of your capacity. What would happen if you assumed that you had at least 60 percent more capacity than you ever believed? You may not be a Navy SEAL, but there's more in you that you've never tapped. What if it's not 60 percent? What if it's only 40, or 25, or even 10 percent? Wouldn't that still change your life? Believing there's more and working to tap into it could be a first step in reimagining your capacity and embracing a no-limits life.

What's Holding You Back?

Are you ready to take the capacity challenge? I bet you want to increase your capacity, and you desire to achieve more. And you probably love the idea of increasing your potential. But do you still have doubts? Maybe it would help you to take a free capacity assessment developed to help you gauge where you currently stand when it comes to capacity. If so, I encourage you to stop right now and assess yourself at www.CapacityQuiz.com. The last few paragraphs of this chapter can wait. Your capacity can't.

Maintaining the status quo is easier than accepting the capacity challenge. If you wanted to, you could find plenty of reasons *not* to strive for your potential. But that shouldn't stop you.

When I was a kid, I heard stories from my mother's side of the family about Henry Ford. My mother's uncles knew him pretty well. In the mid-1890s, Ford began building his first vehicle made with bicycle parts and a combustion engine. He worked on it in a shop behind the rental house where he and his wife lived. He believed that people's capacity for travel could be increased. Of course, he faced his share of doubters. People thought he couldn't do it. Others advised against it because they believed there weren't enough roads built to accommodate a vehicle that powered itself. But Ford was undaunted.

In 1896, Ford completed his project. He named his vehicle the Quadricycle. However, he'd made one small miscalculation. It was too big to fit through the doorway of his shop. So what did he do? He knocked bricks out of the wall to get it out. He wasn't going to allow the door's lack of capacity to limit *his* capacity.

Ford, of course, went on to found the Ford Motor Company in 1903. His belief in unlimited capacity helped him take car manufacturing from a slow, expensive, meticulous, hand-built process to a fast, efficient, automated process that put the automobile within reach of everyday people. By 1924, the company had produced 10 million cars. Three years later, it had produced more than 15 million.

Trying to build your life without removing your limitations and increasing your capacity is like building a car in a small shed and being unwilling to knock out the wall to get the car out on the road. All locked up, your capacity can't really go anywhere. Remove the limitations, and the world is open to you.

Capacity Awareness Questions

1. In which abilities and choices listed in this chapter would you like to increase your capacity and reach a higher level?

2. How would your life change if you were to increase your capacity in those areas? Describe how that would look and feel.

3. What is your strategy for developing greater self-awareness? Who will you enlist to help you learn, change, and grow?

2

Blow Off the Caps That Limit Your Life

A few years ago I met a wonderful man named Nick Vujicic at one of the John Maxwell Team events where we train and certify coaches and speakers. Paul Martinelli, the president of the John Maxwell Team, had brought Nick in to speak.

Nick is inspiring. He's got a fantastic attitude, a great sense of humor, and a warm and loving spirit. Though he's only in his early thirties, he has already written and published five books, acted in two movies, performed in a music video, appeared on *Oprah*, and spoken to hundreds of millions of people around the world, often filling stadiums.

Not impressed? Would you be if you knew that Nick has no arms or legs?

Nick was born without limbs, and he had a very difficult time growing up. He was bullied. He felt lonely. And he even contemplated suicide when he was eight years old. But he persevered. He drew on his faith, the love of his parents, and his desire to make a difference. He would not allow himself to be defined by his limitations.

He made the most of everything he had. In his book *Life Without Limits*, Nick writes:

> Helen Keller, who lost both her sight and hearing in childhood but became a renowned activist and author, said that there is no such thing as a secure life. "It does not exist in nature.... Life is either a daring adventure or nothing." Risk, then, is not just part of life. It *is* life. The place between your comfort zone and your dream is where life takes place. It's the high-anxiety zone, but it's also where you discover who you are. Karl Wallenda, patriarch of the legendary high-wire-walking family, nailed it when he said: "Being on the tightrope is living; everything else is waiting."[1]

> The place between your comfort zone and your dream is where life takes place.
> —*Nick Vujicic*

Nick believed his purpose was to speak to audiences, to become a motivational speaker, yet he had no experience, no resources, and no invitations. He decided to begin calling schools and offering to speak about bullying, dreaming big, and never giving up. He received fifty-two rejections. But on his fifty-third try, a school finally said yes and offered to pay him $50. He was ecstatic. Then he realized that it would take a two-and-a-half-hour drive just to get to the school. Undaunted, Nick offered the money to his brother Aaron to drive him there. As it turned out, Nick spoke to only ten students for five minutes. Five hours of driving for five minutes of speaking. He felt foolish.

But then the next week the phone started ringing. School after school asked him to come and share his story. And those requests grew. They're still growing. Today, more than a decade later, Nick receives 35,000 speaking requests a year.

Nick advises people to dream big and be a little foolish. He says, "If we went by the world's definition of who I'm supposed to be because I look weird... 'Well, surely, this guy can't have a productive life, surely, he doesn't have a sense of humor. Surely, he can't love life.' We stereotype people in this world. And so... if the world thinks you're not good enough, it's a lie, you know. Get a second opinion."[2]

Recognize Your Value and Increase Your Capacity

I want to be the person to give you that second opinion: You have great value. You have great potential. Not only are you good enough, but you have the ability to get even better and to achieve greater significance in your life. I echo the words of Nick, who says, "If God can use a man without arms and legs to be His hands and feet, then He will certainly use any willing heart."

Catherine B. Ahles, public relations professor and vice president for college relations at Macomb Community College, observes, "We spend most of our twenties discovering all of the hundreds of things we can be. But as we mature into our thirties, we begin to discover all of the things we will never be. The challenge for us as we reach our forties and beyond is to put it all together—to know our capabilities and recognize our limitations—and become the best we can be." I believe her advice is valuable, but I also think that we are not limited by our season of life. You can begin to put some things together before your twenties. And if you're past your fifties, you can still increase your capacity. As I mentioned in the last chapter, that starts with developing self-awareness. More specifically, you need to become aware of the caps of your life, and recognize which caps you can't remove and which ones you can.

Caps You *Can't* Remove

I believe you can live a life with no limits, that you can go further than you believe and can do more than you've ever dreamed. But that doesn't mean that you don't possess limitations. We all do. Some caps cannot be removed. When Nick was a child, he prayed to God that he would grow arms and legs. Obviously, it didn't happen. He had to acknowledge that limitation and learn to live with it. But he didn't let it limit him.

Think about some of the caps in your life that you need to acknowledge and accept:

Birth Caps

You had no control over your birth, nor can you go back in time and change it. You just have to live with some things:

• **Your Place of Birth:** You may love the place you were born, or you may hate it. That doesn't matter. It is what it is.

• **The Year of Your Birth:** I hear people say they were born in the wrong time. They wish they were born in the Middle Ages or in the Old West. They may *feel* out of place, but they're not. Have you heard the saying "You can only be where you are"? Well, you also can only be *when* you are. You were born exactly when you were supposed to be. And for my part, I'm glad to have been born when I was. I'm not sure how I would have survived if I had been born during America's pioneer days.

• **Your Birth Family:** You don't get to choose your parents, birth order, siblings, or upbringing. Good or bad, you have to live with it and make the best of it.

- **Your Birth Characteristics:** You cannot change your genetic makeup, your race, your bone structure, or your height. You want to dunk basketballs, but you're only five feet seven? Pick another sport or develop the skills of slam-dunk champion Spud Webb. You need to learn to adapt.

When you're feeling discouraged, think of Nick. He's only three feet three inches tall. He has only a small foot with two toes, but he swims, goes fishing, paints, and types forty-five words a minute.

Life Caps

We don't have any control over how our life begins, but there are also many things that happen to us in our lives that we cannot control. We suffer accidents or illnesses. We lose people we love. We discover that we don't have the talent or ability to fulfill a dream. I call these "life caps."

My father was marked by the death of his mother when he was six years old. I think he was constantly aware of what he had missed. It showed in the way he treated our mom and how he wanted us to treat her. For example, growing up, we were expected to do the dishes. If we grumbled, Dad would say, "I would have loved to do dishes for my mom."

Losing your mother hurts. I lost mine when I was in my sixties, and I still miss her. We all have life-cap stories, some big, some small. We have our nicks and dents.

Mark Twain reportedly said that the two greatest days in people's lives are the day they are born, and the day they find out why. Part of the process

> Part of the process of fulfilling your purpose is becoming aware of the things you can't change that limit you, so that you can direct your attention toward the things you can maximize to increase your capacity.

of fulfilling your purpose is becoming aware of the things you can't change that limit you, so that you can direct your attention toward the things you can maximize to increase your capacity.

Caps You *Can* Remove

Nick Vujicic says, "The biggest temptation I believe is to feel comfortable, to feel like you've worked through all of that here on Earth, and are satisfied with this life."[3] I think that's the problem for too many people who aren't as successful, productive, and fulfilled as they would like to be. They mistakenly think they've worked through their issues, they've reached their capacity, and there are no new mountains they can climb. They settle. And they get comfortable.

Let me tell you: You're not even close to your capacity. You haven't come close to reaching your limits. Neither have I. I'm about to turn seventy years old, I've dedicated the last forty-five years to personal growth, and I'm still amazed by the gains I am able to make. I'm not done getting better, and if you're willing to believe you have more capacity and work at making the most of it, you'll be amazed by the gains you can make, too. To get started, you need to remove the two main types of caps people have on their lives.

Caps That Others Put on You

The first type of limitation comes from the caps that others put on us. The best story I know of this is recorded in the Old Testament. God told Samuel the prophet that he was to go to Jesse in Bethlehem and there he would anoint one of Jesse's sons as the next king of Israel.

When Samuel arrived, he asked Jesse to show him his boys, because one of them was going to be king. I bet Jesse and his wife got excited.

I bet they speculated about which one it would be. Maybe they thought the way Samuel did: When Jesse lined up his boys, Samuel saw the oldest, Eliab, and thought, *He looks like a king.* But Eliab wasn't the one God wanted. Neither was the next son. Or the next. Samuel looked at seven sons, and said, "None of them is the one. Is this everybody?"

In fact, there was one more: David. Jesse hadn't considered him king material and hadn't even called him in from the fields. Jesse had thought of every one of his boys *except* David. Jesse didn't believe David had it in him. They had to send somebody out to the pasture where the sheep were to get David and wait for him to get there. The boy showed up, dirty, smelly, and out of breath, looking less like a king than anyone else in the family. Who knows, David might have even known Samuel was coming that day, and had been told he wasn't welcome at the party. Yet lo and behold, he was the one God wanted. Nobody there saw David's potential, but God did.

David had much greater capacity than others gave him credit for. Time after time people discounted him. Not only did his brothers think he wasn't king material, but they also thought he wasn't soldier material. On the day that Jesse sent David to the battle lines with food and supplies for his brothers, Goliath was taunting the army of Israel, asking them to send a champion to fight him.

David was angered by Goliath's disrespect for God, but the moment David started asking questions about what would be done for the person who took on Goliath, David's oldest brother mocked and criticized him. It was like they were saying, "Why are you here? This is for men." David was undeterred.

When King Saul heard that finally someone was willing to fight the giant, he sent for David. But when Saul took one look at David, he thought David wasn't champion material. He tried to talk David out of facing Goliath. When David was still intent on doing battle, Saul tried to put his armor on the boy. But six-foot-five armor for a

240-pound man doesn't work on a five-foot-six, 140-pound shepherd. David took off the armor and faced Goliath in his regular clothes with nothing but a sling and stones. Goliath took one look at him and thought he wasn't hero material, either. But that didn't matter to David. He took the giant down.

David did go on to become king. He brought together all the Hebrew tribes into the nation of Israel, conquered his enemies, and established his throne, which he passed to his son Solomon, said to be the wisest king who ever lived.

That's a dramatic story of a great leader who had many caps put on him by other people. But we all have caps put on us—both great and small—by others. I remember one put on me in fifth grade. I wanted to play the trumpet, so my parents rented a trumpet for me. I was excited as I went to a music teacher for my first lesson. But she took one look at my mouth and said, "Your mouth isn't shaped right to play the trumpet. You'll never be able to do it." She told my parents that I should play the clarinet. But I didn't *want* to play clarinet. I wanted to play trumpet. Guess what? My parents traded in the trumpet and got me a clarinet. I've always wondered what would have happened if I had just been given a chance to play the trumpet. I think I would have loved it.

Today, I am unwilling to surrender my potential to someone else. I'm unwilling to allow others to put caps on me and define my potential. I fought too hard to get where I am to let others control where I am going.

> I fought too hard to get where I am to let others control where I am going.

People have put caps on you. You're not even aware of some of them. But you don't have to let their lack of belief define you. Be open to the possibilities that are in you! Later in this chapter, I'll discuss how you can remove these caps.

Caps You Put on Yourself

Perhaps the caps that limit us most are the ones we put on ourselves. Author, speaker, and coach Michele Rosenthal writes about an incident that happened to her in elementary school, which prompted her to put a cap on herself that she continues to deal with today:

> In fourth grade I was placed in an advanced math group with four other students.... Being part of this special group felt good; when it came to math I was calm, confident, and competent.
>
> One day the teacher announced a math quiz: twelve addition problems (simple equations containing four numbers each) to be done in six minutes. "These are very easy," the teacher explained. "If you can't get all twelve correct, then you're just plain stupid." Stupid? Not me. I set out to answer all twelve problems correctly. This was our first timed math test, and I quickly discovered I didn't know how to judge how long to spend solving each problem. I tried to add as fast as possible but never felt I could trust the resulting sums. I began to panic. My brain froze. The numbers swam. I couldn't think. By the time the teacher told us to put down our pencils, I had placed numbers in each answer box but I knew they were all wrong.
>
> The next day our tests were handed back. At the top of mine, written in enormous red numbers: "−12"—complete and total failure. I walked home carrying my test, crying all the way.
>
> When I look back I can tell you that was the day I formed and accepted the belief, "I can't do math." It's a belief that continues today.[4]

We all put caps on ourselves. But we don't have to leave them in place. We don't have to be limited by them forever. I think back to some of the caps I put on myself:

Looking for Approval from Others

When I started in my career, I was a people pleaser. I wanted to be everybody's favorite, and I didn't like rocking the boat. That's not a good mind-set if you want to be a leader. I had to learn how to remove that cap. I had to be willing to do what was right or what was best for the organization, even if it made people unhappy or I received criticism. It took me a few years to work through this, but I did it. Every time I wanted to do the easy thing that would please others, I tried to think of the vision I had for the organization and the people, and it helped me to make better decisions.

Living in a Limiting Environment

Too many people simply accept whatever environment they're born into. They think it's normal, and they start to believe they don't have any other choices in life. When that happens, they've created a self-imposed cap on their life. For example, I grew up in a small town in a very conservative environment, where leadership wasn't valued or taught. The expectation was that if you worked hard and were a good person, that was enough. It wasn't for me. I wanted to make a difference, and when I began to learn about leadership, I realized that I needed to move from that environment if I wanted to keep growing, learning, and expanding my potential. When I was in my early thirties, that was what I did. I removed that cap from my life. If I hadn't, it would have remained on me, and that would have been my own choice once I'd realized I could do something about it.

Having Few Expansive Models of Success

I started planning to go into ministry starting when I was seventeen years old. When I was a senior in college and was getting ready to become a pastor, I sat down and wrote out my career goals in a church administration class. I remember writing that I wanted to someday lead a church of five hundred people. To me that was a bold goal, because a church of five hundred was the largest I'd ever seen or heard of.

About two years out of college, I came across a book by Elmer Towns called *The Ten Largest Sunday Schools and What Makes Them Grow.* I remember reading the first chapter and thinking, *Wait. This church has more than five hundred people in it.* I didn't even know such a thing existed! The same was true of the next church, and the next. All ten churches in the book had more than five hundred people in them. The book started to change the way I thought. I suddenly had models of growth beyond anything I'd ever seen.

That was the day this cap on my life became loosened. It prompted me to try to interview the leaders of the ten churches Elmer Towns wrote about. That further loosened the cap, until finally, it came off and my thinking and expectations changed for myself, my leadership, and my desired impact.

The Process of Loosening My Leadership Cap

I think that's the way many self-imposed caps come off for most of us. They don't just blow off in one moment. We expose ourselves to new ideas and successful people, and the caps begin to loosen. And when they get loose enough, then they come off.

If I look back and think about what I went through in removing the cap put on me by myself and others in the area of leadership, I see a process that went something like this:

• **Exposure**—In 1973, I read Elmer Towns's *Ten Largest Sunday Schools*. All those churches had more than five hundred people, and I realized that leading a church larger than that was possible.

• **Example**—In 1974, I interviewed two of the ten pastors in that book. They said I could be successful. I started to believe it myself.

• **Expression**—In 1975 I read *See You at the Top* by Zig Ziglar. This made me realize I needed to become intentional to reach my potential.

• **Experiment**—I started a program at my church where I bought buses that would pick people up and bring them to services. I named each bus after a book of the Bible starting with Genesis. I made it to Ruth—that's eight buses—before the gas shortage made it impractical. But I had broken through barriers.

• **Experience**—In 1975, my church had the fastest-growing Sunday School in the state of Ohio.

• **Eureka**—In 1976, I heard Lee Roberson, the founder of Tennessee Temple University, say, "Everything rises or falls on leadership," at a conference in Chattanooga. I understood the importance of leadership in my life for the first time.

What caps do you need to loosen so that you can blow them off and start increasing your capacity? Are you limited by complacency?

> "You cannot be comfortable in your own skin without your own approval."
> —*Mark Twain*

C. S. Lewis identified complacency as a human being's mortal enemy. Do you not like who you are? Mark Twain said that you cannot be comfortable in your own skin without your own approval.

What are the caps that are holding you back? You need to identify them and get to work loosening them. (If you need help with this, you can go to www.CapacityQuiz.com to take the free assessment.)

I Believe in You

I want to be a cap remover in your life because I want you to become more successful and significant. I'd like to help you reach your potential and achieve your dream. Being a lid lifter and cap remover is the greatest role I could hope for in another person's life. Helping you begins with my belief in you. You may be thinking, *You don't even know me!* That's true. I wish I could, but I don't know the specifics of your story. But I know that as a human being, you have huge potential. Every person does, so that means *you* do. You specifically. You may be facing challenges.

> "Don't put your life on hold so that you can dwell on the unfairness of past hurts."
> —*Nick Vujicic*

Others may not believe in you. You may have a tough past. That doesn't take away what you can do or who you can become. As my friend Nick Vujicic says, "Don't put your life on hold so that you can dwell on the unfairness of past hurts."

Some people and organizations try to hype you up. I'm not trying to convince you to act confident without knowing what to do. You can't be *hyped* to success. But you can be *helped* to success. You can be taught how to grow. You can be shown how to win inside victories that lead to outside victories. The idea of "if you believe it you can achieve it" doesn't last. Contrast that with "if you achieve it you can believe it." That does last, and it brings genuine confidence.

When I was just getting started, people believed in me. They believed in me more than I believed in myself and before I believed in myself. And they backed up their belief with opportunities they gave me. It has been said that it's wonderful when the people believe in their leader. It's even better when the leader believes in the people. But it's *best* when the people believe in themselves.

People in my life believed in me, and that helped me believe in myself.

As I was growing up, every day my dad and mom told me how much they believed in me.

When I was in high school, Coach Neff believed in me. In every basketball game, when we got to the fourth quarter, he would say, "John, look at me. It's your time. I'm counting on you."

In my twenties, Leonard Fitts, my first overseer when I became a pastor, was the first person to say he saw leadership in me. And Bob Klein, another of the leaders, said, "I pray for you every day because I think you have the greatest potential in our organization."

When I moved to California in my early thirties, Chuck Swindoll, the best-known pastor in church circles, introduced me to other pastors at a conference and told them I was marked to do great work for God. To this day, I don't know how Chuck even knew who I was or why he believed in me.

The list goes on and on. They believed in me so thoroughly and encouraged me so much that I worked harder and started to believe in myself, too.

If you don't have others who believe in you, then let me be the first. I believe in you. And I want the best for you. I want you to believe in yourself. I can loan you my belief, but that only works for a short time. To be successful, you *must* believe in yourself. You can be successful if others don't believe in you, but you cannot be successful if you don't believe in yourself. And to make a change, you must take action and do the right things that will allow you to possess self-belief.

> You can be successful if others don't believe in you, but you cannot be successful if you don't believe in yourself.

I want to help you believe and give you a path forward to increasing your capacity so that you can make the most of whatever potential you have. The way your life has gone up to now? It doesn't matter. Write a new story with your life. As Nick Vujicic says, "Life may not be going well for you now, but as long as you are here, as long as you press forward, anything is possible. Hold on to hope."[5]

That's great advice. Hold on to hope as you turn the page, and let's get ready to get to work.

Capacity Cap Questions

1. What are the life and birth caps that you cannot change? List them.

2. What caps have others put on you that you want to remove? What must you do to begin loosening those caps?

3. What caps have you put on yourself that are limiting your capacity? What must you do to begin loosening those caps?

PART II

Ability: Develop the Capacities You Already Possess

We often talk about *capacity* in the singular. But what if we're thinking about capacity the wrong way? Thinking of capacity as one thing is too limiting.

In the previous two chapters on awareness, I discussed how our capacity is not set. It's expandable. In this section I want to talk to you about how we can make the most of the abilities we have.

After awareness, the second step to changing our capacity is to recognize that we have many capacities. You have dozens, maybe even hundreds. Each capacity is based on your talents and choices. Right now, I want to focus on the top seven capacities that rely more on talent than choices, though both are involved:

Energy Capacity—Your Ability to Push On Physically
Emotional Capacity—Your Ability to Manage Your Emotions
Thinking Capacity—Your Ability to Think Effectively

People Capacity—Your Ability to Build Relationships
Creative Capacity—Your Ability to See Options and Find
    Answers
Production Capacity—Your Ability to Accomplish Results
Leadership Capacity—Your Ability to Lift and Lead Others

Everyone possesses these capacities, and every one of these capacities is significant to a person's success. By continually maximizing today's capacity in these areas, you will increase tomorrow's potential.

Before we dive into the specific capacities, I want to say one more thing about them. They don't develop in isolation. They work together. It may be helpful to think about this idea in two ways. First, your capacities build in layers. This creates a great foundation that you can build your life upon. It's like constructing a house on layers of solid rock instead of building it in soft sand. It can carry weight. You can build a large, weighty structure that has the potential to stand for a long time.

Second, they connect to one another. Each time you increase a capacity, it has the potential to synergize with another capacity and increase your potential. For example, if you increase your energy capacity so that you can push on physically, and you increase your leadership capacity, which is the ability to lift and lead others, your overall effectiveness increases. Where you once ran out of energy and stopped engaging with people when you really needed to, you'll learn to push through and be at your best as you interact with them.

As you develop your seven core capacities, explore your options. Look for ways to expand your ability. You will be amazed by the compounding effect you will experience and the increased potential that will result.

3

Energy Capacity—Your Ability to Push On Physically

Several years ago, I read a story called "A Thousand Marbles" by Jeffrey Davis, and it left a really strong impression on me. It was about an older gentleman who had placed hundreds of marbles in a jar, each one representing the Saturdays he had left if he lived to his normal life expectancy. It was a reminder to him that his time was limited and that he should make the most of it.

When I read that story, I was in my midsixties, and I was thinking a lot about the next several years of my life. At that time, I had just agreed to start two new businesses, the John Maxwell Company and the John Maxwell Team, and I believed that I should give them everything I had up to the age of seventy.

Having read the marble story, I asked Mark Cole, my CEO, to have a jar filled with marbles, each representing a week of my life until I would turn seventy. I asked him to put the jar in the office at the John Maxwell Company and to remove one each week as a reminder to the staff that my time with them would be limited. Together during that time, we would work on building my legacy. I did this because I wanted to have a good succession plan for the organizations, I didn't want to outstay my effectiveness, I wanted to transition well, and I wanted my companies to maximize the time they had with me.

I believed that I was doing the right thing. But as time passed, I discovered there was a problem: I wasn't winding down. I didn't want to quit. I was enjoying my work more than I ever had. Further, I was experiencing my greatest success, I was receiving more opportunities than at any other time in my life, and my companies were growing fast and starting to reach their potential. I wasn't sure what to do.

Everything changed when I spent some time with my friend Bill Hybels, senior pastor of Willow Creek Community Church. It was at Exchange, a leadership experience put on by the John Maxwell Company every year. We were on St. Thomas in the Virgin Islands, and Bill and I were chatting. At Exchange the previous year, I had brought the jar of marbles to the event, and during one of my sessions, I had spoken about how I was counting down the time I had left.

Bill had heard a podcast of that talk. As we sat on a sailboat in St. Thomas, Bill stared me down. And as only Bill can, he said, "John, have you lost your marbles?" Bill's a few years younger than I am, but he was like an older brother scolding me. "You can't *quit*! You can't start *counting down*. You've got way too much to do. You've got way too much to give. What is *wrong* with you?"

It was like a slap in the face.

And it woke me up.

Bill was right. I needed to quit counting marbles. That was scarcity thinking. I'd always approached life with an abundance mind-set. Why was I trying to limit myself? There was nothing in the world I wanted to do more than what I was currently doing. I wanted to pour myself and my energy into making a difference for as long as I was able.

The next year at Exchange in Atlanta, I again asked my staff to bring the jar of marbles to one of my sessions. This time when I spoke I took it, and I dumped the whole jar onto the floor. I declared my intention to keep working, keep adding value to people, and keep making a difference for as long as I had the energy to do so. And in order to do that, I needed to do four things:

- **Reengage:** It's difficult to gear up again when you're geared down. It's like stepping out of the stands, putting on your old uniform, and getting back into the game. But that was what I needed to do. I had to give more time and attention to my companies.

- **Reinvest:** If I was going to help my companies, I couldn't be half-hearted. I had to reinvest emotionally, physically, and financially.

- **Reinvent:** Yesterday's success won't bring success tomorrow. If I wanted to help my companies maximize their capacity, I would have to help them reinvent themselves. We would either improve and try to become the best or we could get out of the business.

- **Replenish:** I knew I also needed to do a better job of replenishing myself through exercise, better eating, recreation, and rest.

I immediately began to make changes. The result? I had a new surge of energy. And I also learned a lesson: it's better to manage your energy than to manage your time.

> It's better to manage your energy than to manage your time.

Why You Should Focus on Energy Instead of Time

There are many capacities that we can increase, but there's nothing we can do to expand time. The number of minutes in a day, days in a week, and weeks in a year are set. Even our time here on Earth is fixed. Our days are numbered.

That's why we need to focus on our energy. That's something we can influence. In their book *The Power of Full Engagement*, authors Jim Loehr and Tony Schwartz assert, "Energy, not time, is the fundamental currency of high performance." They go on to explain,

> The ultimate measure of our lives is not how much time we spend on the planet, but rather how much energy we invest in the time that we have. The premise of this book—and of the training we do each year with thousands of clients—is simple enough: Performance, health, and happiness are grounded in the skillful management of energy.... The number of hours in a day is fixed, but the quantity and quality of energy available to us is not. It is our most precious resource. The more we take responsibility for the energy we bring to the world, the more empowered and productive we become. The more we blame others or external circumstances, the more negative and compromised our energy is likely to be.[1]

If we want to get more done and make a greater impact on the world, we need to increase our energy capacity.

A former CEO of General Electric, Jack Welch, put a great emphasis on a candidate's energy when he hired leaders. He valued stamina over many other qualities, because he believed it was important for leadership sustainability. He also valued a leader's ability to energize others and motivate a team to be productive.

I appreciate energy. I grew up in a house *full* of energy. Dad was always working and was often on the road helping others. Mom was industrious in taking care of our home and all of us. My brother Larry worked from the time he was in his early teens. As for me, I was never able to sit still. Too many times my teachers would say,

"John never stops talking and he walks around the room while I'm teaching class." I suspect that every morning when I got out of bed, my parents probably said, "Uh-oh. He's up."

The Three *R*s Applied to Energy

Over the years I've noticed that people who reach their capacity do not sit back and wait for things to happen to them. They go out and make things happen. That takes energy. It also takes a sense of purpose and focus. How should you focus your energy? For years I've taught people the 3 *R*s that I use for prioritizing:

Requirement—What I have to do
Return—What I do well
Reward—What I love to do

However, I've never related the concepts to energy. Here's how it works: Doing what rewards you almost always gives you energy. The same is true for doing what gives us a high return. However, for most people, fulfilling requirements is not energizing—unless your requirements line up with return and reward. If you have the power to align all three of those, you'll always be energized by your work.

How can you do that? You can change jobs. You can talk to your boss and see if what's required of you can be adjusted. Or you can learn to distinguish between what *has* to be done for the organization and what *only you* could do for it.

In my career, I had an energy turnaround when I started to make that distinction. Not everything that had to be done had to be done *by me*. If something was necessary but I didn't have to do it personally, I delegated it. If it was unnecessary, I had the power to remove it from my requirements. Maybe you do, too.

Over the years as I've gotten more control of my own calendar, I've continually worked to align my 3 *R*s. The more they have gotten in sync, the more energy I've possessed. Today I am required to lead, communicate, and create. That's it. Because those three things are aligned with my passions and talents, I have an abundance of energy—even at nearly seventy.

Questions That Help Me Maximize Energy

Even if you don't have the power to change what's required of you on the job, there are still ways to maximize your energy. I want to give you strategies for managing and increasing your energy capacity based on five questions. If you can answer these questions and take action based on your answers, you'll see your energy rise dramatically.

1. The Plugged-In Question—"When Am I Fully Charged?"

If you travel a lot, as I do, you spend a lot of time in airports. When I traveled, I used to see people sitting on floors near power outlets so that they could keep their phones and other devices plugged in. But more and more, I see power stations situated among the seats at departure gates. Airports have recognized that people need energy. They want to plug in.

I wish more people were as intentional about plugging in personally as they are about plugging in their phones and laptops. If they were, they'd see new levels of productivity and satisfaction in their lives.

Author and researcher Tom Rath opens his book *Are You Fully Charged?* with the following words about the impact of energy on our lives:

When you are fully charged, you get more done. You have better interactions. Your mind is sharp, and your body is strong. On days when you are fully charged, you experience high levels of engagement and well-being. This charge carries forward, creating an upward cycle for those you care about.[2]

Tom goes on in the book to describe the three key conditions required for a person to experience a "full charge" in their day:

- **Meaning:** Doing something that benefits another person

- **Interactions:** Creating far more positive than negative moments

- **Energy:** Making choices that improve your mental and physical health[3]

Tom Rath's words stimulated me to ask myself the question, "What fully charges me?" I give you my answers below, because I believe they will stimulate you to think about what charges you up.

> Ask yourself, "What fully charges me?"

Living in My Gift Zone

Whenever I am leading, creating, or communicating, I'm fully charged. I'm using my best gifts to do the things I really care about. I was created to do those things, and when I do them, I say to myself, "I was born to do this." What activities make you feel that way?

Investing in My Family and Friends

Few things in life give me greater joy than helping those closest to me experience togetherness; create memories; and learn, grow, and mature as they find themselves. I love sharing these experiences with the people I love. That's why every year Margaret and I are very intentional about taking our entire family on a trip with us. We grow together, create memories, and become better people—and a better family. What kinds of interactions fill you with energy?

Adding Value to Others

I love people, and every day I look for ways to add value to them. That's true for team members, clients, and strangers. Helping others fills me with energy and validates my calling. What activities done for others strengthen your sense of purpose and energize you?

Taking Good Care of Myself Physically

I have to confess that I have not always taken good care of myself. For too many years I neglected exercise, proper rest, and healthy eating. However, over the last few years I've come to realize that taking care of myself and my health are not selfish acts or time wasted. These are matters of good stewardship. I was put on this earth to help others and use my gifts to make a difference. I won't be able to do that if my health is shot—or if I'm dead. What can you do to improve your physical health and give you more physical energy?

Being a Catalyst to Growth and Building

> "There is no passion to be found in playing small—in settling for a life that is less than the one you are capable of living."
> —Nelson Mandela

A friend once told me that "growth is happiness." I agree. My life has been filled with happiness and energy as I developed people, built companies, enlarged possibilities, and expanded capacities. Nelson Mandela was right:

"There is no passion to be found in playing small—in settling for a life that is less than the one you are capable of living." What bold endeavor can you embark upon that will energize you?

Possessing God Awareness

As I write these words I am looking out at the ocean. On my desk within my view of that vast body of water is a plaque that reads, "O God, thy sea is so great and my boat is so small." I am a person of faith, so it reminds me of God's greatness, which not only humbles me, but also helps me to depend on Him. It reminds me of God's presence within and causes me to want to follow Him and seek His guidance. And it makes me aware of God's unconditional love for me. All of these thoughts energize me. If you're a person of faith, how can you better connect with God to be energized by Him?

That's my list of things that charge me up. What's on yours? If you don't know, then take some time to figure it out. That way you can be intentional about becoming fully charged.

2. The Depletion Question—"What Wears Me Down?"

Some of us were raised believing that we can accomplish *anything* as long as we try hard enough. But that's not true. While I believe our potential is unlimited, I also recognize that we cannot be our best in areas where we have no talent. No matter how hard I try, I cannot become a professional ballet dancer.

Gallup has proven with their studies on disengagement in the workplace that the anything-is-possible myth has led to many people spending years fighting uphill battles by doing what they're not good at. That's exhausting. Why spend your life trying to be what you're not, instead of trying to be more of who you are naturally? Why not figure out what your natural strengths are and develop those for the benefit of yourself and others? It's the difference between going with the current and swimming against it. The first increases your speed and effectiveness while the second depletes your energy. The first makes you shine. The second makes you have to grind (work through unpleasant situations and tasks to get things done). If you grind away in areas of weakness, you'll just get worn out. However, if you shine in your strengths but with the strength and tenacity of a grinder, you'll go far.

Another thing that wears most people down is dealing with change. The gymnast Dan Millman wrote, "The secret of change is to focus all your energy not on fighting the old, but on building the new." Even taking that advice, most people still find change depleting. It takes mental, emotional, and physical energy to create change. And the will and discipline needed to sustain change are resources that are more limited than most people realize.

What depletes you? Do you know? Have you paid attention to what sucks the life out of you? Do you avoid those things? It's important to recognize what depletes your energy and take action to defend against them.

3. The Proximity Question—"How Accessible Are My Energy Pluses?"

I discovered the Proximity Principle right after I graduated from college. That June, Margaret and I got married and moved 250 miles away from home. I was ecstatic to start my new life with Margaret, but within a couple of weeks I realized how much energy I had always received from my parents. Both of my parents were energy connectors. My dad's positive attitude and confidence were contagious, and as a young person, I was energized whenever I was around him. My mom loved me unconditionally and was always ready to listen to me.

In those days there were no cell phones, long distance calls were expensive, and Margaret and I had no money to make those calls. So we had very limited contact with my parents. That was quite an adjustment for me, because my energy level went down dramatically.

Tom Rath says that research shows that proximity matters a lot. He states, "Your well-being is more dramatically affected by the people you see every day, people who live within a few blocks of your house, people who live within a few miles, than it is by distant connections."[4]

People are not the only energy pluses we have in our lives. Almost anything can boost your energy as long as it touches you in a positive way. The key is being intentional about keeping those things in proximity to you.

For years I have been intentional about having energy pluses close to me so that I can quickly access them when I need an energy shot. For example, when I'm getting ready to speak and I want a shot of mental energy, I look at my iPhone and read a couple of inspirational quotes. When I need energy to keep writing, I look at the bookshelf in my office that holds the books that have changed my life. It reminds me that what I'm doing is likely to help someone. When my schedule feels heavy and I have a hard time focusing on the big picture, I pull out my folder that contains my written goals for that year. When I'm physically dragging, I go to my exercise room and work out. When I'm feeling down, I call someone in my inner circle.

All these things lift me up, and you need to figure out what lifts you up, too. Look at these categories and see if any of them might be possible energy sources for you:

Music—The songs that lift you
Thoughts—The ideas that speak to you
Experiences—The activities that rejuvenate you

Friends—The people who encourage you

Recreation—The fun events that invigorate you

Soul—The spiritual exercises that strengthen you

Hopes—The dreams that inspire you

Home—The family members who care for you

Giftedness—The talents that activate you

Memories—The recollections that make you smile

Books—The messages that change you

If you find the things that are energy pluses for you, I think you'll be amazed by how much your energy capacity can increase.

4. The 100 Percent Question—"When Do I Need to Be Full of Energy?"

It's vital to increase your energy as much as possible. It's also crucial to use the energy you have wisely. Use it when you need it, and conserve it when you don't. And know the difference between the two.

I learned to ask myself this question when I was eighteen. As a college freshman, I needed a job. My friend Steve Benner suggested we apply at a grocery store to be stock boys. Sounded good to me, so we went to the store and talked to the manager.

"Boys," he said, "follow me to the back of the store." He quickly turned and walked briskly to the back of the store. I remember thinking that he sure seemed in a hurry. Steve was on his heels, while it took me a few seconds to catch up with them. At the back of the store, we filled out our applications, shook the manager's hand, and waited for his call.

The next day Steve found out that he was hired. I got a call, too—saying I wasn't.

That entire day I couldn't figure out what happened. *How come Steve was accepted and I wasn't?* I wondered. The next day I could stand it no more. I went to the store and asked the manager why he didn't hire me.

"You didn't walk fast enough to the back of the store," he answered. "I'm looking for boys that show energy. Steve did, and you didn't!"

Wow. I was pretty sure I would have done a better job than Steve, yet he got hired because he hustled. As I walked out to my car, I realized that hustle beats talent when talent doesn't hustle!

> Hustle beats talent when talent doesn't hustle!

Since then I've made it a priority to marshal my energy when I need it, because it's impossible to be full of energy the entire day. So every day I look at my calendar and determine the times that will be what Jeffrey Gitomer calls "showtime," the interactions when what you say, do, and think are crucial to your success or that of your business.

My calendar is full tomorrow, but as I review it, I see that I have three showtime events. At 10:00 a.m. I'll meet with Mike Matheny, the manager of the St. Louis Cardinals, and twenty high-capacity leaders in that baseball organization. I need to be at 100 percent as I share leadership principles that will add value to them. At 2:00 p.m. I'll meet with Mark Cole, the CEO of my five organizations, and we'll talk about three critical issues, including how to train 50,000 leaders in Guatemala who will teach leadership values to 250,000 people there. And at 6:00 p.m. I'll meet with Rob Hoskins, president of One Hope, as we prepare to meet with donors and share our vision of training five million kids in leadership over the next five years. Our belief is that these donors will give $30 million to this initiative.

When *won't* I need to be at 100 percent tomorrow? When I give blood at the lab at 7:30 a.m., when I have lunch, when I drive to Fort Lauderdale, and when I'm shaking hands at a formal reception in the evening.

You need to know when it's showtime every day in your life. No matter what hour of the day it occurs or how many of them you have on a particular day, at those times you need to show up and give 100 percent of your energy. That's the only way you'll reach your capacity.

5. The Margin Question—"Where Is the Space for Things I Need but Haven't Planned?"

Finally, the last question you need to ask yourself to maximize your energy has to do with having margin in your life. By margin, I mean extra time to breathe, think, and make adjustments. Not only does having margin provide space for you to grow; it also gives you the opportunity to recharge.

I have to confess, this is a continual challenge for me. I'm weak when it comes to creating margin. For too many years I have over-scheduled myself. The good news is that I am highly productive. The bad news is that I lose opportunities because I have no margin.

For example, this year I missed two opportunities to play at the Augusta National Golf Club because I didn't have any margin. And I wanted to revise my book *Developing the Leader Within You* this year, but I couldn't because I didn't have margin. But I'm learning. I have already planned to give myself space for opportunities in my schedule next year.

Several years ago I read an article in *Harvard Business Review* on the management of energy. In it the authors pointed out that people need margin for many aspects of their health and effectiveness. They need time to recover from difficulties and regain their emotional footing. Without that margin, people become negative. They wrote:

Without intermittent recovery, we're not physiologically capable of sustaining highly positive emotions for long periods. Confronted with relentless demands and unexpected challenges, people tend to slip into negative emotions—the fight-or-flight mode—often multiple times in a day. They become irritable and impatient, or anxious and insecure. Such states of mind drain people's energy and cause friction in their relationships. Fight-or-flight emotions also make it impossible to think clearly, logically, and reflectively. When executives learn to recognize what kinds of events trigger their negative emotions, they gain greater capacity to take control of their reactions.[5]

Do you give yourself space in your schedule for the unexpected, and to recover psychologically and emotionally? I still find it hard to do. In *The Touch of the Earth*, Jean Hersey writes, "It's extremely important not to have one's life all blocked out, not to have the days and weeks totally organized. It's essential to leave gaps and interludes for spontaneous action, for it is often in spontaneity and surprises that we open ourselves to the unlimited opportunities and new areas brought into our lives by chance."[6] Those gaps also allow us to use our energy more wisely.

Fortunately, I am doing better at creating margin in the area of my health. I now have a trainer who keeps me accountable for physical exercise and a doctor who helps me manage my weight. I'm doing better at resting and recovering. I'm working out more, and my strength and energy capacity are good. I'm still learning and trying to grow in this area as well as others, such as my schedule.

How much have you thought about your energy capacity? Have you assumed that your energy capacity is fixed? That you can't change it? If so, you need to change your mind-set. Start paying close attention to what increases or decreases your energy, and begin making adjustments to what you do. Reduce the energy depleters as much as you can. Tap into things that increase your energy capacity. And manage your energy for the things that matter most to you. Trust me—it will change your life.

Energy Capacity Questions

1. What are the activities, people, tasks, and places that sap your energy?

2. What are the activities, people, tasks, and places that give you greater energy?

3. In what areas of your life are you not maximizing your energy and the energy of the people around you?

4

Emotional Capacity—Your Ability to Manage Your Emotions

In 1969 when I started my ministry career in rural Indiana, pastors were expected to provide counseling services to the people of their congregations. I had taken a few classes in this area in college, and I wanted to help people. So as the new senior pastor, I took this on.

Sometimes the sessions went well. However, many times they did not. I have to own my part in that. I have little natural gifting as a counselor. When someone presents me with a problem, I want to present them with a solution. And an action plan. And I don't want to revisit the problem with them until they've executed the action plan.

That's not the way you're supposed to do counseling. And it's one of the reasons I gave it up.

But I was not the only problem in these less-than-perfect sessions. There were other problems, which I can see clearly now as I look back on that time:

- Most people do not see themselves as they really are.

- Many people don't want to resolve their problems; they just want someone to listen to them talk.

- Some people are not emotionally strong, and as a result, they do not cope well with life's difficulties.

Back then, I couldn't understand why everyone wasn't emotionally strong. And I didn't have a good strategy to help people increase their emotional capacity. But now I do. And I want to share that with you. If your emotional capacity isn't high, this will help you to increase it. If your emotional capacity is naturally high, then perhaps you can use these tips to help others on your team or in your family.

How to Increase Your Emotional Capacity

Before we dive in, let me first explain what I mean by emotional capacity. Emotional capacity is the ability to handle adversity, failure, criticism, change, and pressure in a positive way. All of these things create stress in our lives. I've found that the inability to deal with stress or emotional pressure takes a lot out of people. They give up, break down, or do unhealthy things to try to escape the pressure. However, emotionally strong people are able to manage their emotions and process through difficulties. That allows them to increase their capacity and moves them closer to reaching their full potential.

I've known and talked to a lot of people who have a high emotional capacity, and I've observed what they do. If you can adopt the following seven practices that I've observed in emotionally strong people, you will increase your emotional capacity.

1. Emotionally Strong People Are *Proactive* in Dealing with Their Emotions

The first and maybe most important thing that emotionally strong people do is take an active approach to their emotions. They never say, "That's just how I feel. I can't help that." They are never victims of their own feelings.

Researcher and teacher M. Asch said in her book *Perspectives on Applied Psychology*, "Remember, motions are the precursors of emotions." That means you *can* do things to influence your own emotions. Maybe you can't control them completely, but you can change them through your actions. One of my favorite examples of this was written by author and speaker Og Mandino. He said,

> If I feel depressed I will sing.
> If I feel sad I will laugh.
> If I feel ill I will double my labor.
> If I feel fear I will plunge ahead.
> If I feel inferior I will wear new garments.
> If I feel uncertain I will raise my voice.
> If I feel poverty I will think of wealth to come.
> If I feel incompetent I will remember past success.
> If I feel insignificant I will remember my goals.
> Today I will be master of my emotions.[1]

I'm not sure that I will ever be "master of my emotions," but I will always get in motion in an attempt to head off my damaging emotions.

Here's what I know. All of us are hit in the gut by unwanted surprises, blindsided by negative relationships,

> "Motions are the precursors of emotions."
> —*M. Asch*

and knocked down by the blow we didn't see coming. There are times when we want to tell the world how unfair life is. But only by taking action can we pull ourselves out of the pits we find ourselves in. Hoping, wishing, denying, crying, cussing, fussing, moaning, blaming, and waiting only keep us in the pit. The faster we can recover from the shock of the emotion, process through it, and move toward action, the quicker our recovery time will be. And the more emotionally strong we will become. The choice is always ours. We either continually work on mastering our emotions, or we will be continually mastered by them.

2. Emotionally Strong People Do Not Waste Time Feeling Sorry for Themselves

Perhaps you've heard the joke about a woman who complained to her best friend, "The whole world is against me!"

Her friend tried to comfort her. "That's not true. The whole world isn't against you," she replied. "They don't even know you yet."

It may be corny, but it illustrates a common characteristic of people who feel sorry for themselves: they negatively exaggerate their entire situation.

At a recent conference, I shared with a group of leaders that you can't moan and lead at the same time. That truth also applies to success. You can't complain and get ahead at the same time. Moaning about your troubles and moving in the right direction rarely happen together. Former Navy SEAL Eric Greitens writes in his book *Resilience*:

> Many of life's annoyances just have to be ignored. That doesn't mean that we suppress, ignore, or deny every pain. Serious pain has to be confronted. But one mark of resilience is learning to tell which pain deserves our attention. Paying

attention to every pain, all the time, doesn't lead to resilience. It usually just leads to whining.[2]

> "One mark of resilience is learning to tell which pain deserves our attention."
> —*Eric Greitens*

The way you deal with difficulties and avoid feeling sorry for yourself can be as unique as you are. I love the way PGA pro golfer Richard Lee handles adversity on the course. He and I met and became friends at the AT&T Pebble Beach Pro-Am. I've had the privilege of playing in that tournament a few times, twice with Richard. One year we made the playoffs! I will never forget the thrill I had on the first tee on Sunday when I received a golf umbrella that read, I MADE THE CUT AT THE AT&T PRO AM. It's one of my prized possessions. Not many amateurs can say that. The other time we did terribly, finishing near the bottom of the standings.

The year we did poorly, we went to dinner after we failed to make the cut to console ourselves and recover from our poor play. During dinner, one of the questions I asked Richard was "What's the best advice you have ever received?"

"Welcome the ball," he answered. That intrigued me. Everyone around the table wanted him to explain that.

"I play golf for a living," he said. "Every shot is important to me. Any shot can either make me or break me in a tournament.

"Early in my career my mother-in-law could see how when I had a bad shot, I would get really disappointed. And my negative emotions would start to fill my mind and hurt my play.

"One day she said to me, 'Richard, you will always have days when you make bad shots. Every golfer does. As you walk toward your ball you have a decision to make: Will I dread seeing the lie of my ball and begin filling my mind with negative thoughts and my body with negative emotions? Or will I welcome the ball and be glad I am a golfer and realize that I have an opportunity to make a great recovery shot? If you always welcome the ball regardless of your lie, you will more often make good recovery shots.' "

Richard looked at us and said, "Wherever my ball lies, I walk up to it and welcome the ball. It has made a great difference in my game."

What a great way to think of dealing with adversity: making a recovery shot!

In life, every one of is is faced with "bad lies." What will be our response when things are not working out, when bad breaks come our way, and when life isn't fair? What will our mind-set be as we "find our ball"? We can let the bad lie ruin our attitude, or we can welcome the ball.

This reminds me of something I learned in the first Dale Carnegie course I took when I was in junior high school. I was taught to ask myself, "What is the worst that can happen?" If you can ask yourself that question and then prepare to accept it, you can hit a good "recovery shot." If it's as bad as the worst, you can deal with it. If it's not as bad as you anticipated, then all the better.

3. Emotionally Strong People Do Not Allow Others to Control Their Relationships

When I began my career as a leader, I thought being effective meant making everyone happy with me. And because I had pretty good relationship skills, I was pretty good at making others feel good and picking them up when they were down. But I was a people pleaser, which meant that other people's behavior was really in control of my life.

Then one day one of my mentors, Elmer Towns, told me something that really got my attention: "John, the weaker person usually controls the relationship." He went on to explain that emotionally strong people usually have the ability to adjust to difficult relationships, while the weaker person can't or won't.

The implications of this are huge. If you are the emotionally stronger person in a relationship, but you are unconscious of the relationship's dynamics, you conform to the other person's way of relating. However, if you *are* conscious of the dynamics, you can choose to passively adapt to the other person, or you can take action to try to influence the dynamics or to distance yourself from the other person.

> "The weaker person usually controls the relationship."
> —*Elmer Towns*

Education professor Leo Buscaglia said, "The easiest thing to be in the world is you. The most difficult thing to be is what other people want you to be. Don't let them put you in that position." I began to look at my relationships differently that day. If a weaker person usually controlled my relationship with them, I had to take action or else there would be many times I would not reach capacity. Dysfunctional people want others to function on their level. Average people want others to be average. High achievers want others to achieve.

This sent me on a journey of discovery. First, I tried to look objectively at the people I was trying to please. Where were they headed in life? What were their motives? Did they understand the bigger vision? Were their desires in the best interests of others? Second, I looked for positive models of leadership, growth, and success. What did they do? What were their priorities? How did they fulfill their vision? How did they treat others? When I examined both groups, there was no comparison. The people I admired showed me the way forward. I learned from them and followed their modeling. The more I did that, the less I wanted to please people whose goals and vision didn't line up with mine. And in some cases, I had to let go of old relationships to embrace a new way of living and leading.

Relationships are complicated and can be difficult to navigate. One of the ways that I can keep proper control of my life and not allow others to take that control is to understand that I wear different hats in my life: husband, father, friend, businessperson, and leader. The hat I have on determines the way I interact in the relationship. I'm continually making relationship choices throughout the day based on the hat I'm wearing.

Recently I came across a story by psychologist Henry Cloud that illustrates the idea of different hats beautifully:

> A man started a company and built it into a very large enterprise, and was planning to hand over the reins to his son at retirement. One day, he was walking through the factory and observed his son angrily berating an employee in front of other employees. He looked at his son and motioned for him to come to his office.
>
> "David," he began. "I wear two hats around here. I am the boss and I am your father. Right now, I am going to put my boss hat on. *You're fired.* You are done here. I will not have that kind of behavior in my company and will not ever tolerate employees being treated that way. I have warned you about this kind of thing before, and you are still doing it. So, I have to let you go."
>
> Then he said, "Now, I am going to put on my father hat."
>
> After a moment's pause, he continued. "Son, I heard you just lost your job. How can I help you?"[3]

Emotionally strong people honor their relationships while at the same time guarding against letting others control them, especially in difficult relationships,

4. Emotionally Strong People Do Not Waste Energy on Things They Cannot Control

I have always admired Nelson Mandela. Several years ago I took a tour of Robben Island with a journalist and a former prisoner who knew Mandela. I saw the rock yard, the cave where Mandela and his fellow prisoners would meet to discuss ending apartheid, the exercise yard, and the eight-by-ten cell where Mandela spent eighteen of his first twenty-seven years in prison. I got to spend about fifteen minutes alone in that cell. I lay down on the mat that was in the cell and spent time looking through the bars imaging myself in his place, dreaming of freedom. I walked away thinking, *You can't imprison greatness. You can't lock away a dream.*

I talked quite a bit with the reporter that day. The continuing theme of our conversation was that Mandela did not allow the things he could not control to control him. That was how he could bring good out of bad and focus on what could be rather than on what was.

That evening in my hotel room, I wrote the following:

Lessons Learned from Nelson Mandela
Our surroundings need not control our spirit.
People who devalue us do not determine our value.
Dreams can be birthed during the daily grind.
Out of our brokenness, we can be made whole and bring
healing to others.

Controlling what you can and not wasting energy on what you can't is one of the most important lessons we can learn in life. One of my mentors, consultant Fred Smith, would often say to me, "You must understand the difference between a fact of life and a problem. A fact of life is something you cannot control or fix. A problem is something you can fix." I've never forgotten that great advice.

> "You must understand the difference between a fact of life and a problem. A fact of life is something you cannot control or fix. A problem is something you can fix."
> —*Fred Smith*

Emotionally strong people don't waste their energy when they are stuck in bad traffic, lose their luggage, or get caught in a storm. They recognize that all of these factors are beyond their control. Instead, they focus on what they can control.

When I turned sixteen, my father tried to impress this upon me. As we got into the car for me to go take my driver's test, Dad put a book in the glove compartment, and said, "Son, there are times when you are driving that a train will cause you to stop and wait. When that happens, pull out this book and read it. Don't let what you can't control waste your time." From that time on, I've always tried to carry a book or other resource with me that I could use to help me grow any time I was forced to wait. And I've taken responsibility for the things I can control:

- **My Attitude**—Only I will determine how I think or feel.
- **My Time**—Only I will determine how I spend time and whom I spend it with.
- **My Priorities**—Only I will determine what is important in my life and how much time I give to these essentials.
- **My Passion**—Only I will identify what I love and what I was created to do.
- **My Potential**—Only I will determine where I commit myself to grow.
- **My Calling**—Only I will answer to God someday for my purpose.

I will devote my energy to these things. At times this may cause people to be unhappy with me, but I won't be unhappy with myself.

Only I am responsible for how I steward these areas and the energy I give them. And only I will answer to God for them.

5. Emotionally Strong People Do Not Keep Making the Same Mistakes

It's been said that the definition of insanity is doing the same thing over and over but expecting different results. When we think about it logically, we should expect the same results from the same actions, yet many people find themselves in ruts doing what they've always done but wishing for something different. How exhausting! Why does it happen? Because they never take the time to stop, figure out why their efforts aren't getting positive results, and change course.

One of the ways successful people keep their emotional capacity high is by avoiding falling into this trap. Sure, they make mistakes. But they take the time to learn from them. They don't follow the old rule of business, which says, "When it's over, it's over." Instead, they follow a different rule: it's not over until you've learned from it.

One of the principles I've embraced for many years is the idea that reflection turns experience into insight. Acting on this belief has helped me to grow, gain wisdom, and maintain a high emotional capacity. How do I do that? By doing the following:

> Reflection turns experience into insight.

Review by Myself

Every evening I set aside time to reflect and ask myself questions. I think of this as an appointment with myself. One question I always ask myself is "What mistakes did I make today?" I do this because my mistakes are fertile ground for learning. Most people fear mistakes more than they love learning. I love learning more than I hate making mistakes.

Think to Myself

Emotionally strong people look first at themselves and what they need to change when reflecting. They don't focus on others or their circumstances. So after I identify my mistakes, I ask, "What can I learn from what I did wrong today?"

Talk to Myself

The most important conversations you and I have each day are with ourselves. Self-talk has a great impact on us. This is where we can coach ourselves to remain positive while looking at our negatives. One of the things I always do is remind myself that I'm learning and growing from my mistakes and that each effort gets me closer to becoming the person that I was created to be.

Direct Myself

The next step in the process of avoiding making the same mistakes is to set yourself in the right direction. Speaker Jim Rohn said, "One of the best places to start to turn your life around is by doing whatever appears on your mental 'I should' list." As I observe my mistakes and learn from what I've done wrong, I determine the right direction I need to go to leave that mistake behind. This goes on my "I should" list.

Take Action Myself

I don't carry the weight of my "I should" list very long. It's been my practice to try to immediately move every task from my "I should" list to my "I did" list. Life is already stressful enough. We don't need to be carrying the extra weight of too many "I shoulds" around with us.

Emotionally strong people are honest with themselves. The discipline of reflection is what I do to try to keep myself honest. That's important because, as poet James Russell Lowell remarked, "No one can produce great things who is not thoroughly sincere in dealing with himself."

> "No one can produce great things who is not thoroughly sincere in dealing with himself."
> —*James Russell Lowell*

6. Emotionally Strong People Don't Allow the Highs or Lows to Control Their Lives

As a child, I was taught this proverb: "He who rules his emotions is greater than he that takes a city."[4] I don't know how hard it is to conquer a city, but I do know how hard it is to rule my emotions. And that's what I work to do. I want to control my emotions, not allow them to control me.

I once saw a story about a guy who got to play a round of golf with PGA great Sam Snead. On the first hole, Snead made a terrible score, a seven—three strokes over par. As they exited the green to go to the next hole, Snead was unruffled. "That's why we play eighteen holes," he said.

His round ended that day four under par. He didn't allow a low to control his emotions or his game.

In my early career as a leader, one of my mentors said, "There are not two good consecutive days in a leader's life." How true. After almost seventy years of life, I might even say there are not two good consecutive days in any person's life. Every day contains something negative that threatens to wear us down emotionally.

You probably know that we shouldn't let those things take us down too low, or we can become discouraged. But are you also aware that you shouldn't let your highs take you too high? Success has a tendency to make us complacent. We start to assume that everything will automatically stay good, so we might rest on our laurels and try to protect what we have. We can begin to feel entitled, lose perspective, and stop working hard. In the end, the highs and lows can rob us of reality and prevent our activity.

How do I do limit the impact of my highs and lows? I practice the twenty-four-hour rule. Simply stated, I limit the effect of any emotional high or low to the twenty-four-hour period that follows the occurrence. If I have a great success, I celebrate for twenty-four hours. My team and I give each other high fives, we relive the victory, we compliment one another, but only for a day. Then we get back to work. We know that yesterday's success won't bring us tomorrow's success. *Today's work does.*

If I have a difficult time leveling myself out, I do things that will give me a more realistic perspective. I will go through Jim Collins's book *Built to Last* and then look at all the companies that started strong but then failed. I will list all the things that could go wrong if I don't continue to make positive changes and improvements in my life. Or I'll look at the challenges that still lie ahead.

Similarly, if I experience a great failure, I allow myself twenty-four hours to feel bad, sing the blues, wear black, and grieve. Toward the end of my emotional time limit, I'll begin doing things that will bring me back to a level of emotional stability. I'll spend time with a positive friend. Play a round of golf. Share with someone the lessons I learned in my downtime. Focus on the good things in my life. Or help someone.

Action is the key. Whether dealing with highs or lows, taking action helps me to get back on track and regain control of my emotions. That's how I stay emotionally strong.

7. Emotionally Strong People Understand, Appreciate, and Grow Through Their Struggles

Many people resist change, want immediate results, and hope for a life devoid of problems. However, those desires make a person emotionally weak. Why? Because life involves struggle. Emotionally strong people expect difficulties and learn to appreciate the growth they bring. As Lolly Daskal, founder and president of Lead From Within, writes,

> It's human nature to resist change—particularly when it comes in the form of adversity or challenges. But change is inevitable, and developing the trait of resilience helps us not only survive change, but also learn, grow, and thrive on it. Resilience is the capacity to cope with stress and adversity. It comes from believing in yourself and, at the same time, in something bigger than yourself. Resilience is not a trait that people are born with; it involves behaviors, thoughts, and actions that can be learned and developed in anyone.[5]

Emotionally strong people do not expect immediate results. As they approach life, they know they are in it for the long haul. As they face struggles, they do so with energy and fortitude. They understand that genuine success takes time. They try new things and fail. They run into obstacles but persevere. They keep going, keep working. They focus on the right decisions they need to make, and make them quickly. They realize that they may change their direction overnight, but they won't arrive at their destination overnight. They keep their eye on the big picture, and they don't quit. They personify the attitude of Eric Greitens, author of *Resilience*, who wrote,

You will fail. Especially in the beginning. You will fail. And that's not just OK, it's essential. Without resilience, the first failure is also the last—because it's final. Those who are excellent at their work have learned to comfortably coexist with failure. The excellent fail more often than the mediocre. They begin more. They attempt more. They attack more. Mastery lives quietly atop a mountain of mistakes.[6]

> "Without resilience, the first failure is also the last—because it's final."
> —Eric Greitens

Greitens believes that as human beings, there are some things all of us must do to live well: breathe, sleep, drink, eat, and love. But he also believes that we struggle. We need challenges to master and problems to solve in order to be at our best. We can do that only when we master our emotions and appreciate our struggles.

Being an emotionally strong person who has high emotional capacity is about being able to start fresh every day and function with a clean slate emotionally. We can't hold on to old emotional baggage and remain emotionally resilient at the same time.

Recently I was reminded of the importance of that ability to start fresh when I came across an idea expressed by Steve Jobs, who essentially said that we must learn to erase the board of our achievements and allow ourselves to become beginners again. I needed to take that advice this month as Margaret and I packed our things in preparation for a move. We were evaluating everything and trying to determine what to eliminate.

For about a month I looked over everything in my old filing cabinets. In them were over forty-five years of material I had filed for future use in writing and speaking. As I tried to process what I would take in the move and what I would get rid of, I realized these files had become a security blanket for me. As long as I had those files, I knew I'd have material to fall back on. But recently I had been challenging myself to write and speak more out of my own life experiences, to go deep inside of myself and pull out thoughts and ideas, not reach for my files.

> "Erase the board of your achievements and allow yourself to be a beginner again."
> —*Steve Jobs*

So I had a decision to make, and for me it was an emotional one. Those file cabinets represented forty-five years of intentional collecting of thoughts and ideas. As I looked through each folder, I could remember why I filed items, how much I loved them, and how I had used them to help others. But as much as I wanted to keep them, I wanted to grow even more. I ended up saving fewer than ten folders. The rest I gave away.

No longer will I look to the files for help. Now I just ask the God who made me to keep remaking me. I kind of like what he is doing. I'm discovering that moving from security to risk, from the known to the unknown, requires courage and faith. And emotional capacity.

Emotional Capacity Questions

1. In the past, have you considered yourself to be emotionally strong or emotionally weak as a person? Why?

2. Which of the seven practices of emotionally strong people are you best at doing?

3. Which of the seven practices of emotionally strong people is most difficult for you and why? What could you do to improve in that area?

5

Thinking Capacity—Your Ability to Think Effectively

My father grew up in Georgetown, Ohio, during the Great Depression. Ever industrious and a hard worker, he always found jobs. As a teenager, he managed to get work running errands for the only three wealthy families in town. And during his employment with them, he made a life-changing discovery. The members of those three families thought differently than his own family and differently than all the other people he knew in town. What was more, the thinking habits of the people in those three families were similar to one another.

> Successful people think differently than unsuccessful people.

While still in high school, he came to this conclusion: successful people think differently than unsuccessful people.

That conclusion drove Dad to study successful people, to read books that would help him to think positively, and to work at increasing his ability to think effectively. And he taught those lessons to my brother Larry, my sister Trish, and me, and challenged us to become good thinkers.

As a result of Dad's encouragement and my own study of successful people, I've come to the same conclusion about good thinking. I believe success is difficult, if not impossible, to achieve without it. That's one of the reasons I've written so much about it. It's foundational. In fact, I opened my book *Thinking for a Change* with some thoughts about thinking that I'd like to share with you. They will help you understand why I believe thinking is so important:

1. **Everything begins with a thought.**

Life consists of what a man is thinking about all day.

—RALPH WALDO EMERSON

2. **What we think determines who we are. Who we are determines what we do.**

I have always thought the actions of men the best interpreters of their thoughts.

—JOHN LOCKE

3. **Our thoughts determine our destiny. Our destiny determines our legacy.**

You are today where your thoughts have brought you. You will be tomorrow where your thoughts take you.

—JAMES ALLEN

4. **People who go to the top think differently than others.**

Nothing limits achievement like small thinking; nothing expands possibilities like unleashed imagination.

—WILLIAM ARTHUR WARD

5. We *can* change the way we think.

Whatever things are true...noble...just...pure...lovely...
are of good report, if there is any virtue and if there is anything
praiseworthy; think on these things.

—PAUL THE APOSTLE

How to Increase Your Thinking Capacity

Like other high-energy people and most leaders, I have a natural bias for action. And success in achieving goals certainly requires action. But a bias for action has its limits. I discovered a long time ago that if I wanted to increase my overall success capacity, then I needed to increase my thinking capacity.

Here is the process that I use to expand ideas and improve my thinking on a daily basis. If you can learn this process, it will make your thinking more thorough. As your thinking improves, the number of good ideas you have will increase. And as you take action on those ideas, your life will become better. Great lives are created by taking good actions on great ideas.

> If you want to increase your overall success capacity, then you need to increase your thinking capacity.

1. Think the Thought—Value Your Thinking

Most people do not recognize the value of good thinking. They have thoughts, but they let them go and don't do anything with them. However, when you value good thoughts, it makes all of your thinking more valuable. That is the starting point of increasing your thinking capacity.

Because I value good thinking, I am constantly asking myself questions to help me discover and develop ideas, such as:

Where Can I Find an Idea?

Becoming a better thinker means having the right mind-set. Two people can see the same things, go through the same experiences, have the same conversations, yet one walks away with a flurry of great thoughts and the other without a single new idea. To increase your thinking capacity, you need to become an idea digger. That's how I think of myself. I'm *always* looking for ideas and trying to mine them. To me, when two things happen, it's a great day: when I've added value to someone and when I've found a good idea.

> It's a great day when I've added value to someone and I've found a good idea.

How Can I Use It?

A lot of people come across an idea, and recognize that it's a good idea, yet don't do anything with it. They don't follow through. That's a shame, because ideas are like muscles. You use them or lose them.

I remember back when I was leading a church in San Diego, I was mentored for a few years by Charles Blair, who led a church in Denver, Colorado. Charles once talked to me about the importance of first impressions, and he said, "I build this church on good first impressions."

What a great idea, I thought. *How can I use that?* It forced me to think about how the first impression of my church wasn't even *in* the church. It was in the parking lot. So I made sure the parking lot attendants were fantastic. I equipped them with the idea, "You are the first impression for everyone who comes to the church." When you get a good idea, you need to think to yourself, *How can I use it?*

How Can I Maximize the Idea?

There isn't a single idea that starts out as good as it can be. Every idea can be taken to another level and can be applied in a way that maximizes it. Going back to that same experience I had with Charles Blair's advice, we ended up maximizing the idea of the first impression by using it to improve a lot of things in the church. We retrained all of our ushers so that they would make a great impression. We looked at our buildings and the impression

> There isn't a single idea that starts out as good as it can be.

they made on people. We retrained our children's workers. We maximized the idea by helping people in every area of the organization present themselves better and give visitors a positive experience.

Any time you have an idea that can add value to others, you should take note of it and plan to give it more thought. Ask yourself, "Where can I maximize that idea?" If it will help your organization, apply it there. Also pay attention if the idea meets you where you are in your life journey, if it will help you become better in one of your strengths, or if it will help you to grow and get better. When you get one of those ideas, pay attention, and prepare to go to step two.

2. Write Out Your Thought—Clarify Your Thinking

University president and United States senator S. I. Hayakawa believed, "Learning to write is learning to think. You don't know anything clearly unless you can state it in writing." I think there's a lot of truth to that. Writing makes you think things through. It forces you to articulate the thought. And it makes your thoughts visual.

That doesn't make it easy. Nobel Prize–winning novelist Ernest

Hemingway is famous for saying how bad the first draft of anything is. It may take you multiple tries to get something coherent written. I know that was usually true for me when I started my writing career. When I wrote my first book, *Think on These Things*, I threw away ten pages for every one I kept. But trust me: putting your ideas down on paper will be worth the effort.

3. Find a Place to Keep Your Thoughts—Capture Your Thinking

Do you know what people's number one time waster is? It's looking for things that are lost. That's why you need a good system for capturing your ideas. And it's why my first goal when I have a good thought is not to lose it.

As I mentioned in a previous chapter, I've been an avid filer for most of my career. For years I always kept two books in my briefcase: whatever book I was reading, and a notebook to capture my ideas. Today, I still carry a book, but I use my iPhone to capture and review my thoughts.

While I'm at it, I want to also encourage you to find a place to *find* your thoughts. What do I mean by that? You need to condition yourself to think in certain places. Early in my life, I had a thinking rock. As I got older, I wanted a place that was a little more comfortable, so I designated one particular chair in my office as my thinking spot. It doesn't matter where it is—just pick your place, spend time there, and good thoughts will show up.

That reminds me of a story I once heard about Charles Kettering, the founder of Delco. He once bet a friend of his one hundred dollars that he could make him buy a bird. The friend thought the idea was absurd, so he agreed to the bet.

That Christmas, Kettering bought the friend a beautiful, elaborate, and very expensive birdcage and had it delivered to the man's house. It was set up right by the front door so all his guests would see it.

The friend understood Kettering's strategy, but he had no intention of getting a bird for the cage. However, every time that guests visited the man at his home, they would admire the cage and remark about how beautiful it was. And they would always ask, "Where's the bird?"

Finally, the friend got so sick of the question that he gave in and bought a bird. The moral of the story? When you have a designated place for something, whatever it is, there is the sense within you that it needs to be filled. And you'll find yourself doing what it takes to fill it. That holds true for your thinking.

4. Rethink Your Thought—Evaluate Your Thinking

The next step is perhaps the most critical of the thinking process, because this is where you cull the bad thoughts and set the good ones on track to be improved and become great ideas. Have you ever awakened in the middle of the night with an idea? It happens to me all the time. Before smartphones, I used to keep a special pad of paper next to my bed that had a light and pen incorporated into it. When you pulled the pen out of its holder, the little light would come on automatically and shine on the paper. I thought it was fantastic, because I was able to write down my ideas without waking up Margaret. Now I record those ideas in the Notes app on my iPhone.

While I love having a system for capturing thoughts I get in the middle of the night, there's still a problem: looking at what I've written again in the morning. A lot of times, the idea isn't nearly as good as I thought. In the light of day, most of my midnight ideas are not worth pursuing. But that's okay. The only thing worse than not having a way to capture great ideas, and thus missing them, is capturing a bad idea and trying to make it work. If it's not good, let it go.

Most of the time, I have pretty good instincts about whether an idea is any good. The good ones still speak to me after twenty-four hours. The bad ones don't. If you're not certain how to evaluate an idea, ask yourself these questions. They work for me:

- Does the thought still speak to me?
- Will this thought speak to others?
- How, where, and when can I use this thought?
- Who can I help by delivering or implementing the thought?

If you don't have positive answers, the idea's probably not worth taking to the next step of the thinking process.

5. Verbalize the Thought—Express Your Thinking

To get the most out of an idea, you need to not only think it through, but you also need to talk it out. Both are necessary, but the order in which you do it depends on how you're wired. For example, I like to think things through first. Some people may be surprised by that, because I'm known as a communicator. But I've always wanted to think something through completely before presenting it. That got me into trouble when Margaret and I first got married. She wanted us to discuss and solve problems together. I wanted to solve problems and then tell her about it afterward. I had to learn to express what I was thinking earlier.

Early in my leadership career, I also held on to ideas and didn't talk about them until I had solutions all figured out. Like many young leaders, I didn't want to share a problem without offering a solution because I worried that I'd look dumb to the people I was leading. What I didn't realize was that if my solution wasn't any good, I'd look dumb anyway.

I'm still learning about the need to talk through ideas. For two decades, I've worked with Charlie Wetzel on my books. Most often I write outlines for the chapters of a book and give them to Charlie. He does the wordsmithing, adds original stories, and takes the book through the entire editorial process with the publisher.

Charlie is similar to me in that he likes to solve problems on his own. Early in our working relationship, when he came up against a problem while writing a book, he'd work too long on it in isolation. I had to insist that he call me to talk it through, which he now does. Verbalizing the ideas brings them into great clarity quickly for us.

A couple of years ago I discovered another level of value in talking through ideas. It occurred when I was working on my book *Intentional Living*. I wrestled with the idea of that book for two years while trying to land the ideas. And at one point I hit a wall. During that season, I was fortunate to meet Laura Morton, a writer and television producer who has worked with many celebrity clients on their books. I spent hours with her interviewing me. Her questions drew out stories and forced me to articulate ideas that really helped me with the book.

If you want to take your ideas to another level, you need to talk them out. Here's why:

Talking Expresses Your Heart

Writing about an idea gives your thinking intellectual weight. It creates clarity in your thinking. Talking about an idea gives it emotional weight. It connects your thinking to your heart.

Have you ever noticed that you can think about a tragic time from your past pretty rationally, but when you try to tell someone else about it, you get flooded with emotion and get choked up? That's the heart connection that occurs when you express those ideas.

Talking Expands Your Idea

Many times when you try to elaborate on an idea verbally, you expand it. You give it greater life and clarification. Some of that comes from having to express it. Some comes from the nonverbal feedback you receive from listeners when they don't understand what you're saying. Some comes from answering questions people ask you about your idea. All of these things help you improve your idea. They also help you expand your thinking capacity for the future.

Are you wired as a natural talker or a natural thinker? Start with whichever comes naturally to you. But be sure to include both solo thinking time and talking time with others to get the best out of your thinking capacity.

6. Put the Thought on the Table—Share Your Thinking

As I mentioned, early in my career I was reluctant to share unformed thoughts with others because I thought it was the leader's job to solve all the problems. But as I gained leadership experience I made a discovery. I didn't have the capacity to think great thoughts all by myself. This became painfully obvious when I attended an idea exchange of leaders in my field. The older and more experienced leaders were very open, sharing both ideas and problems, and as they put their thoughts on the table, others helped them come up with better ideas.

This process may seem obvious to you, but it was a eureka moment for me. It was at that time that I began sharing my ideas and asking others for help. It transformed my leadership and greatly expanded my thinking capacity. It was like adding one plus one and coming up with three!

It has become rare for me not to bring a thought to the table and share it with members of my team. For example, when I wrote *The*

21 Irrefutable Laws of Leadership in 1997, I took the concept to a small group of good thinkers, and we batted around ideas on what constituted a law of leadership. And once we landed on a list of laws, I got their feedback on the wording for each. We worked on the choice and wording of the laws for five months before I wrote a single word of the book. And without their help, the book would not have been nearly as good or successful.

I want to encourage you to share your thinking with others to take it to another level. To do that, follow these steps:

- **Bring a good thought to the table.** It doesn't have to be a great thought, but it needs to be a good one.

- **Share your desire for others to improve on your thought.** You need to want better thoughts more than you want the credit.

- **Ask everyone to participate.** People should know that they're either at the table or on the menu.

- **Ask questions.** Nothing stimulates improved thinking more than questions.

- **Let the best idea win.** When the best idea wins, you win!

When you bring a good thought to the table with a small group of good thinkers, they will always make your thoughts better. Just make sure you bring good thinkers to the table, and as my friend Linda Kaplan Thaler says, make sure you have one person who can recognize a great idea. Do that, and you'll always walk away with a better idea.

> When you bring a good thought to the table with a small group of good thinkers, they will always make your thoughts better.

7. Practice the Thought—Take Your Thinking for a Walk

Once an idea has been put on the table and improved by a key group of people, it's time to take the idea out and let more people see it. I think of this as being like taking a dog for a walk in the park. People see it, react to it, and make comments.

I do this a lot in my speaking. When I have an idea that I've been working on, I'll take it out and practice it with an audience. I did this when I was thinking about the idea of *failing forward*. People responded so positively to that phrase that it became a book. More recently, I said to an audience, "Everything worthwhile is uphill." There was an audible response from people and I could feel the energy in the room go up two notches.

You learn a lot when you present an idea to people who don't know you or who won't automatically give you the benefit of the doubt. If the only person who ever hears your ideas is your mother, you'll think all of them are good. Present them to strangers and skeptics, and you'll find out where you really stand.

A few years ago, I was working on a concept for a book that I just couldn't land with people no matter how hard I tried or how I contextualized it. The idea was *transformation*. Nobody got it. To be honest, I had a hard time defining it. I just couldn't seem to define it in a way that made sense. Finally that idea turned into *intentional living*. I was able to describe it as taking actions intentionally to add value to others, and that made sense to people. They also understood that if what they did aligned with their purpose, they could achieve significance.

It's always easier to think an idea than to practice it. An idea always sounds better when it hasn't been challenged. But an unchallenged idea is rarely able to live in the real world. That's why you need to take it for a walk and see what happens.

8. Question the Thought—Expand Your Thinking

I explained earlier in this thinking expansion process how we need to evaluate our thoughts by asking if they still speak to us after twenty-four hours have passed. Now at this point, it's important for us to question our thinking again.

After practicing a thought, it's time to ask, "What did I learn from practicing it?" and to judge whether the idea is still viable. We should never be so in love with a thought that we don't question it.

A couple of years ago, one of my organizations partnered with a popular magazine to coproduce a digital resource to help people become more successful. As we developed the idea, both organizations thought it was a million-dollar idea. But it never gained the traction or had the impact we'd hoped for. Perhaps we didn't ask enough questions on the front end. However, after the launch and the disappointing results, I guarantee you that we started asking questions. We wanted to discern why we missed the mark, learn from our mistakes, and change the way we did things in the future. My discovery? The more questions you ask on the front end, the fewer questions you have to ask on the back end.

> The more questions you ask on the front end, the fewer questions you have to ask on the back end.

Why was that so important? It was more than just avoiding a future failure. The process of questioning expands your thinking, your capacity, and your potential. We now know a few things we should do and a half-dozen or more things we shouldn't. And we're better for having gone through the painful process.

9. Embrace the Thought—Own Your Thinking

Something powerful happens when a person moves from *believing* in an idea to *owning* an idea. Believing in an idea can be good, but it's very limiting. When you *believe* in an idea, it's like investing in an endeavor with someone else's money. You give it a try and you hope it works. However, when you *own* an idea, it's like putting your own money into an investment. You do what it takes to make it work. The greater the investment, the more you feel that it *has to work*.

In 2015 when I launched my book *Intentional Living*, I wanted to get it into the hands of people any way I could, because I believed that it could change their lives and transform communities. To do that, my team and I got creative. We hired outside marketing companies. We created Intentional Living programs to help people and included a free book with them. We invested in technology platforms. And we gave thousands of books away. All of that cost a tremendous amount of money and time.

Why did I dedicate so much energy and so many dollars to the effort? I owned it. I wanted to do everything I could to get out the message that intentional actions coupled with the desire to add value to people would make a difference and lead to a life of significance. I believe it down to the bottom of my soul.

I believe in the message of intentional living so strongly that I'm still investing time and money to share it. In 2016 with the help of my organizations, I led an effort in Paraguay to train eighteen thousand people to lead roundtables (small discussion groups) on values and intentional living in their communities. To accomplish that, two hundred John Maxwell Team certified coaches and I went down to Paraguay, paying all our own expenses, and volunteered as trainers of Paraguayans in businesses, government organizations, educational institutions, and communities in and around Asunción.

As I write this, more than seventy thousand people have gone through roundtables in Paraguay to learn about intentional living, and that number is growing every day. I hope to launch similar efforts in other countries in the years to come. But that process would never have happened if my organizations, a group of my coaches, and I hadn't fully embraced the idea and taken ownership of it.

10. Launch the Thought—Implement Your Thinking

When you launch an idea, you need to be clear about what you want people to know and what you want people to do. When I described to the coaches the things we would be doing in Paraguay, I also included the launching of the idea in my description. The people knew what they were supposed to do, and they did it.

The launch is the greatest test of any idea. The implementation demonstrates an idea's real value—or lack of value. When it works, it's powerful, because everyone sees it. That was true in Paraguay. Virtually everyone knew about it. The coaches' efforts were shown on the news and written about in the papers. And people all over the country, from

> **The launch is the greatest test of any idea.**

the president's office, to the chambers of congress, to the neighborhood restaurants, were talking about it. And it also started grabbing the attention of people in other countries.

11. Land the Thought—Make Your Thinking Work

Launching an idea is very rewarding. But the results come with the landing. It's similar to the way gymnastics are scored. I've watched quite a few gymnastics competitions over the years because two of my granddaughters competed, and Ella, Steve and Eli's younger daughter, is particularly talented and was ranked pretty highly. At a meet, the tumbling passes and the aerial vaults of the best gymnasts always got lots of oohs and aahs from the audience, but their twists and turns in the air didn't bring high scores unless the athletes stuck their landings.

The landing always matters. Not too long ago, a group in the military offered to let me skydive with them. I have to say, I was intrigued by the idea. I thought it would be very exhilarating. However, I was more concerned about the landing than I was the jumping. I believed they would keep me safe on the jump. But I have bad knees, and I wasn't sure I could take the impact of the landing, so I had to pass.

By the time you're reading this, we will know whether all our efforts in Paraguay have landed. We'll know if we were able to transform communities and help the country become better. I certainly hope we've added value to them, and they will be in a better place to help one another.

12. Upgrade the Thought—Mature Your Thinking

When a thought lands and makes a positive difference, the temptation is to celebrate and move on. I'm all for celebrating. Wins can be hard to come by, and when we do experience a win, we should thank the people who helped to make it happen and give them the credit they deserve. But if we do that without looking for a way to upgrade the thought, we've missed a great opportunity.

Growth requires your thoughts to be continually upgraded. I'm always trying to get better. The better I get, the more I have to give. My desire is that what I am teaching today will be better tomorrow.

As I mentioned, people in other parts of South and Central America are watching what's happening in Paraguay. And they're sending me invitations to come to their countries to train people to promote values and intentional living. I hope to accept many of those invitations. And when I do, I hope we will have already upgraded the ideas we used in Paraguay, and they will make the process even better.

If you want to increase your potential, maximize your capacity, and be successful, develop your thinking. High thinking capacity and the ability to sustain your thinking will give you a higher return than being smart or working hard. The difference between average thinkers and good thinkers is like the difference between ice cubes and icebergs. Ice cubes are small and short-lived. Icebergs are huge, and there is much more to them than meets the eye. Their capacity is enormous.

Thinking Capacity Questions

1. Do you have a system for capturing your ideas? If yes, how well is it working for you? If not, what could you do to begin recording your ideas so you don't lose them?

2. Who are the people you bring to the table to improve your ideas? How well are they helping you? What can you change to get them to help you more?

3. Do you have a greater bias toward action or toward thinking? What would happen if you were able to harness both?

6

People Capacity—Your Ability to Build Relationships

When I turned forty in 1987, I felt that I was reaching a kind of halftime, and I decided to take an inventory of my life. I have to admit, I wasn't satisfied with what I discovered. Although I had set my priorities, worked hard, and stayed focused on achieving results, I wasn't making the impact I had hoped for. My conclusion? My focus was too much on myself and reaching my potential, and not enough on connecting and working with others.

That experience helped me realize that reaching my capacity was not just about me doing my very best. It was about my relationship with others, how we could work together, and how our gifts could complete and complement one another. A decade later, the memory of this experience prompted me to write Law of the Inner Circle in *The 21 Irrefutable Laws of Leadership*, which is, "A leader's potential is determined by those closest to him."

For the last thirty years I have placed my relationships with key people at the top of my priority list. That changed my focus from *me* to *we*. The result? Beautiful, productive, long-term relationships that have greatly improved my life—and my capacity.

I'm Grateful for the People in My Life

The importance of these relationships in my life was highlighted for me in 2015 when my literary agents, Sealy and Matt Yates of Yates and Yates, took me out to a special dinner in Las Vegas to celebrate twenty-five years of an incredible working relationship. We laughed as we told stories about each other and the funny things that had happened over those years. We cried as we shared how our relationship had positively shaped all of our lives. We expressed our love for each other, promising to make the next twenty-five years even better than the first. We made toasts, presented gifts, gave hugs, and expressed what it meant to do life and work together.

That evening my heart was full, and I reflected on the many significant relationships in my life. I thought of Margaret, to whom I have been married for forty-eight years. Linda Eggers, my assistant, who has served me beautifully for thirty years. Charlie Wetzel, my writing companion, who has helped me write more than ninety books during the last twenty-three years. David Hoyt, my speaking agent, who joined me right out of college and has worked with me for nineteen years. Mark Cole, the CEO of all my companies, who started in the stockroom seventeen years ago and has now become irreplaceable.

These people are the reason I am enjoying so many blessings in my life. And thinking about this reminded me that the most important decision in my business life was to develop great long-term relationships with people who could help me make a difference. Relational capacity is key to personal and professional success.

How to Increase Your People Capacity

In 2004 I wrote a book called *Winning with People* out of the conviction that people can usually trace their successes and failures to the relationships in their lives. We are defined by our relationships.

> People can usually trace their successes and failures to the relationships in their lives.

Maybe up until now your relationships haven't been as positive, rewarding, and productive as you'd like them to be. That's okay, because you can learn how to build better relationships and increase your relational capacity.

I've spent some time thinking about the things I've done that have enabled me to establish and enjoy long-term relationships with others, and these seven steps can help you to develop stronger relationships with others.

1. Value People Every Day

I have a passion for adding value to people because I truly value people. The seed for valuing people was planted into my life by my father, Melvin. When I graduated from college, I asked him to give me advice as I began my career. He said, "John, every day, intentionally value people, believe in people, and unconditionally love them." Those words have been the North Star that has guided me for more than fifty years.

You cannot increase your people capacity unless you value people and care about them. If you don't like people, don't respect them, and don't believe they have value, it stands as a barrier to your success with them. You can't secretly look down on others and build them up at the same time. However, if you value people, it shows through. And it makes the development of positive relationships possible.

2. Make Yourself More Valuable in Your Relationships

What's the fastest way to make a relationship better? Make yourself better so that you have more to give. That requires an abundance mind-set. That's the belief that there's more than enough for everyone and people always have the potential to find or create more. Because I believe that, I know that the more I give, the more I will have to give. I started to adopt that attitude years ago when I heard Zig Ziglar say, "If you will help others get what they want, they will help you get everything you need in life."

Try improving yourself and your situation with the purpose of giving to others, and see what happens. As you give, I guarantee that your ability to give more will increase. It will motivate you to give of your thoughts, time, assets, relationships, influence, and giftedness.

Out of this abundance mind-set, I work at adding value to people every day. And I ask a lot of questions to discover how I can better add value to others. That's why I'm a feedback fanatic. There is no better way to show people you value them than by asking for their opinion. I do this constantly, because I care about what people think and because knowing what's important to them helps me to help them. For example, before every speaking engagement, I always ask the host what I can say or do to help them and add value to their organization. Communicating is about adding value to people in the audience, not about adding value to yourself.

> There is no better way to show people you value them than by asking for their opinion.

The more you know about people and the more you improve yourself, the more you can make a difference in the lives of others. When I celebrated last year with Sealy and Matt Yates, one of the things they thanked me for was sending other authors to them. And when Church of the Highlands pastor Chris Hodges, a very close friend, played golf with me not long ago, I asked him what he was most passionate about these days. His face lit up as he talked about the college he had founded. "That has my heart. We're training kids to be leaders and make a difference in this world."

I love Chris. He has been a great friend who has added value to me and EQUIP, my nonprofit organization. I try to do whatever I can to add value to him, so I offered to give him a day in which I would speak at an event in Birmingham, so that he could raise funds for the college and add value to his community. And that's what we did. After much planning and groundwork, I spoke for Chris, and he was able to raise over $700,000 for the college. It was so rewarding to do something of value for someone I love.

A friend once told me long ago, "John, you need to improve yourself. You're not good enough to stay the same." He was right. I wanted to get better so that I could be good. I still do. And that should be your goal, too. Get better so that you can help the people around you to get better. Whenever you make yourself more valuable, you can give more value to others, and increase your relational capacity.

> A friend once told me long ago, "John, you need to improve yourself. You're not good enough to stay the same."

3. Put Yourself in Their World

Several years ago while traveling to speak at a convention, I came across this quote by author and professor Leo Buscaglia: "Too often we underestimate the power of a touch, a smile, a kind word, a listening ear, an honest compliment, or the smallest act of caring, all of which have the potential to turn a life around." Later that day I went onstage and spoke to a very large audience and had a very successful session. I left the stage to a standing ovation. I was feeling pretty good about myself, but then the Buscaglia quote came to mind and it made me realize that I had been thinking entirely about myself. My focus was entirely wrong.

As I spoke that day, I had invited people to come to me in my world. I realized that instead, I needed go to them and put myself in their world. I was scheduled to sign books for people later that same day, so I decided that would give me the opportunity I sought. I would make that time all about the people I met. I ended up spending two hours signing books, personalizing them by writing in people's names, smiling and shaking their hands, talking to them, and thanking them for coming. I watched each person's face as I did my best to make him or her feel appreciated and important.

That evening as I reviewed my day, I wondered, if I had the opportunity to ask those people what specific part of that day together they had enjoyed the most, what would they say? I felt certain they would choose the time when I signed books and valued them as individuals. That's one of the reasons I've made signing books a priority whenever I speak. I understand the truth of Leo Buscaglia's words, "Too often we underestimate the power of a touch."

It's also why, whenever possible, I try to walk around and connect with people in the auditorium before I'm scheduled to speak. When I travel internationally, the hosts usually try to separate me from the crowd. But I always want to go into their world and shake hands if I can. I make it my goal to walk slowly through the crowd. People are more receptive to my message when I've come to them first.

Are you familiar with the phrase "It's lonely at the top"? I don't like it. It's the sign of disconnection. I tell leaders that if they're lonely at the top, it means no one is following them. They need to get off their mountain or out of their ivory tower, go to where their people are, and spend time with them. People don't care how much you know until they know how much you care.

Make yourself available to the people in your life. And be alert to ways you can go to them when they need it. Sometimes you don't even need to say a word. Just be there. Just let others know what they mean to you. A couple of years ago, a friend of mine named Kristen suddenly lost her son. She was understandably devastated. It happened when a group of us were gathered together for an event. Mark Cole, another friend named Dianna, and I went to Kristen's hotel room. All I could do was put my arm around her. She needed the touch of a friend. We didn't say anything to her for a long time. We just wanted to be with her and let her know we cared. That's something any of us could do for a friend.

4. Focus Your Relationships on Benefiting Others, Not Yourself

As I write this book I am planning my seventieth birthday. I want to do something special with all of the people who are special to me, so I'm asking those people what they would like to do with me to help me celebrate. They get to pick the month and the activity, and then we'll do it together. I want to fill this milestone birthday year with fun things each month that my friends love. I did the same thing the year I turned sixty. Almost a decade later, my friends still talk about what we did together during their month.

To build great relationships, you need to want more *for* people than you want *from* people. The people who want more for others and give more than they take are pluses. The ones who want and take more than they give are minuses. That's simple relational math. I determined that I wanted to be a plus with people. With those closest to me, I want to be a plus *plus*. My desire is to make five relational deposits for every relational withdrawal I make from the relationship. I don't always succeed, but it is my goal.

It has been my joy for the last twelve years to serve as a teaching pastor at Christ Fellowship in West Palm Beach, Florida. Tom

Mullins, the founding pastor, and his son Todd, who is now the lead pastor, are great friends of mine. We have traveled the world together, shared great experiences, and made many memories. I preach for them on holidays and "off" Sundays to help them. However, I never take for granted the privilege they've given me of being on their staff and doing a few sermons a year. I never want to take advantage of them. In fact, I believe I should remain on the staff only if I am continuing to add value to them and the congregation. So each year I sit down with Tom and Todd and offer to resign my role as a teaching pastor. I make it clear that I don't believe that our relationship alone is a good enough reason for me to be on their staff. In fact, I usually ask if it's time for them get someone younger and more relevant for the congregation.

So far each year they have asked me to stay on the team, but they know that the next year we will meet again and discuss the situation. And one of these days, they will accept my resignation because it will benefit them. And if anything, it will enhance the relationship we have.

I never want to take any relationship for granted. I never want to assume that a relationship gives me privileges that are not mine. Assumption is a killer in relationships. It needs to be replaced with *awareness*. If you want to increase your relational capacity, you should be continually aware that relationships never stay the same. And they never stay alive on their own. They need cultivation. And you have to keep being intentional about adding value to continue being a plus in another person's life.

5. Be a Consistent Friend in Your Relationships

I believe the ability to be a good friend is something that is often undervalued and overlooked today. Eric Greitens, in his book *Resilience: Hard-Won Wisdom for Living a Better Life*, recalls the words of Greek philosopher Aristotle to describe what it means to be a good friend. Greitens writes,

> Aristotle points out that your deep and true friends—sometimes he calls them your "perfect" friends—can also be pleasant and useful, but they don't have to constantly work at it. And neither do you. You aren't fearful that your true friend will lose interest. With your closest friends, it's often enough to simply be together.
>
> Aristotle argues that such friendships are an end in themselves. It's not that we pursue them because they will help us to live an excellent life; we make time to create such friendships because they are *part* of an excellent life. In fact, Aristotle suggests—and I also believe—that we can't live our best lives or become our best selves without these kinds of friendships. The best friends support us, challenge us, inspire us. And we can do the same for them.[1]

What is the key to relationships like the ones Greitens describes? They are built upon consistency. Relationships that are volatile and continually up and down are not easy. They provide no relational "rest." There is nothing pleasant about being in relationships that are continually high maintenance. You can't be good friends with people when you have to walk on eggshells or where any conversation could lead to the end of the relationship.

To be the kind of friend Aristotle described, we must be dependable and consistent. We must be trustworthy. Our friends must know that they can depend us.

When I speak to the people who come to the conference each year to become certified as John Maxwell Team speakers and coaches, I often tell them, "Hi, my name is John, and I'm your friend." I want them to feel my friendship from the very beginning, and I want them to know they can depend on me.

I've worked very hard to become consistent and dependable with the people who rely on me, and I want to share a few tips that have helped me over the years:

I Believe the Best About People

Poet Rudyard Kipling is credited with saying, "I always prefer to believe the best of everybody—it saves so much trouble." He was right. I try to see people as they could be, not necessarily as they are. When you believe the best in people, you don't feel the need to correct them or try to fix them. I often smile when I see people trying to fix others. I think, *Don't they realize that they're not perfect, either?* I only have enough time to try to fix myself—that's a full-time job!

> "I always prefer to believe the best of everybody—it saves so much trouble."
> —*Rudyard Kipling*

Believing the best in others is always the right thing to do, even if it means you may not always be right. My high belief in people may be way off sometimes, but lacking belief in others is not going to help them or our relationship. People are more apt to change because another person believes in them than when people *don't* believe in them.

I Don't Allow Other People's Behavior to Control Me

Too often people allow the actions of others to impact their own attitudes and emotions. They let others' inconsistency make them inconsistent. But you need to understand that when that happens, you've allowed it. As humans we have the capacity to create and control our own attitudes and emotions. We need to make that choice for ourselves every day. Otherwise, people will control us.

Let me share with you what I do that helps me not to get sucked in by the behavior of difficult people. I associate two numbers with everyone I meet. The first is my *belief* number for them. I refer to this as putting a ten on people's heads. I see everyone as a potential 10 (on a scale of 1 to 10). I choose to do that so that I'll treat every person well. I also know that most people rise to the level of our expectations for them, so by seeing everyone as a 10, I'm making room for every person to rise to that level.

The second number I associate with people is based on my personal experience and interaction with them. I call this my *experience* number with them. While I choose in advance to make the belief number a 10, the experience number is derived from their behavior. In my interaction, if the person treats others well, keeps his word, adds value with people, has high competence, and so on, the number will be high. If the person is self-centered, dysfunctional, abusive, and negative, then the number will be low. As I gain more experience with the person, the number continually changes. If in my experience the interactions are negative and the person's number is low, I choose to have less interaction with that person. That's how I keep others from controlling me.

I Place High Value on Relationships Even in Difficult Situations

Dealing with people is sometimes difficult. As a leader, I have occasionally had to fire an individual. Letting someone go may be the right thing to do for the organization, but we should also make sure to do the right thing for the person relationally. I always ask for an exit interview to learn from the difficult experience we had, and to let the person know that I'm willing to always be a friend.

If possible, I seek to continue the relationship. Sometimes the person doesn't want that. That's okay. I cannot determine what they are going to do. I can only determine what I am going to do, and what I will do is remain a friend to them.

I Unconditionally Love People

Unconditional love is the greatest gift we can give another person. It allows someone to feel secure, be vulnerable, sense their worth, and discover who they really are. How do I know that? My mother unconditionally loved me! That was what her love did for me. And that's what I want to do for other people.

I once heard President George W. Bush say to his daughter, "I love you, and there's nothing you can do to keep me from loving you, so stop trying." I laughed and then reflected that unconditional love can be tested, but it always passes the test.

I believe that all people long to have a consistent friend who loves them, believes in them, and is continually there for them no matter the circumstances. If you're willing to be that kind of person for others, not only will it expand your people capacity, it will also give you a more satisfying life.

You may also be thinking, *I can't do this with everyone, because some people are just difficult.* That's true—for all of us. Debbie Ellis calls such people porcupines in her book *How to Hug a Porcupine*. When I was a pastor, we called such people EGRs—extra grace required. But we can all use extra grace from time to time. Maybe those who face the greatest challenges are the ones who have difficult people in their families. A friend once told me, "My family is a circus, and every day there is a different clown." Family life is ground zero in learning how to deal with difficult people.

The advice of cartoonist Michael Leunig? "Love one another and you will be happy. It's as simple and as difficult as that." It *is* both difficult and simple. In the end, our goal should be to treat others better than they treat us, to add value to them in a greater capacity than maybe they expect. I love the way Brian Bethune described Nelson Mandela. The South African statesman was a fantastic example of someone with high relational capacity. Bethune said of Mandela, "He was greater than his enemies deserved; greater than the leaders of foot-dragging Western countries who later rushed to eulogize him; greater than his family, squabbling about his legacy. 'Deep down in every human heart,' he wrote..., 'there is mercy and generosity.' "[2] I don't see that in myself every day. But I'm striving to cultivate it.

6. Create Great Memories for People

It has been my observation that most people do not maximize the experiences they have in life. To do so, two things are essential: intentionality on the front end of the experience and reflection on the back end. So anytime you can help another person to do those things, it becomes special for them, and it often creates a positive memory for them.

As I write this, Margaret and I are on a skiing vacation with our children and grandchildren—okay, they're skiing, while I'm enjoying the view from the hotel. This is our second year at this ski resort. Last night during dinner, I asked two questions. One prompted reflection: "What was your favorite memory from last year?" The answers to that question brought warmth, laughter, and connectedness as each family member shared. The second question was designed to encourage intentionality: "What one thing are you going to do this year that you didn't do last year?" Again, the responses were beautiful, yet different. We listened to one another describe experiencing, trying, and learning new things. It was fun to hear how we all wanted to get out of our comfort zones. When dinner was over, everyone was happy, and I guarantee you, they will remember that meal. Why? Because by asking those questions, I was creating a memory for my family through intention and reflection. And I try to create memories for many people, not just my family.

I recently read about a man who kept a Thanksgiving journal for his wife. What a great idea. So starting that day, I kept a Thanksgiving journal for Margaret. I paid attention to the things my wife was doing that touched my heart. I also recorded the attributes, characteristics, and qualities I appreciated in her, writing them down secretly every day. By the end of that year, I'd filled an entire journal.

When the following Thanksgiving rolled around, I surprised her by giving her the journal. It made her cry, and she told me it was the best gift she'd ever received. What was most interesting is that the whole process affected me even more than it did her. Creating the journal prompted me to look for all the positive things I could find in my wife, which directed my focus away from anything negative. It was a great win for both of us.

This has been a common theme in my life. The memories I intentionally create with others often bless me more than the people I create them for. Whenever I am with people, I am continually asking myself, "What can I do or say that will make this experience memorable for them?" It may be as simple as saying, "I remember when you said this to me," or "I'll never forget when we did this together." What am I doing when I say these things? I'm showing people how much value I place on them by telling them that what they say and do is worth remembering.

Last year I was invited to have dinner at the home of golfer Jack Nicklaus and his wife Barbara to celebrate New Year's Eve. I was the newbie in the crowd and soon learned that for thirty years the same group of friends had gathered on New Year's Eve at the Nicklauses' home. Close to midnight, I noticed that everyone was gathering out on the patio, so I followed them out. We then watched Jack and Barbara ring a bell on that patio as the clock struck midnight. One by one, each person rang the bell to usher in the New Year and then received a hug from Barbara and Jack, who stood nearby. What struck me as wonderful was that for thirty years, ringing that bell and receiving a hug from the hosts was a tradition that created a great memory, one that they all looked forward to each year. Jack and Barbara made New Year's Eve special to all their friends.

Most of us have traditions and memories on special days, but I want to challenge you to make memories out of everyday experiences. How can you do that? Every time you are with people, ask yourself these questions:

- What can I say that will affirm those with me?
- What question can I ask that they will find interesting to discuss?
- What can we do that will be different and fun?
- What do I know that they would want to know?
- Do I have a secret of my own that I can tell them?

All of these can lead to great memories, and I have to tell you that the last one about a secret really works. Sharing something private is an act of inclusion; it invites others into your life, and it lets people know that you value them. Try it. Say, "Can I share something with you that I have never shared with anyone else?" Bam! You've got their attention. The secret doesn't have to be big. And of course, it must be something you have permission to tell. The appeal to the people you're with is in the fact that you told them first.

Many little things done repeatedly with high intention are better than big things done only occasionally. You can make big or small moments special for others, but you have to be intentional about it.

7. Move toward the Relationships You Desire in Your Life

The final way I suggest that you increase your people capacity is to put yourself in the position to meet and spend time with the right people. Use the Power of Proximity Principle, which is, "Get next to ten people who can take you to the next level."

> Use the Power of Proximity Principle: "Get next to ten people who can take you to the next level."

I started doing this at age twenty-four. As a young pastor I wanted to build a successful church. As I mentioned earlier, one of the books that greatly influenced me was *The Ten Largest Sunday Schools and What Makes Them Grow* by Elmer Towns. As soon as I read the book, I knew I wanted to meet the leaders of the ten large churches he wrote about. But how could I do that? I needed to meet Dr. Towns. I figured that since he wrote the book, he must know those ten leaders.

It took some searching, but I obtained Dr. Towns's speaking schedule and decided to attend a conference where he would be speaking in Waterloo, Iowa. At the conference I met him and shared my desire to connect with those ten leaders. With his help, I got appointments with two of them. After I met those two, they helped me get appointments with the other eight. Those meetings helped me as a young leader and set me on a path for success.

Ever since then, I have practiced the Power of Proximity. I always want to spend time with people who know more than I do, and whenever I'm with someone I respect and have gotten to know, I ask them, "Who do you know that I should know?" That question has given me a greater return in life than any other. The greatest way to know who you should know is to ask someone who knows you.

I want to encourage you to be intentional and show initiative by moving toward the relationships you desire in life. If you wait for the right people to meet you, you won't meet the right people. I didn't wait for all the stars to align before I took action, and neither should you. Find one star and start moving toward it.

What kind of person should you try to connect with? I'll give you some advice I learned one evening at dinner with Margaret and our friends Paul and Vicky Saunders. That evening we were discussing the question "What's the best advice you ever received?" At one point in the conversation, Paul said, "I'm always asking advice from people who are ten years older than me, and the question I ask is 'What have you learned about yourself and life that I need to know?'" That stoked my curiosity, and I asked him to explain. What he then shared was filled with great common sense.

He explained that he targeted people far enough ahead of him that they had knowledge and experience he didn't possess, but close enough to his age that they still related to what was important to him. "If I go beyond the ten-year gap," he said, "I find that they forget what I need to know or feel it is not important. I want them to be close enough to me to know where I am in life, but far enough ahead of me to have experienced what I probably will experience over the next few years." You could use that as your rule of thumb as you begin to seek out people to help you learn and grow.

Why is it so important for you to move toward the relationships that you need in your life? Because you need "who luck" to reach your relational capacity. That's a concept I learned from Jim Collins, the author of *Good to Great*. He shared with me that the most important luck we can have in life is who luck. He explained, "Who you meet in life and develop relationships with will greatly determine your success in life."

I know I've found that to be true. Without Harvey I would have never met Lou. Without Scott I would have never partnered with

Paul. Without Joy I would have never enjoyed a creative conversation with Pat. Without Dave, I would have never heard Linda or started creating with her. Without Dan, I would have never connected and collaborated with Kevin.

Who do you know that knows someone you should know? You are only one person away from the who luck that you need in your life. Don't allow yourself to say, "I will never be successful because I haven't met the right person." Instead say, "Success is within my control, and I will look for other people who can add to it."

People capacity really does make a huge difference in a person's life. And your people capacity will go to a new level once you realize how much you need the right people in your life. Philanthropist Andrew Carnegie declared, "It marks a big step in your development when you come to realize that other people can help you do a better job than you could do alone." You receive the help of those people when you're willing to say, "I need you." In my early days I might say, "I want you," but not "I need you," because I still thought I could do things on my own if I had to. But after a while, I discovered that I couldn't be successful alone, and had to have the help of others. Then I was willing to say, "I need you." And I learned that people really only desire to help someone who can't make it without them.

I know that this can be challenging for some people. You may be someone who isn't naturally good with people. You may be thinking, *I'm not a people person.* If that's true, then this capacity category may not be a natural strength. But you can still become better and increase your capacity. One of the most effective ways to do this is to ask people with strong relational skills to help you. Let them complement and complete you. Remember, you can draw people to you by saying to them, "I need you."

My son Joel is brilliant. Not just smart—brilliant. Ask him anything and he can give you an answer. And he is highly gifted in the area of technology. He has become a successful young businessman, and I'm very proud of him. However, he is not a natural people person. Although he has worked hard to improve this area, he has also worked hard at bringing people around him who complement and complete him. You can do the same.

The more you value people, put yourself into their world, seek to add value to them, and be their friend, the better your life will be. Not only that, but doing these things will increase your people capacity, improve your potential, and improve your life. Just remember, helping people is always worth the effort.

People Capacity Questions

1. When you interact with people, where is your focus? Are you usually thinking about how you can help them, or how they can help you? What must you do to make benefiting others the focus of your relationships?

2. Which of the people in your life would describe you as a consistent friend? Which would you not? What must you change to become a consistently positive friend to everyone?

3. What relationship do you desire to move toward to improve your life and capacity? What is the first step you must take to facilitate the connection?

7

Creative Capacity—Your Ability to See Options and Find Answers

In 1965, I was a freshman in college. One day in my Psychology 101 class, we were tested for creativity, and when I got back the results, I was shocked to learn that I had tested at the bottom of my class.

I was devastated.

I've taken a lot of tests in my life. I have three college degrees. But of all the tests I've taken, this low score was my greatest discouragement. I knew I was going to be communicating to people in my career, and the idea of being a boring speaker was unthinkable to me. What do you do to become creative when you're not a creative person?

Walking away from that class, I had two thoughts. First, I would never reach my capacity unless I increased my creativity. And second, I *would* find a way to become creative, no matter what it took.

Fast-forward fifty-plus years. Today, many people tell me that they consider me to be pretty creative. My team often comes to me to discuss creative options and find creative solutions. And I'm known for my creativity when communicating. All of these things are evidence that I've made great improvement in this area. And so can you.

Developing your creative capacity can greatly improve your life. People who have creative confidence make better choices. They set off more easily in new directions. They are better able to find solutions to seemingly intractable problems. They continually see new possibilities and effectively collaborate with others to improve the situations around them. A person who develops creative ability discovers newfound courage to approach big challenges.

Keys to Increasing Creative Capacity

Is it true that some people are born highly creative? Of course. There are the rare few who breathe to create and are gifted to change the world in that regard. In fact, some argue that all of us are born creative, but most of us lose that creativity as we grow up. Novelist Madeleine L'Engle said, "All children are artists, and it is an indictment of our culture that so many of them lose their creativity, their unfettered imaginations, as they grow older."

You can rekindle the creativity that's already in you, plus cultivate new pathways of creativity. If I did it, so can you.

I want to walk you through the eight keys to increasing creative capacity that I've used to go from bottom of the class to top of my game. Embrace each of them, and you will immediately see an increase in your ability to see options, solve problems, and find answers.

1. I Believe There Is *Always* an Answer

The words *reactive* and *creative* are made up of exactly the same letters. The only difference between the two is where we place the *c*. The first decision I made on my journey toward greater creativity was to change my *c*—that is, how I see challenges. I determined to believe that there is *always* an answer, not matter what the question or situation was. It meant practicing possibilities. It meant changing the question from "Is there an answer?" to "What is the answer?"

That change in mind-set has brought me criticism from some people because they see it as stubborn. But that attitude has served me well. And I've had it confirmed in me when I've heard people like Amazon founder Jeff Bezos say, "I'm a genetic optimist. I've been told, 'Jeff, you're fooling yourself; the problem is unsolvable.' But I don't think so. It just takes a lot of time, patience and experimentation."[1] Creativity is changing the question from "Is there an answer?" to "What is the answer?"

> Creativity is changing the question from "Is there an answer?" to "What is the answer?"

Why are creative people like Bezos willing to give time, patience, and experimentation to "unsolvable" problems? Because creativity always takes time, patience, and experimentation. You just have to enter into the process believing there is an answer.

Holding this belief has led to some fantastic experiences and given me some great stories. For example, one year Margaret, my brother Larry, his wife, Anita, and I went on a cruise, and one of the stops was in Melbourne, Australia. We hired a van with a guide and were on a city tour when we passed Rod Laver Stadium, and our guide said the semifinals of the Australian Open were being held that day between Roger Federer and Andy Murray.

"Stop the van," I said. "I want to get off. I think I want to go watch that."

I had gone to the U.S. Open up in New York City, and I'd always thought it would be fun to go to Wimbledon, the French Open, and the Australian Open—the rest of the major four tennis tournaments. And I knew the boat didn't leave port until eleven o'clock that night.

"Do you have tickets?" the guide asked.

"No, I don't have tickets."

"You won't be able to get in, because it's sold out," she said. "And most tickets are held in families for generations here, and they're just passed down. It's not possible for you to get a ticket."

"That's okay," I said. "Just let me out here."

"You want us to wait so that you can continue the tour after you find out they're all sold out?" she asked.

"No, you go on ahead without me."

"Text us when you get in," Larry said to me before the van pulled away from the curb.

I walked up to the ticket window and said, "I'd like to buy a ticket for the semifinals." When they explained that there were no tickets available, I pointed inside the fence where I saw literally thousands of people mingling around and asked, "You mean all of those people have tickets to get into the match?"

"No, most of them don't have tickets to the match. They paid thirty dollars to get on the grounds. They'll watch it on the big screens."

I paid the thirty dollars to get inside. It was the first step in solving the "unsolvable" problem.

I found another ticket window inside the grounds, and tried again. Again I was told there were no tickets for the match for sale. "But if you go over to that other window, they may have some return tickets if somebody has turned theirs in."

I went over to that window and said, "I would like to buy a ticket that somebody isn't going to use this evening."

"I'm so sorry, but that is not going to be possible," the man said.

"Don't you have any?" I asked.

"Yes, I do. Right now I have twelve," he replied. "But you see that line of about two hundred people?" he said, pointing. "They're waiting for them. And at most, there will be about twenty tickets available. People just don't return them."

I walked clear to the back of that line, but I thought, *There's no chance here.* So I started exploring my options. First, I walked up to the front of the line to see if I could make friends with somebody there who might be willing to help me. I was going around talking to people and kind of feeling them out, but it didn't look good until I talked to the fifth or sixth person. After talking for a while I said, "Boy, I really would love a ticket. If you get tickets and get one for me, I'll give you three times the price. I just want to get in," and the person said, "Okay, I'll do that for you."

I was feeling a bit better, but I wanted to have a backup plan. I just wanted to make sure that I got in. So I went to an usher at one of the gates and asked, "When the match starts, will there be any people who don't show up in your section?"

"That's possible," he said.

"If someone doesn't show, would you let me buy that seat?"

"Well, first of all, I would have to wait until the first set was over, because sometimes people come late."

"That would be fine."

"You hang around here, and let's see what happens after the first set," he said.

I had my second option in place. I figured that I might not get in for the whole match, but I could get in for part of it. I continued looking around for other possibilities. I talked to a lot of people, but I kept hearing the same thing: "You can't get in if you don't have a ticket." I must have heard that fifty times.

So I started looking around for a scalper, but I quickly found out that it was against the law there to sell tickets for a profit. Still I didn't give up. Remember, I believe there's *always* an answer.

It was getting close to time for the semifinals to begin, and I had been at it for more than two hours. At that point I was beginning to worry that I might not get in. But suddenly, while I was still looking around trying to solve the problem, a woman singled me out. She must have passed fifty other people as she walked straight up to me and said, "I have to leave. There's an emergency. Would you like to buy my ticket?"

"I would love to buy your ticket," I answered.

I saw the face value and asked if I could pay her more. She said, "I don't want you to pay me more. I just want you to buy my ticket, and I'll be happy." We were both happy.

As I walked into the stadium, I wondered where the seat would be. The ticket wasn't all that expensive, so I thought I'd be somewhere up in a top section. But when I went through the gate, they directed me downward, and I kept going down. I ended up only twelve rows above the court. Wow.

I'd been there only a little while when someone tapped me on the shoulder. It turned out to be my friend Nabi Saleh, chairman and CEO of Gloria Jean's Coffee, based in Australia.

"John, how in the world did you get this seat? This is where the season ticket holders sit!" he said. It turned out that Nabi's family had had season tickets for over forty years. He laughed as I told him the story.

I can tell you, I had the time of my life. And I don't know if it was more fun actually watching the Australian Open, or just knowing that I had used my creativity and defied all the odds to get in.

As you read this story, you may be thinking, *I haven't been to Australia, and I don't have extra money to buy sports tickets at the spur of the moment.* My answer is that creativity is a mind-set. You have to believe that answers and solutions are out there if you're willing to keep fighting to find them. If I had listened to the tour guide, I never would have gotten out of the van. If I hadn't gotten out of the van, I never would have found out there was a thirty-dollar ticket that would get me

> Creativity is a mind-set. You have to believe that answers and solutions are out there if you're willing to keep fighting to find them.

onto the grounds. If I hadn't bought the thirty-dollar ticket, I never would have been able to talk to anyone in a position to get me a ticket, and I never would have gotten the ticket that eventually got me in to see the match. Each door you open leads to another door. *One* of those doors will eventually lead to an answer.

2. I Believe There Is *More than One* Answer

My favorite word is *options*. However, that has not always been true. In my younger years I was always quick to give people what I thought was *the* answer to any question they asked. I was confident, opinionated, and certain about everything. Ask me about raising children, and I would give you the answer. Ask me about how to grow a church, and I'd tell my way, which I was certain was the right way. Ask me which was the best NFL team, best leadership book, best place to live, best way to do anything, and I could give you my one right answer.

Then I had children of my own and discovered that I had few answers. And I met church leaders more successful than I was, who were succeeding in a different way. And of course my pick often didn't make it to the Super Bowl. And on and on it went. Slowly, with exposure to new ideas, self-evaluation, and hard-won maturity, I began to realize that for almost everything in life, there is more than just one answer.

Today as I near seventy, I have fewer certainties than I did at thirty. And I'm very comfortable with that. In my younger years, my approach would be to dig deep to fight for the one "right" answer. Today I think broadly and search for as many possible answers as I can find. Only when I develop a long list of options do I line them up and ask, "What is the *best* option?" I take great comfort in finding several effective ways to get things accomplished and seek to discover as many options as possible.

If you're a leader, you may want to adopt a practice that I've used with my staff. Whenever people on my team come to me with a problem, I ask them to prepare at least three solutions to that problem. I do that to help them to become more creative, more open-minded and willing to consider different ideas and opinions. If they can become flexible and demonstrate the ability to adapt to fluctuating situations, they will be more effective and productive. I know from my own experience that I became more creative when I began to believe there was always an answer. That creativity multiplied dramatically when I discovered that there are many answers.

3. I Believe That Everything and Everyone Can Get Better

Creative people, whether they are artists, inventors, businesspeople, or teachers, believe there are always better ways to do things. And they search for them. Monte Haymon, former president and CEO of Packaging Corporation of America, advised,

> Don't cap your expectations! What you define as impossible today is impossible only in the context of present paradigms. But maybe we should let William Wordsworth have the last word on this subject of the untapped promise that lies within us all. Speaking of his fellow humans, he said simply, "We are greater than we know." It's true for us as individuals, as institutions, and as a society. We can only guess at our true potential. And we can only achieve it if we get past the paradigms and unleash our imaginations.

> **"Don't cap your expectations!"**
> —*Monte Haymon*

At my age, I have to deal with both reality and possibility. The reality: I am getting older and can't do everything I once did. The possibility: I am getting better, including in the area of creativity. Will that always be true? Or will there be a day when I wake up and have no more creative ideas? I hope not, because as a writer and speaker, I need to remain creative. The good news is that while in my late sixties, I wrote my first children's book, grew companies that are adding value to others every day, and discovered a way to transfer values by teaching them via roundtables, which may actually lead to the transformation of nations. That gives me confidence, and I no longer ask myself if I'll ever run out of creativity. Instead, I ask, "Will I have enough time in my life to respond creatively to all the opportunities before me?"

When you believe that everyone and everything can get better, it gives you confidence that you can help people and make a difference. And it inspires you to keep looking for ways to solve problems and pursue opportunities.

4. I Understand That Questions Help Me to Be More Creative

Questions always spur creativity. Why? Because questions cause you to explore, to seek out. The phrase "what if" is one of my favorites, because it's the start of a question that will lead to sometimes breathtakingly creative answers.

A few years ago I wrote a book called *Good Leaders Ask Great Questions*. In it, I describe some of the questions I ask myself as a leader, and some of the questions I ask my team members to make the whole team better. Today, I want to share some of the questions I ask that help us to become more creative.

How Can We Make Things Better?

If you're already successful, this is a fantastic question to ask yourself and your team. Anytime we're successful, there is a temptation to be lulled into a feeling of false security, to believe that we have arrived. But the greatest detriment to continual success is relying on past success.

> The greatest detriment to continual success is relying on past success.

The legendary coach John Wooden once shared with me that every day he asked himself the question "How can I make my team better?" Think about this: Wooden won ten national championships and was the most successful coach in the history of college basketball, yet he wasn't satisfied. He kept asking that question and found creative ways to help his team.

What Can I Do to Become Better?

I am obsessed with becoming better every day. I don't spend time thinking about any honors I've been given in the past. I'm grateful, but I also recognize that awards are given for what we've done yesterday. The question I ask myself is "What am I doing today?"

In my lifetime, I have reinvented myself five times. What's been consistent is that I write and speak on success, personal growth, leadership, relationships, and significance. But my companies and my roles with them have remained fluid to meet the needs of people and stay relevant with my message. If I want to keep improving and expanding my influence, I have to keep improving myself and my team.

Are the Right People at the Table?

In the chapter on People Capacity, I explained Jim Collins's concept of who luck. The people around you make all the difference when it comes to creativity. You need people who are willing to prepare as well as to dream. And you need people who are willing to be as tenacious as you are in searching for answers. That's why my friend, advertising genius Linda Kaplan Thaler, says that it's in the second hour that the best ideas come out. But as she also says, you need to make sure you have people at the table who can recognize a great idea and run with it.

How Can I Connect Things with Creativity?

My biggest creative breakthrough occurred when I discovered that creativity is about connecting things. As a young theologian who would speak several times a week, I realized that I needed to read and file quotes and ideas every day so I would always have material for my lessons. As I accumulated more material and more knowledge, I began to ask more questions about how and where I could use my material. There was a point after years of gaining knowledge at which I began to connect ideas with one another, and what I knew with what I was doing. When that happened, my life opened up, and I began to think more strategically and creatively.

This graphic by Hugh MacLeod shows the impact that connections make between knowledge and experience.

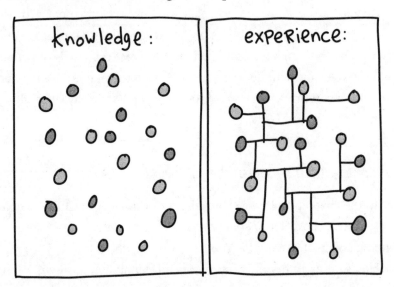

As Steve Jobs said, "Creativity is just connecting things. When you ask creative people how they did something, they feel a little guilty because they didn't really do it; they just saw something. It seemed obvious to them after a while."

For years, when I've tried to create or innovate, I have focused on a particular idea and then looked for ways to make connections to it. I call this connection creativity. With an idea fixed in my mind, I look for ways to connect it with experiences, people, quotes, stories, opportunities, questions—anything I can think of.

Recently I've been wanting to attract more builders—people who can drive business units and initiatives to success—to my companies. Every day I'm looking for builder thoughts, stories, characteristics, examples, experiences, advice, and questions. Everything that I do in this regard is to strategically connect what I know with new ways to accomplish what I desire.

My personal creativity has been stimulated more by making connections than by anything else. If you want to increase your creativity, begin looking for connections.

5. I Am Comfortable with Half-Baked Ideas

When I was young I held on to ideas way too long before I shared them with others. Why? I wanted them to be "presentable." I didn't want to fail. I didn't want my ideas to be rejected. And I wanted credit. Back then looking good was more important to me than getting good.

The catalyst for my change came when a man I greatly respected came to me with an idea and asked my opinion. He said, "I just started thinking about this idea and I wondered if you could jump-start me."

Me? Jump-start him?

He shared his new idea and we talked for about an hour. Toward the end of our conversation, I asked him, "Why did you share your idea so quickly?" His response staggered me: "The sooner I can get other perspectives on my thinking, the closer I come to finding my answer."

His confidence and insight inspired me to change the way I did things. And it also prompted me to develop my three-*E* formula for creativity:

Exposure of an idea to the right people
+ **Expression** from their different perspectives
= **Expansion** of that idea beyond my personal ability.

If you want to increase your creative capacity, I suggest you use this formula, too.

Today I'm in love with half-baked ideas, and am willing to ask for them as well as share them with others. Why? Because when we do, we gain at least these three benefits:

We Increase Our Odds of Being Successful

If you want to accomplish many things, you have to try many things—even if you feel they're not quite ready. Dan Ariely, Duke University professor and author of *Irrationally Yours: On Missing Socks, Pick-up Lines, and Other Existential Puzzles*, says that if you try thirty new things this year, you might find that you racked up fifteen good experiences. But if you wait to try things only when you're sure of success, you might experience only three good things.

We Gain More Practice with Creative Ideas

Keeping our imaginations sharp is essential to creative thinking and problem solving. That requires practice. Unfortunately, as we get older, most people practice creative thinking less and less. We stop using our imaginations. Stephanie Carlson, professor and director of research at the University of Minnesota's Institute of Child Development, says there are reasons our natural creativity wanes as we mature. One of the biggest is that when children are in school, they are forced to turn their attention to logic, reason, and facts, and they spend more of their time and brain power in reality—and less in imagination. As a result, they get out of practice.[2] Working with half-baked ideas forces us to use our imaginations and practice creative thinking.

We Become More Comfortable with Our Misses

If you throw a lot of ideas at the wall, you will have many hits and misses. And that's good. You can't succeed if you don't try. And if you try repeatedly and miss but realize you're no worse off for having tried and failed, it gives you confidence to keep trying.

Creative people fail, and the best fail often. They're like children who try an idea before it's formed, and if it doesn't work, they move on to the next idea. And they keep moving on until they find one that works. If you want to be more creative, get used to missing the mark.

As the founder of five companies, I need to be an example of a creative leader who is not afraid to miss. If I am more tentative than decisive, more cautious than creative, I will not develop a creative culture. And any organization that doesn't innovate is destined to die. Professor David Hills of Stanford University says, "Studies of creativity suggest that the biggest single variable of whether or not employees will be creative is whether they perceive they have permission." As the leader, I have to model that permission.

> "The biggest single variable of whether or not employees will be creative is whether they perceive they have permission."
> —David Hills

6. I Am Comfortable Letting Go of What I Embraced Yesterday

Margaret and I had an interesting dinner conversation with Bob and Ann Hammer recently. Bob is the chairman, president, and CEO of Commvault, a company that creates firewalls and other data protection solutions for large companies. One of the things Bob does is hire people to try to defeat their own software. He knows that when they get close to breaking in, the company had better be ready to roll out the next solution. What grabbed my attention was something Bob said: "We stay in business because we continue to create. Nothing that worked yesterday will work today."

Bob knows that to be successful, he has to let go of what worked last year. He has to continually create to be successful. The only difference between him and us is that he recognizes it, and often we don't.

When we work hard on something, we usually have a hard time letting it go. Author and creativity expert Roger von Oech said, "It's easy to come up with new ideas; the hard part is letting go of the things you have loved and that worked for you two years ago, but will soon be out of date." Nobel Prize–winning author William Faulkner called this process killing your darlings. Here are some examples of things I had to let go of:

I used to have a monthly tape club. The lessons helped hundreds of thousands of people and sold millions of tapes. Today I don't have it. I had to kill my darling.

I used to talk a lot about my success and how I accomplished so much. Now I talk more about my failures and my struggles. I had to kill my darling.

I used to start my lesson-writing process by first going to my files and pulling together material, but now I try to write from my heart. I had to kill my darling.

I could continue. My history is filled with a lot of dead darlings. Is yours? When was the last time you said good-bye to something that was special that no longer works today?

> When was the last time you said good-bye to something that was special that no longer works today?

Often I have been asked how I can let go of things so quickly and easily. My reply: "In the beginning, it wasn't quick or easy." But over time, I have been able to move on and let go because I've learned some lessons:

- **It's easier to let go of something if you're going to get something better.** You don't let go just for the sake of letting go. You let go only because tomorrow looks better than yesterday.

- **People usually cut their losses too late.** My brother Larry, who is a fine businessman, taught me many years ago about cutting losses. He would say, "John, try to let your first loss be your last loss." I haven't always done that well, but I have gotten a lot better.

- **Excellence is possible only with creative dissatisfaction.** If we're satisfied, we don't try to get better. At the other extreme, if we embrace dissatisfaction but without a desire for excellence, we just become miserable or depressed. However, when you couple dissatisfaction with the desire for improvement, you become innovative.

- **You can't fall in love with structure.** When your security is structure, rules, and regulations, you stop being creative. I love the way Richard Branson, founder of Virgin Group, puts this: "People often remark to me that it's great how Virgin thinks outside the box. They are genuinely surprised when I tell them, 'Actually we don't! We just never let the box get built in the first place.'" You can't love both boxes and creativity.

Are you willing to let go of some things you love? If not, you're going to have a hard time being creative and becoming any better than you are today.

7. I Ask Creative People to Help Me

I mentioned in the previous chapter that I always like to bring peo-ple around the table to help me. That includes the times when I'm trying to be creative. For example, as I began working on this book, I asked a group of good thinkers and innovators to help me explore the idea of *capacity*. Some of the ideas were great. Some were good. Many were terrible. That's what you get when you try to do something creative. And that's okay. You have to deal with the misses to get the hits.

When you ask creative people to help you, your goal isn't just to have people come together for a creative think session. Your goal is to have the *right* people in the meeting. What are the qualities of the right people? Here is what I look for:

- **Fluency**—the ability to generate a number of ideas so that there is an abundance of possible solutions
- **Flexibility**—the ability to produce many different kinds of ideas in varied categories for any given problem
- **Elaboration**—the ability to add to, embellish, or build from an idea
- **Originality**—the ability to create fresh, unique, unusual, or different ideas
- **Complexity**—the ability to drill down and conceptualize dif-ficult, intricate, or multifaceted ideas
- **Boldness**—the willingness to be daring, try new things, and take risks
- **Imagination**—the ability to invent, see, and conceptualize ingenious new ideas
- **Security**—the willingness to appreciate others' ideas and not protect their own
- **Values**—the ability to think and create in accordance with my values and priorities

These are the people who can help you create. Leave out analysts, critics, editors, educators, and implementers. Otherwise the group's creative wings will be clipped before you are ever given any room to fly.

8. I Give Myself Creative Retreats

While I love bringing together a group of creative people to brainstorm, I also love spending time by myself thinking. Why? Because we need inspiration from within as well as from without. Solitude is the other side of the coin in creativity.

Creativity flourishes in solitude. For me it is essential. You will become as creative as the amount of time you set aside for it. I try to schedule time every day as well as planning extended times weekly, monthly, and yearly. There is a relationship between scheduling a time to be creative and being inspired to create.

Years ago I discovered that if I do the right thing regardless of whether I feel any inspiration, then I will become inspired because I did the right thing. The key to increasing your creative capacity is to schedule time for it, and then expect to be more creative during that time. The discipline of developing the habit gives you the results you desire. Perhaps that's why many authors including William Faulkner have been

> "I write only when inspiration strikes. Fortunately, it strikes every morning at nine a.m. sharp."
> —*William Faulkner*

quoted as saying things like this: "I write only when inspiration strikes. Fortunately, it strikes every morning at nine a.m. sharp."

This morning I scheduled time to be at my desk working on this chapter. It is hard to describe how excited I felt when I walked into my office, picked up my four-color pen, and began writing to you on my legal pad. As I write these words, I'm filled with anticipation that these words will help you increase your creative capacity. I am the only one in my office, but I am not alone. In my imagination, I am with you, sharing the things that have helped me, and I feel certain they will help you. As you read this page, we are taking a journey together, one that I believe will help you blow the lid off your capacity.

Why do I believe this? Because hundreds of times I have been on the receiving end of this process, reading words from another person's hand and heart. I've felt connected with those authors and been grateful for the help I was receiving. But I only benefitted because they took the time to be alone and write.

What do you have to give that you can create only in solitude? If you're like me, you need time alone to think and create for yourself and others. That creative time of retreat can give you the greatest ROI—return on investment—in your life.

My life has been dedicated to leadership, and my observation of leaders is that most do not schedule enough creative thinking time alone. Most leaders have a bias for action, and too often solitude gets pushed off their calendars because action calls out to them. But when that happens, not only do the leaders suffer. So do their people, because their leaders aren't at their best and most creative. People deserve a leader who emerges out of solitude with solutions.

There you have it. These are the things that have helped me transform from the guy with the lowest creativity score in the class to someone who has leveraged his creativity every day for fifty years to earn his living and try to make the world a better place.

If you desire to increase your creativity capacity, you can do it. You can train yourself to see possibilities. You can learn to find answers. You can become someone who always offers options. And you can work with others to become inventive and innovative. If you can harness that with productivity, which is the subject of the next chapter, you'll *really* be able to increase your capacity.

Creative Capacity Questions

1. When it comes to problems, challenges, and obstacles, do you believe there is *always* a solution? Explain your answer.

2. Do you find it difficult or easy to let go of old successes and solutions? Why? How could you leverage a stronger faith in the future in order to let go of the past?

3. Are you better at pulling together a group of creative people to get ideas, or at retreating into solitude to think? What could you do to improve in the area where you currently don't do as well?

8

Production Capacity—Your Ability to Accomplish Results

As I think about the seven capacities I'm challenging you to develop in this section of the book—energy, emotional, thinking, people, creative, production, and leadership capacities—I recognize that talent and natural ability come into play with all of them. But of the seven, production capacity can be increased the most regardless of the level of giftedness a person possesses. Production capacity can be increased dramatically and immediately if you are highly intentional about it. If you're willing to work at it, you can be successful.

> Production capacity can be increased dramatically and immediately if you are highly intentional about it.

No one has ever had to work at *limiting* their capacity. That happens naturally. The world tries to talk us out of working hard. We convince ourselves that we can't get ahead. We feel down, and we watch our lives go downhill. There are even people who will tell you that others have put you there, that the system is rigged, that successful people have pushed you down and have gotten to the top by stepping on you.

Well, I have good news for you. I'm successful, and I don't intend to push you down. Instead, I want to help you get up and get going and live a productive life. Your production capacity is within your own control, and I believe that what you are about to read can change your life—if you let it.

Everything Worthwhile Is Uphill

I want to begin by telling you the truth: everything worthwhile in life—everything you want, everything you desire to achieve, everything you want to receive—is uphill. The problem is that most of us have uphill dreams but downhill habits. And that's why we have a cap on our production capacity.

> Everything worthwhile in life—everything you want, everything you desire to achieve, everything you want to receive—is uphill.

Take a look at the difference between a life of downhill sliding and uphill climbing:

DOWNHILL SLIDING	UPHILL CLIMBING
Nothing Worthwhile	Everything Worthwhile
Low Self-Esteem	High Self-Respect
Negative Momentum	Positive Momentum
Losses	Wins
Low Morale	High Morale
Not Making a Difference	Making a Difference
No Improvement	Self-Improvement
Aimless	Purposeful
Empty	Fulfilling

If we compare those two lists, we know we don't want a downhill life. But are we willing to work for an uphill life? That's the question. So I'll say it again: Everything worthwhile is uphill. I want you to let that really sink in. I want you to feel the implications of that statement. To help with that, let's look at the components individually:

> *Everything* is inclusive. It means total, all-encompassing. Nothing is excluded.
>
> *Worthwhile* is a good word. It means desirable, advisable, appropriate, good for you.
>
> *Uphill* is demanding. It means the experience is going to be grueling, exhausting, rugged, punishing, strenuous.

The word *everything* holds promise. We like that. The word *worthwhile* is attractive. We want what's worthwhile. But *uphill*? That's challenging. Many of us do not want to deal with that.

Downhill is easy. It has no requirements. It doesn't take any effort. It's like feeling the effects of gravity, which continually pull us down. You can *slide* downhill—in your sleep. A downhill lifestyle is characterized by unintentionality, complacency, inconsistency, and excuses. There is no big-picture vision for the future, only instant gratification.

Uphill is hard. Moving uphill requires intentionality, energy, determination, hard work, and consistency. It requires you to keep an eye on the big picture, be determined, demonstrate character, and put in the time. The right thing to do and the hard thing to do are usually the same thing.

> **The right thing to do and the hard thing to do are usually the same thing.**

More and more people resist doing the right thing because it's hard, so they choose the easy thing. They go downhill instead of uphill.

Have You Considered Your Production Capacity?

Civil rights activist Benjamin E. Mays observed, "The tragedy of life is often not in our failure, but rather in our complacency; not in our doing too much, but rather in our doing too little; not in our living above our ability, but rather in our living below our capacities."

The challenge every person faces in the area of capacity is changing from what you have done to what you are capable of doing. That's what I want to encourage you to do. I want to challenge you to become an uphill climber. Perhaps you find that intimidating. Maybe you've not done as well in the past as you'd like to. And you find it difficult to move forward in this area. If so, let me ask you this: If you won't do it for yourself, will you do it for your family and friends? The life you choose for you doesn't begin and end with you. What you do influences others.

If you feel like your life is going downhill instead of upward toward the accomplishment and rewards you desire, you need to change the way you approach productivity. First, you need to own your current level of productivity, whatever it is. You need to see your past productivity as your responsibility alone. Next, you need to learn to embrace uphill practices and habits that will help you to increase your capacity.

I want to help you with productivity. And I'm going to try to do that by acquainting you with a friend of mine named Paul Martinelli. He is the president of the John Maxwell Team. Every day he climbs uphill and leads thousands of certified coaches to climb with him. I've met few people in my life with his ability to produce. In 2011, he started with nothing but an idea. He approached me along with mutual friend Scott Fay and said, "John, let's start a world-class coaching company." It was something I'd never considered before.

And to be honest, I wasn't sure I wanted to do it. I didn't know if I wanted to lend my name to people I didn't know personally, and I wasn't sure if we could deliver a certification of high value. But Paul was very persuasive, and we decided to partner together. I would give the program my name and teach the coaches my values, and Paul would do all the other work.

Let me tell you, in just six years, Paul has done wonders. He has taken the John Maxwell Team from zero coaches to more that fifteen thousand coaches. He's grown it from his headquarters in South Florida and spread it to 145 countries around the world. Before he started, he taught a few masterminds (discussion groups) himself to business people he knew personally. Now the coaches are leading masterminds all over the world, and nearly a million people have gone through a mastermind led by a certified coach. And starting from zero dollars, Paul estimates that the coaches have generated nearly a billion dollars in revenue in their businesses. If you're a businessperson, I bet I've got your attention now! But you don't have to be in business to learn from Paul or appreciate his story.

Starting the Uphill Climb

Paul grew up in Mount Lebanon, an upper-middle-class neighborhood in Pittsburgh, Pennsylvania, with an older sister and two older brothers. Theirs was a single-parent home, because Paul's dad left when his mom was pregnant with him. The community they lived in was nice, but they were very poor. You know how some people say, "We grew up poor, but we never knew it"? Paul says, "We grew up poor, and we *knew* we were poor. We felt it every day."

Nobody gave Paul much of a chance, because he had a speech impediment. Back in those days, the school system treated him like he was disabled. His friends made fun of him and called him stupid. Paul dealt with that by working. He spent his childhood delivering the morning paper, delivering the evening paper, collecting bottles, selling lightbulbs door-to-door, raking leaves in the fall, and shoveling driveways in the winter. He did whatever he could to make an honest buck.

Paul used his money to help his family. He told me about two of his proudest memories. The first came at Christmas. When Paul was little, he, his mom, and his siblings would wait every year for his father to bring them a Christmas tree. They never knew when he would bring it, and when he did (often not until Christmas Eve), he just left it on the porch. One year Paul thought, *Why do we need to wait until Christmas Eve to get our tree?* So Paul went out and bought the family's tree. He was *nine.*

A few years later, Paul's brother David was running track in high school, and he was a bit of a track star. But he didn't have any money to buy real track shoes. That was right when Nikes were coming in. Paul went out and bought his older brother a pair of Nikes for thirty-eight dollars. He was always doing things like that.

Dropout

By the time he was fifteen, Paul was pretty discouraged with school and decided he'd rather just work. So he dropped out and started work on a roofing crew. But he also joined the Guardian Angels, a group of citizen-volunteers who patrolled the streets to discourage crime. The New York City–based nonprofit organization had been founded in 1979 by Curtis Sliwa. When Guardian Angels started a Pittsburgh chapter, they recruited tough kids who wanted to help people. Paul was one of them.

It took no time at all for Paul to rise up. He quickly recruited a hundred young people into his chapter. He was so good at recruiting and fund-raising that he soon became the number two man in the organization and traveled the country with Sliwa.

When the Guardian Angels wanted to start a new chapter in a city, they sent Paul to lead it. He opened chapters in Chicago, Minneapolis, Atlanta, Jacksonville, Tampa, and Miami. The last chapter he opened was in Palm Beach, where he eventually relocated. That was during the height of the crack cocaine epidemic, and the Palm Beach area was where a lot of the drugs came into the country.

Entrepreneur

Paul enjoyed his role with the Guardian Angels, but after seven years, the entrepreneurial bug bit him again, and he decided he wanted to start his own business. At Thanksgiving dinner with the entire extended family, over the turkey and lasagna (it was an Italian-American Thanksgiving) he decided to announce his decision.

Back when he had quit high school, his mother had been so angry with him that she had kicked him out of the house. But she and the rest of his family had been proud of the work he was doing with the Guardian Angels. When he made the announcement that he was going to quit the organization to start his own business, time stopped. Paul says it was like everyone at the table dropped their fork at the same time and just stared at him.

"What, are you crazy?"

"What kind of business are *you* going to do?"

"I'm going to start a cleaning business," Paul answered.

"A cleaning business! Do you remember what your room looked like when you lived at home? What do you know about cleaning?"

Paul says it was like he suddenly became invisible, and they started to plan his life for him.

"*Mamma mia*," said his grandmother, "let's call Ro." She meant Paul's cousin Rose, who worked at the post office. They thought they would save him by finding him a government job.

Undaunted, Paul started his own business at age twenty-two. During the day, he went door-to-door at office buildings, cold-calling to try to get clients to hire this company to clean their offices. At night, he went out and did the cleaning himself. He started with two partners, but in less than a year, they had dropped out. Paul was on his own.

For sixteen years, through many ups and downs, Paul led his company, At Your Service, and grew it into a highly profitable business. He learned a lot of lessons during that time and developed principles of productivity, which I'll share with you in a moment. But by the time he sold the business, he had one hundred full-time employees cleaning 150 locations every night, including offices, restaurants, country clubs, movie theaters, imaging centers, hospitals, and even a zoo. Paul's motto was "If it stood still, we cleaned it."

While he was learning and growing, Paul decided that he wanted to help others become more successful in their careers. So he started to teach them from a book that had changed his life: *Think and Grow Rich* by Napoleon Hill. He found it so rewarding that he found an organization that trained and certified him as a speaker. And he started speaking and training people while still running his cleaning business. Within months, he became the most successful entrepreneur in that network of speakers. The organization's founder discovered this and wanted to hire Paul to run his conference business, so Paul sold At Your Service and changed careers. Five years later, he approached me about starting the John Maxwell Team.

Nine Principles of Highly Productive People

I find Paul's story remarkable. It illustrates the power of perseverance and productivity. Of his early years, Paul says, "Even though all my programming said you've got to play the cards you were dealt, there was a part of me that knew that I could take those cards and throw them back in the center of the table of life. I just didn't know how to do that. But I just knew all my life that there was something more for me, that I could change my life. I did not know how to articulate that. I didn't know what that meant. I didn't know how to do it, but in my heart there was a part of me that knew it was possible."

Paul found a way, and I want to share that way with you. Paul's principles can be applied to anything you want to accomplish, whether it's a business, a nonprofit organization, a home remodel, a sports team—you name it. If you want to increase your production capacity, take these ideas to heart:

1. Visualize the Perfect Outcome

Stephen R. Covey advised in *The 7 Habits of Highly Effective People* that we should always begin with the end in mind. Paul takes this idea one step further. He calls this "creating a mental model of perfection." He doesn't just want to know where he's going. He wants to visualize the *perfect* outcome with as much detail as he possibly can. Before we launched the John Maxwell Team, Paul had the end product mapped out in his mind: the teaching team, the number of trained and certified coaches, the number of cities with licensed partners—all of it. He wants to know what perfection looks like, so he can strive to achieve it.

Paul likens this to what a master gardener does. In his mind, he has an image of what a perfect tree looks like. When he goes to prune a tree, he keeps that picture in mind and goes to work. You can see the results of this in bonsai trees that have been carefully cultivated into ideal forms, or in topiaries where a shrub has been sculpted to represent a geometric form or the shape of a familiar character.

Do you have a vision for what you want to accomplish? Have you created a mental model of perfection for what you desire to achieve? If not, you need to work on that. It's your starting point. Put as much detail to it as you can. Will it actually *be* perfect? No. But that idea is where you need to start.

2. Start Working Before You Know How to Achieve the Vision

Paul's productivity process starts with the idea of perfection. However, the next step would appear to be in exact opposition to that. Paul calls this suspending the requirement of knowing how. Paul says, "I think for me what makes me productive is that I'm willing to do what I know to do, and not get hung up on what I don't know to do." In other words, begin. Do something, anything.

> "What makes me productive is that I'm willing to do what I know to do, and not get hung up on what I don't know to do."
> —*Paul Martinelli*

"There are so many people who are not productive because they've already made an inventory of everything that they cannot do," Paul explains, "and that becomes a 'because.' 'I can't because I don't know this.' 'I can't because I don't have the resources.' 'I can't because I don't have the time.' 'I can't because I don't have the money.' 'I can't because I don't have the contacts.' What I've learned to do is just take whatever I *do* know and allow that to be causative."

When you want to accomplish something, you have to have a vision for what you're trying to do, but you also have to be willing to take action in the face of uncertainty. You need to tap into your thinking capacity to know what you're shooting for, but you also need to have a bias for action to be productive. You have to be willing to take a step, probably a small step.

Most people want to start with one bold certain leap. They want a big head start, a quantum leap. But Paul points out that there are very few quantum leaps. If we're willing to take one small step, ten small steps, one hundred small steps, then we may have a chance to make a leap later. It may look like an overnight success to others, but we know it's the result of many small successes. And you don't achieve those unless you're willing to take that *first* uncertain step.

Paul gave me a humorous example of this from his childhood. When he decided to shovel snow to make money, he went to his garage and found a shovel, and off he went, knocking on doors. If you grew up where it snows, like I did in Ohio, you know what a snow shovel looks like. It's big and wide and has a curved blade to make it easy to pick up lots of snow. What did Paul have? A shovel made for digging holes in the garden.

"I laugh now," says Paul. "I didn't have a snow shovel. Everybody else had these very nice snow shovels. I didn't have that. I found an old spade in our garage. I didn't know that there were seven different types of shovels. I just knew that I had a shovel, and that I was going to go out there and get to work. That's what I did."

That's the mind-set you must have to become more productive. Whatever you have—or don't have—you're willing to start, regardless of how little you know about how you're going to get where you want to go.

3. Fail Fast, Fail First, and Fail Often

This next step also seems to fly in the face of the idea of striving for perfection. To be productive, you have to be willing to fail. A lot. One of the things I admire about Paul is that he tries new things and just keeps moving. He doesn't let something that doesn't work bother him. A key to Paul's thinking is that he doesn't think of his

> "Fail fast, fail first, and fail often."
> —*Paul Martinelli*

efforts as right or wrong, as successes or failures. He asks himself whether what he did got him closer to his vision of perfection. If it did, it's a win. If it didn't, he focuses on the feedback he's getting from what didn't work. Then he makes adjustments and tries again, immediately.

Are you willing to fail? Are you willing to fail repeatedly? Are you willing to learn from what didn't work? That's what will be required for you to blow the cap off your production capacity.

4. Stay Focused Longer Than Other People Do

Paul learned a lot of lessons as a budding entrepreneur during his childhood. One of the most important was how to stay focused. "As I look back," says Paul, "I realize that I stayed focused longer than most people. When all the other kids would go out to shovel snow, most kids would do it for thirty minutes and maybe earn three or four dollars. Then they would quit. I had the ability to stay focused, regardless of the distractions, to the exclusion of outside conditions or circumstances. That was what was giving me the results."

That still gives Paul results. It will give you results, too. Paul started out working hard because people told him he wasn't smart. Now he recognizes how smart he is, but his work ethic is still intact. So I have to ask: How long do you stick with something to make it work? And how hard do you work at it while you're doing it? Do you stay focused? Here's the thing you need to learn from Paul's example. He initiates *many* tries at *one thing*, not *one* try

> To increase production capacity, initiate *many* tries at *one thing*, not *one* try at *many things*.

at *many things*. That's an approach anyone can adopt, regardless of talent, intelligence, resources, or opportunity.

5. Take Inventory of Your Skills and Resources

About two years into his cleaning business, Paul hit a wall. "I was doing what I'd been told my whole life," says Paul. "I was told that if I worked hard and did honest work that things would be okay. I was working hard. I was doing honest work, but things weren't okay. I would get a new account, then I would lose two others. I would get an employee well trained, and then he would leave to earn twenty-five or fifty cents an hour more somewhere else. It was the proverbial 'one step forward, two steps back,' and I didn't know how to change it. I was stuck. And let me tell you: stuck stinks."

Back then Paul didn't know how to navigate himself out of his problem. So he started to think about himself and his skills. He realized that he needed to grow. "If you are not growing," Paul says, "you are not living at your full capacity. If you are not fully expressing your full capacity, it registers in your spirit as stuck and it stinks. The reason why it stinks is because it's so contrary to who we are as human beings."

One of the books Paul read was *Psycho-Cybernetics* by Maxwell Maltz. It made him realize he had created his own lid on his capacity. He had created a negative expectation for himself without realizing it. "I thought, *If you are a high school dropout, you should never be able to go that far*," says Paul. "But after reading Maltz I thought, *Huh, I'm the one that really controls the ability to expand what I produce*. It had never occurred to me that I had created all those limits on my own capacity. I expected only a limited level of success, for a certain level of happiness, and I in fact was looking for the rest of the world to try to change that for me, and that was never going to happen."

One of the illustrations in Maltz's book pointed out the difference between a thermometer and a thermostat. Paul had been a thermometer that simply reported on his condition. But he turned himself into a thermostat, which *changes* the conditions. If you want to be more productive, you need to take charge of your own productivity. You need to become a thermostat.

6. Stop Doing What You're Not Great at Doing

Coming out of one of his sessions of inventory taking, Paul made a decision. He would not try to become a keynote speaker. That was his original goal when he sold his cleaning business. Paul's a good speaker, but he realized he wasn't a great speaker, the kind who could fill an arena. Nor was he willing to do what it took to try to get there.

Paul recognized that he's at his best as a second in command. It's true that he ran a very successful business himself, but he performed at the highest level in the second chair. He got a first glimpse of that when he worked with Curtis Sliwa in the Guardian Angels. And he's found it to be true working with me at the John Maxwell Team.

You will drastically increase your production capacity if you stop doing what you're not great at and instead focus on what you do best. Find ways to focus your time and attention and work toward eliminating from your schedule anything that doesn't have a high return.

7. Tune In to Your Team Every Day

Paul credits his high production capacity to building a team. "When I look at all my successes," says Paul, "I see teams. Guardian Angels: team of people. At Your Service commercial cleaning company: team of people. The John Maxwell Team: teaching team, sales and marketing team, and the team of certified coaches. Some of these people have worked with me ten, twelve years. Cheryl Fisher has been with us for twenty-two years. I didn't want employees. I wanted a team. I needed teams because I realized my capacity is limited. But when I bring together a team and unify us to achieve a goal, it automatically, exponentially, increases my capacity in ways that I could never do alone. It's productivity squared."

Because Paul recognizes the importance of the team, he is highly intentional in staying connected to his people. Every day he calls somebody to check in with them or drops into their office just to chat. He pays attention to his team's social media. He wants to know how they're doing. "You've got to know the vibe of the tribe," says Paul.

I do this as well. I try to have dinner with key members of my staff, and I take them with me to events so that we can spend time together. I know that those closest to me determine my level of success, so I want to maintain and develop those relationships and add value to my team members whenever I can. If you want to be productive, you need to develop a team, connect with team members, and keep adding value to them.

8. Make Decisions Every Day to Move Yourself and the Team Forward

When Paul starts any endeavor, his first goal is to just get started and make things functional. For example, when he started the John Maxwell Team, he didn't even have a website. But he didn't let that stop him. He did the things he knew how to do, and then worked to make improvements. And that's where he focuses a lot of his production energy. That process requires the ability to make decisions every day.

One of the things I find most interesting about Paul is that he doesn't see decisions as right or wrong, good or bad. He judges only whether or not they move him and the team forward or backward in the journey toward his vision. "There are lots of things that we do wrong, but the decision was still right, because it moved momentum in the right way. Again, I am not attached to failure, so I don't care. The question I ask is 'Does it move us closer in the direction of perfection?' All I am worried about is trajectory. I'm not worried about hitting the mark. I am a futurist. I don't care about the now; the now is going to change. I want to make sure that I am getting the trajectory right. I want to get us moving the right way. If you ask John Maxwell Team members, they'll tell you that one of the quotes I share all the time is 'Jump and build your wings on the way.' "

You will only reach your production capacity if you are willing to make decisions. And Paul's approach to decision making can free you up. When it comes to character and ethical decisions, yes, there is a right and wrong. But when it comes to productivity and achievement, there isn't. Either something works or it doesn't. Either it takes you forward, or it doesn't. If you develop the habit of making quick decisions, trying new things, and judging whether or not they take you forward, you will be more productive.

9. Continually Reevaluate What Could Work Better

Productive people are always working to become better and to find better ways of doing things. That's certainly Paul's goal. He's constantly reevaluating everything. Every time he has hosted the semiannual training event to certify coaches, it has gotten better. Every time he has changed the marketing and sales plan, the results have gotten stronger. Right now, he's redesigning the pretraining process that's included in the certification program. He's also reevaluating the teaching faculty. These aren't things that are broken. They have been highly successful. But he wants to make them better. He's still driving toward that model of perfection he has in his mind.

Paul is motivated by continual improvement. "I phrase it this way," Paul explains. "We have three options in life. We can be historians, reporters, or futurists. The historian wants to remind us of everything in the past and wants to filter everything in the future through that. The reporter is really attached to conditions and circumstances today, and that's just the way it is. The futurist focuses on what hasn't yet been done. He says, 'There is more for us to do. We can do more. We can broaden our capacity. There is more of our potential we can take advantage of.' "

Paul calls this living in the emerging future. I would also describe it as acting today with the intent of making a better tomorrow. The place where today and tomorrow meet is where you can create positive change. The only time you really control is now. You can't change yesterday. You can't control tomorrow. But you can choose what you do today with the goal of those choices making things better tomorrow. Professor Edward Banfield of Harvard University confirmed the importance of a future focus in his book *The Unheavenly City*. He called it a "long-term perspective," and said that according to studies, it is the most accurate single predictor of upward social and economic mobility in America, more important than family background, education, race, intelligence, connections, or virtually any other single factor. If you want to be productive and successful, think of the future, but act today.

I've now known Paul for six years, and I'm amazed not only at his level of productivity, but by the way he continues to increase that productivity. Paul says, "What's the point of potential if there isn't capacity for you to express it?" Believe me, he is expressing it.

> The importance of a future focus or "long-term perspective" is the most accurate single predictor of upward social and economic mobility in America.

Few things will positively impact your potential or your success more quickly and more thoroughly than increasing your production capacity. If you take a cue from Paul, you can do that immediately. Adopt his practices. Repeat them daily until they become habits. And watch what happens.

Production Capacity Questions

1. Is your natural inclination to be a historian, who examines the past; a reporter, who observes and comments on the present; or a futurist, who acts today with the intention of improving tomorrow? What could you do to focus more on the emerging future?

2. Using Paul's story as inspiration, how would you describe your vision of a perfect future? What would you be doing? Describe it in as much detail as possible.

3. What downhill habits do you currently possess that are taking you away from that ideal future? What uphill habits must you cultivate to replace the unproductive ones?

9

Leadership Capacity—Your Ability to Lift and Lead Others

I t's been more than forty years since I realized that everything rises and falls on leadership. From that time, I've worked to become a better leader. Along the way I recognized that leadership is influence, so bettering my leadership meant increasing my influence capacity.

In the 1970s, I heard Earl Nightingale say, "If a person spends one hour a day, five days a week for five years studying a single subject, he or she will become an expert on that subject." My first response was, "Wow! It will only take me five years to become an expert on leadership!"

I made leadership study my focus. After five years, I learned two things: First, I *could* improve as a leader. Second, I couldn't become an *expert* in leadership in only five years. I was nowhere near my capacity. And the more I learned, the more I understood how much I didn't know. That continues to this day. But that just motivates me to want to learn

> The more I learned, the more I understood how much I didn't know.

more! Self-awareness gives me a greater sense of anticipation for further growth.

It's true that I've been given recognition in the area of leadership. In 2014 the American Management Association identified me as the number one leader in business. That same year *Business Insider* and *Inc.* magazines called me the most influential leadership expert in the world. But I don't in any way feel like an expert. What I feel like is a leadership layerer. That may not even be a real word, but it describes what I do. Every time I learn something new, I add it to what I already know about leadership and apply it to my life. And I keep doing that month after month and year after year. Continuous growth in leadership is my goal, with new learning superimposed over the old, which creates greater depth.

Let me give you an example. When my publisher invited me to revise *The 21 Irrefutable Laws of Leadership* for the tenth anniversary of its publication, I happily said yes. I thought it would be a quick process where I would just tweak a few parts of the book, and the mission would be accomplished. I was wrong. When I reread the book, I got discouraged. In the ten years that had passed, I had learned so much more about leadership. I had grown and changed. My leadership had gotten deeper. But the book had stayed the same. What I expected to be minor tweaking became a major revision. I changed 70 percent of the book. I put many more layers of leadership learning on top of what I had previously written.

That was my first conscious realization that new learning creates layers on old ones and compounds greatly when I connected it with what I already knew. That has led me to establish the habit of connecting new learning with past learning. Remember the illustration I shared in the chapter on creative capacity, where creativity connects knowledge? That's how I also think about learning and wisdom. Learning gives you new dots; wisdom connects them. Keep making those connections over time, and it compounds in layers.

Two Sides of the Leadership Coin

I'm continuing to grow in the area of leadership. In chapter 3 I mentioned that the John Maxwell Company does an executive leadership event each year called Exchange. The 2015 edition was held in San Francisco, and one of the keynote speakers was Liz Wiseman, former Oracle executive and current president of the Wiseman Group in Silicon Valley. Liz is also the author of several books, including *Multipliers: How the Best Leaders Make Everyone Smarter.*

At Exchange, Liz spoke on "the Five Disciplines of a Multiplier." When she described multipliers as "leaders who are genius makers who bring out the intelligence in others," I was intrigued. As she talked about each of the five disciplines of a multiplier, I have to admit that I got excited, because I felt as if she was describing me.

- **The Talent Magnet** attracts talented people and uses them at their highest point of contribution. (I thought, *Yes, I do that.*)

- **The Liberator** creates an intense environment that requires people's best thinking and work. (I thought, *Yes, I do that, too.*)

- **The Challenger** defines an opportunity that causes people to stretch. (*I totally do that.*)

- **The Debate Maker** drives sound decisions through rigorous debate. (*I love doing that.*)

- **The Investor** gives other people ownership of the results and invests in their success. (*Wow. I do that, too. That's a 100 percent match!*)

Boy, did I feel good! I began to wonder if Liz would want to put my picture on the cover of her book so that her readers could see what a multiplier looked like.

But before I could offer to let her take my picture, she started talking about how multipliers unwittingly diminish other people:

- **The Idea Guy** intends his ideas to stimulate ideas in others, but the result is that he overwhelms others, who often shut down. (*Oh no! I do that.*)

- **Always On**: intends to create infectious energy and share his point of view, but the result is that he consumes all the emotional space, and other people tune him out. (*Uh-oh. Another one.*)

- **The Rescuer** intends to ensure that people are successful and protect their reputation, but he makes people become dependent on him, which weakens their reputation. (*That's three that I do.*)

- **The Pacesetter** intends to set a high standard for quality or pace, but people become spectators or give up when they can't keep up. (*I've done this more times than I'd like to admit.*)

- **The Rapid Responder** intends to keep the organization moving fast, and does, but the result is that the organization moves slowly because there is a traffic jam of too many decisions or changes. (*Yep. That one, too.*)

- **The Optimist** intends to create a belief that the team can do it, but people wonder if he appreciates how difficult the journey is or acknowledges the possibility of failure. (*That one, too.*)

Wow. As she described and explained the diminishing tendencies of these kinds of leaders, I was humbled. In less than ninety minutes, I went from the top of the world to the bottom of the barrel. I had no idea that my strengths had such strong diminishing qualities in them. Reality set in. Before we even left San Francisco, I brought together several members of my inner circle, admitted that I possessed every one of the the diminishing qualities Liz had shared, and asked them to help me. Since I would not be able to work on all six areas at once, I asked them which one I should start changing. Together they agreed: I needed to temper my optimistic tendency. For the next several months, that was what I worked on. I still have a long way to go, but I'm improving.

The best part? I know it's helping me to become a better leader. It's adding a new layer to my insight and experience. And that will increase my leadership capacity.

Increasing Your Leadership Capacity

My desire is for your leadership capacity to increase as you read this chapter. If you've read some of my other books on leadership, you may be wondering what I plan to teach. I'm going to teach you from the new things I am learning now. Some of what I'm going to share is new thoughts layered on on older thoughts. Some are old thoughts that have spurred new thoughts. I hope all of them increase your capacity as they have increased mine.

1. Ask Questions and Listen to Understand and Find Your People

Recently during an interview, I was asked, "John, what is the main difference in how you lead today at almost seventy versus how you led in your thirties and forties?" My immediate response: "Today I continually ask questions as I lead."

Communication is the language of leadership. Journalist and author William H. Whyte said, "The great enemy of communication, we find, is the illusion of it." For years I had the illusion that as long as I was talking and giving direction, communication was happening. As a young leader, I loved to give answers. I

> "The great enemy of communication, we find, is the illusion of it."
> —William H. Whyte

wanted my team to be impressed with what I knew, and I was mostly interested in getting things done. Before, I was focused on vision. I thought leadership was about me and what I wanted. Today, I want my people to know me, and I want to know them.

Early in my career, my communication wasn't very interactive either. I never wanted to do Q & A. I wanted to teach others what I knew and what I felt was important. Today, I encourage Q & A. Why? Because it's the quickest and easiest way to connect with the audience and meet their needs. For years I had been giving answers to questions nobody was asking!

Slowly I learned that leadership was a two-way street. It took time for me to discover what I later called the Law of Communication: leaders touch a heart before they ask for a hand. For years I bypassed the heart and went straight for the hand. But everything changed when I began asking more questions and started giving less direction. I became intent on focusing on others. Questions are the keys that unlock the door to another person's life, and I began using them to learn about people.

I also ask questions because it helps me find the right people. I didn't know I needed to do that when I was younger. Now I know that to find the people who want to help you as a leader, you need to ask questions and actively listen. Today when I meet someone, my first thought is to wonder what questions I can ask to get to know them and connect with them.

> Before we attempt to *set* things right as leaders, we need to *see* things right.

Questions open up doors and

allow us to connect with others. They place value on the other person. And they give us a different perspective. Before we attempt to *set* things right as leaders, we need to *see* things right. The highest compliment you can give someone is to ask them their opinion.

However, none of that works if you don't listen. If questions unlock the door, listening keeps the door open. Questions start the conversation, but listening encourages it to continue. Listening shows that I want to understand someone before I try to be understood by them. Questions + Listening = Quality Conversation. Quality Conversation = Quality Leadership.

I had to learn how to listen, because I was too intent on talking. Today, I usually ask the other person to talk first and share with me everything they want me to know. I listen intently, keeping my eyes focused on them. I don't interrupt, and I try to give them all the time they need. Why? I want them to feel understood. When they stop, I'll even ask, "Is that everything you wanted to say? If there's anything else, go ahead and share. I have time." Only after they're done will I begin to talk.

Almost all of my leadership cues come from listening to others. To find and understand people, I ask questions, and I listen. Only then can I lead them effectively.

2. Connect with People Before Asking Them to Change

By its nature, leadership is about creating change. As a leader, you are inviting people to change their focus, change their energy, change their skills, and sometimes even their direction in life for the sake of the team and the accomplishment of the vision. How do you get people to trust you for so many changes? The foundation of trust needs to be built on good relationships, and good relationships start with good connection. As I explain in my book *Everyone Communicates, Few Connect*, connection best occurs on common ground.

If you're a task-oriented person, connecting may be something you have to work at to achieve. If you're a people person, building the relationships may come naturally. But making the transition from relationship building to movement requires what I call a *leadershift.* That "shift" is the transition from connecting with people to helping them make the changes necessary for the benefit of the team.

As a young leader, this transition was a challenge for me. I was good only at the relational part. I thought friendship was leadership. The good news was that people liked me. The bad news was that they didn't always follow me. I couldn't get them to move from where we were to where we needed to go.

Recently at a mentoring session sponsored by the John Maxwell Company, coach Matthew Mitchell of the University of Kentucky Lady Wildcats asked me, "John, as a coach, when do I push them and when should I be patient with them?" That's a question that every leader asks himself. My answer is that you push team members in areas of choice, such as attitude, responsibility, and work ethic.

> You can push team members in areas of choice, but you need to be patient with them in areas related to their background, experience, and skill.

But you need to be patient with them in areas related to their background, experience, and skill.

Patience is often required when your team members come from a difficult background. Perhaps they haven't had the same privileges or opportunities that others on the team have had. Lack of experience also requires patience. For example, in college basketball you cannot expect a freshman to make the same caliber of decisions that seniors are making. And less-skilled players require more patience than those with greater skills. The greater the skill, the greater the push. The lower the skill level, the greater the patience.

One of the keys to helping team members make successful changes is to set expectations for them up front. It increases the odds of positive change later in the relationship. As Stephen M. R. Covey says in *The Speed of Trust*, "It is important to focus on a shared vision of success up front. This is a preventative measure. When expectations are not clearly defined up front, trust and speed both go down. A lot of time is wasted due to leaders not clearly defining expectations. Failure to clarify expectations leaves people guessing. When results are delivered they fall short and are not valued." I call this the Expectation Principle: setting expectations on the front end increases the odds of meeting expectations on the back end.

I want to walk you through the six steps I use to set expectations. I believe they will set you up for success as you connect with people and then invite them to change.

Let Them Know You Value Them

The greatest gift a leader gives team members is their belief in them, letting them know that they are valued. It's wonderful when the people value the leader, but it's more wonderful when the leader values the people. Why? For me as a leader, it shows that I care. And the more that I value you as a person, the more I will pour into you. Value assessment determines investment. If I as your leader don't value you, I will try to manipulate you for *my* advantage instead of investing in you for *your* advantage.

> Value assessment determines investment.

So in setting expectations for people, I clearly communicate how much I value them as individual people, not as players. And that means I care enough for them to confront them. I value them too much to allow them to remain the same. Once they know that my expectation for them is birthed out of how much I value them, the environment has been set for the next step.

Identify the Value They Place on Themselves

As I've said, how we as leaders see others determines how much we will invest in them. But how they see themselves determines how much they will invest in themselves. Again, value assessment determines investment. The value you place on yourself determines the level of your commitment to yourself and others. Self-worth is foundational to belief. The moment that your belief in yourself goes up, so can your commitment to help yourself.

If the people on your team don't believe in themselves, as the leader you need to try to help them find that belief. You need to encourage them. You need to speak positive words of affirmation. You need to teach them. And you need to help them put wins under their belt. Does that always work? No. But if their self-worth never rises, neither will their performance.

Tell Them Growth Is Expected

In 2012 I wrote a book called *The 15 Invaluable Laws of Growth*. The very first chapter contains the Law of Intentionality: growth doesn't just happen. If we want to grow, we need to set targets and take action. If we want our people to grow, we need to help them do the same.

As a leader setting expectations for people, you must be ready to answer two questions: What do you want them to *know*, and what do you want them to *do*? As a leader, you want your people to grow, and you want them to know it on the front end. And if they know

> As a leader setting expectations for people, you must be ready to answer two questions: What do you want them to *know*, and what do you want them to *do*?

you will hold them accountable for it, the chances of it happening increase dramatically. One of the greatest mistakes leaders make is sharing expectations without later including accountability.

Show Them Change Is Essential

It is impossible to get better without making changes. No one has ever stayed the same, while at the same time rising to a higher level. Being willing to change is one of the prices we pay to grow.

Good leaders help people recognize and accept that price. They help team members understand that the longest distance between two points is often a shortcut, and that there are no cut-rate methods of growth. They also hang in there with the people who are willing to make those necessary changes to improve and grow. Leaders can't make the changes for them, but they can show them what needs changing, assist them, and encourage them.

Make the Connection a Constant

Recently I was teaching the Expectation Principle to a group of executives. I placed my hand on one executive's back and held it there while I taught. I wanted people to have a visual image of how leaders need to maintain their connection with the people they lead. They must always feel the gentle pressure of the leader reminding them to keep moving forward. Why? Because the moment we remove our leadership hand off most people's backs, their tendency is to settle. When it comes to expectations, leaders can never think, *Set it and forget it.* People rarely lead themselves forward or correct themselves when they get off track.

If you're a parent, how many times have you had to repeat yourself to your kids? Dozens, hundreds, thousands? The consistency of the connection directly affects the consistency of the effort. When we stay connected as leaders, two things are being communicated.

Team members are continually reminded of the effort needed to meet expectations. And the leader knows exactly how they are responding, so that if there is resistance, it can be addressed immediately.

My friend Kevin Turner, former COO of Microsoft and currently the CEO of Citadel Securities, says, "People want to be judged by their intentions, not by their actions." I think that's true. They also want to be empowered. But often what they need most is accountability. Keeping your connection constant and gently nudging them forward provides both encouragement and consistent accountability.

Ask, "Will You Help Me Help You?"

If you have expectations for your people but they don't embrace them, they will never succeed. When you ask people if they will help you to help them, you are able to measure their level of participation and commitment. By getting them to declare the ways that *they* want help to grow and change, you obtain their full buy-in. And if they don't follow through, you can hold them accountable for what they declared they would do. You don't want to spend your time on the type of person that I've heard called an *ask hole*—someone who asks for advice but then never follows it. You want to spend time on people who *want* to change.

3. Demonstrate Transparency Before Challenging People

One of the most valuable things you can do to increase your leadership capacity is to be authentic and transparent with people, and to share your story, especially before you challenge them to attempt something difficult.

I've already explained that it's important for leaders to ask themselves, "What do I want them to know, and what do I want them to do?" I would also add one more question that leaders need to ask: "What do I want them to feel?"

As leaders, our focus is often on the vision, the agenda, the project, our culture, or the next task. All are important, and we need to communicate about them. But I believe a leader's story has great potential to change lives and prepare people to act—as long as that story is an honest one filled with openness and vulnerability.

Too many leaders think they have to project a perfect image to have leadership credibility. They think they always have to put their best foot forward. What they don't understand is that their best foot is a flawed foot. They miss the power of their own stories of imperfection. A leader's story of struggle, growth, and improvement can inspire people and change lives.

That takes courage. Rollin King, founder of Southwest Airlines, once stated, "We adopted the philosophy that we wouldn't hide anything, not any of our problems, from the employees." People respect leaders who tell the truth but who still hold fast to the vision and keep leading the team forward.

> "We adopted the philosophy that we wouldn't hide anything, not any of our problems, from the employees."
> —Rollin King

I experienced the impact of being transparent with members of the team when I invited experienced coaches who are part of the John Maxwell Team to be catalysts for transformation in the country of Paraguay. As I mentioned in chapter 5, the goal would be to train seven hundred thousand leaders in five years. My desire was to ask more than two hundred coaches to give up a week of their time, pay all their own expenses, travel to Asunción, and work twelve hours a day for a week training roundtable facilitators.

But before extending the invitation to them, I first shared the weight of that vision, which I had been feeling intensely and continually. The president of the country had invited me to come. The expectations were high. I knew the journey would be long and hard. The odds of transforming an entire nation were very low. I had never led at this level before, and there were lots of unknowns before us. I knew I was in over my head, and at my age I was uncertain about whether I could finish that project. But I shared all of that with them, and told them that I felt I had no choice. I felt compelled. I was going to lead this project and would rather fail in attempting something big than succeed at something smaller. But to do it, I needed their help. So I asked, "Who will carry this weight with me?"

Two hundred fifty coaches *stretched* to the challenge and said yes—to making cultural adjustments, to giving time and money to be a part of this vision, to carrying the weight that gives the mission integrity. The result? In early 2016, the coaches traveled to Paraguay, and in less than a week, they trained more than seventeen thousand leaders to facilitate roundtables, which mobilized seventy thousand people to learn values and intentional living in those roundtables. Transformation has begun.

If you're a leader, seeing the vision is not enough. You must also *feel* that vision. If you only see it, you may become distracted and lose sight of it. But when you feel it, the vision cannot be easily dismissed. The weight of the vision prompts two indispensable qualities in a leader: consistency and intensity. If you rise to the challenge and carry the weight of the vision, it will mature you as a leader. Then, if you are transparent about what you feel about the vision, followers will be inspired to embrace it.

> The weight of the vision prompts two indispensable qualities in a leader: consistency and intensity.

4. Put Others Ahead of Yourself

The last thing I want to share with you to increase your leadership capacity is a lesson I learned and started practicing in 1976. For forty years I have been continually building more layers on this leadership truth, and I believe if you build on it, you will become a better leader. You need to shift your leadership from *me* to *we*.

In the beginning of my career, my leadership was all about me. All I did was wonder, *Does this person want to hear my vision? Does she want to help my team? Does he want to help me? What can they can do for me?* That changed when my attention began to focus on equipping and empowering others. And for the last twenty years I have focused on serving others and intentionally adding value to them.

I want to encourage you to make that same shift from *me* to *we*, if you haven't made it already. Why? I believe these three factors will make you want to change:

Reality—As the Challenge Escalates, the Need for Teamwork Elevates

My dreams are bigger than I am. Your dreams are bigger than you are. Every worthwhile dream is greater than the individual who initially holds it. When we recognize that truth, it motivates us to ask others for help.

Also, as much as I enjoy mobilizing a team to achieve a dream of my own, I really love to help others achieve theirs. And I've discovered that I can often offer insight on what other leaders need to achieve a dream and am able to help them with it. As a speaker, I'm sometimes in a unique position to do for others what they cannot do for themselves, such as lifting leaders up in front of their people. I love doing that.

Recently I had a chance to do that with Rick Hendrick, the owner of Hendrick Automotive Group and Hendrick Motorsports. I was doing some training for him on behalf of the John Maxwell Company. As part of the training, I also conducted an interview with Rick, during which I took notes. I wanted to lift Rick up in the eyes of his team. So at the end of the session, I told the hundreds of leaders who worked for him that I wanted to share what I had learned and gotten out of the interview that day.

A hush fell over the audience. I knew they were surprised. Mr. Hendrick had brought me in to teach them because I was considered a leadership expert, yet I was sharing what I had learned from their boss. Through this, I was able to let them know how much I respected and admired Rick, and they loved it. It made them want to work just that much harder for him.

Maturity—With One Tiny Exception, the World Is Composed of Others

I define maturity as unselfishness. It's being able to see things from other people's perspective because you value them. It means building ladders so that others can climb, not fighting to climb the ladder yourself. Being a ladder builder means that my success comes from helping others be successful. I may be able to help someone climb all the way up to the top, or I may be able to help someone go up

> I define maturity as unselfishness.

only a rung or two. That doesn't matter. I help people climb as far as they can, and the moment I can't help them climb another step, either because they've passed me by or they need a different kind of expertise, I move myself out of the picture.

I recently did this with someone I greatly respect. She wanted to know why I was taking a step back, so I told her, "If I start to benefit more than you do in this partnership, I won't continue in it." I want to add more value to others than they're adding to me. At the least, I want it to be balanced, but ideally, I'd like to be adding more.

Profitability—Measure Your Success by What You Give, Not What You Gain

Adding value to others has always been a greater desire in me than making money. Probably that's because I started out as a pastor, and I never considered money to be a good measuring stick for my achievements. But no matter what you do professionally, you should judge your success by how much you are able to help others. In the end, life is about people. Never forget it. Take care of your people instead of taking care of your career.

Mark Cole, the CEO of my companies, recently taught a lesson that he said was influenced by working with me for more than a decade. He called his talk "John Maxwell's Life of Compounding Interest of People." In it, he taught three things:

1. Never focus on making money—focus on making people.
2. Never focus on starting companies—focus on starting people.
3. Never focus on growing production—focus on growing people.

I don't believe I can take credit for it, but I certainly agree with it.

If you are willing to do the work to increase your leadership capacity, and you're willing to do it for the sake of others and your ability to add value to them, you will find your life to be greatly rewarding. I know I have. And the people I invest in remind me of why I keep doing it. As I write this, I'm holding in my hand a pen that has the words "You highlight our lives" on it. It was given to me by my staff. That's what I want to keep doing. Adding highlights to others' lives. I want my life to add value to others.

For my sixty-ninth birthday, my friends John and Celeste Li surprised me with an intimate dinner with a few friends. Everyone was so kind, and we had a wonderful time. At one point, Frank Bantz stood and made a toast. He later gave me a copy of it. Here's what he said,

> Our lives are like a breath that we already know,
> However your shadow has caused so many to grow,
> To live life raising leaders is a calling indeed,
> The seeds you have planted grow with astonishing speed.
> Your best writing and wisdom are yet to be done,
> This next season of life will be incredibly fun,
> So as you embark on your sixty-ninth year,
> The Lord has new plans as you continue to draw near.

I don't know how old you are. Now that I'm almost seventy, everyone I meet seems to be younger than I am. But regardless of what your age is, I want to ask you a question: What do you want your life to stand for? As you grow old and draw near to the end of your life, what kind of impact do you want to make on the world? I hope you'll choose to add value to people. And I hope you'll choose to become a leader of higher capacity. The more influence you develop, the greater the positive impact you'll be able to make.

Leadership Capacity Questions

1. How much time and effort do you spend on increasing your leadership capacity? What kind of priority has that been to you up until now? If you're willing to make it a higher priority, what will you do to increase it?

2. How well do you do at connecting with people and challenging them? Are you better at one than the other? How can you improve the one you don't do as well?

3. What changes should you make and what specific action could you take to put others ahead of yourself, especially in your leadership?

PART III

Choices: Do the Things That Maximize Your Capacity

You cannot escape the responsibility of tomorrow by evading it today.

—ABRAHAM LINCOLN

Jim Collins, author of *Good to Great*, says, "Greatness is not a function of circumstance. Greatness, it turns out, is largely a matter of conscious choice, and discipline." The same is true of capacity. Increased capacity comes from making the right choices.

The word *choice* implies that we have other options. And we do. How much capacity do you want in your life? You have the right and the power to choose it. Earlier in this book I introduced you to the capacity equation:

AWARENESS + ABILITY + CHOICES = CAPACITY

Awareness is something we learn. Ability is a gift that we already possess. Choices add to both the things we learn and the gifts we possess.

Before we discuss the ten specific choices that you can make to increase your capacity, I want to give you a strategy that will be useful for all of them. I call it the rule of five. I was introduced to the concept by Mark Victor Hansen and Jack Canfield, authors of the *Chicken Soup for the Soul* books, but I've put my own spin on it.

Let's say you wanted to cut down an enormous tree in your yard. Think of the biggest tree you've ever seen, a tree that makes you think, *That's way too big. I'll never be able to do it.* Huge. How would you approach the task? I suggest you use the rule of five. Every day, go out to the tree with your ax and take five cuts. *That's it?* you may be thinking. Yes, that's it. Here's why it works. If you take those five cuts every day, week after week, month after month, year after year, the tree *will* fall.

You can use that method to accomplish anything over time. Why? Because the rule of five gives you everything you need to accomplish a difficult task:

1. **Intentionality**—What do you want to accomplish? Cut down a tree.
2. **Practicality**—How are you going to accomplish it? Swing the ax.
3. **Focus**—How many trees? Chop one tree, not scar many trees.
4. **Action**—How many swings? Five swings.
5. **Consistency**—How often? Every day.

The results? The tree falls. It may take some time, depending on the size of the tree, but it will fall.

To maximize our capacity, we must choose to be intentional, determine our "ax" (the *how*), focus on one area at a time, and take action every day. That's how we blow the cap off our capacity. My hope is that this book is helping you to find your "ax" and inspiring you to make the choice to keep swinging. Do that every day, and you will have a high return in your capacity.

The next ten chapters of this book will help you to maximize your capacity by making choices in ten key areas. These areas aren't skills or talents; they are life choices. The more you live them and learn to love them, the larger your capacity will be and the greater your success. I want you to know that one of the choices I discuss is spiritual capacity. As a person of faith, I cannot with integrity omit this choice from the book, but I'm aware that you may want to skip that chapter. And that, of course, is fine with me. I value you as a person no matter what. That being said, here are the ten choices:

Responsibility Capacity—Your Choice to Take Charge of Your Life

Character Capacity—Your Choices Based on Good Values

Abundance Capacity—Your Choice to Believe There Is More Than Enough

Discipline Capacity—Your Choice to Focus Now and Follow Through

Intentionality Capacity—Your Choice to Deliberately Pursue Significance

Attitude Capacity—Your Choice to Be Positive Regardless of Circumstances

Risk Capacity—Your Choice to Get Out of Your Comfort Zone

Spiritual Capacity—Your Choice to Strengthen Your Faith

Growth Capacity—Your Choice to Focus on How Far You Can Go

Partnership Capacity—Your Choice to Collaborate with Others

As you explore these areas of capacity, I want to encourage you to make the choices that will help you to become the person you *can* be. Maximizing your capacity through good choices *every day* will help you to realize your potential *someday*. Turn the page to explore the first choice.

10

Responsibility Capacity—Your Choice to Take Charge of Your Life

What is one of the most boring and tiresome words ever? *Respon-sibility.* It's a word you've probably heard repeatedly from every authority figure at every time of your life. There is nothing sexy or exciting about that word, yet it is the first topic that I want to discuss in this section of the book on choices you can make to maximize your potential. Why? Because it is foundational to most of the other important choices we make in our lives.

Not everyone gets this. Many years ago, I came across an article about a man who wanted seemingly everyone else in the world to take responsibility for him, including God! Here's the article:

SYRACUSE, New York (AP)—A Pennsylvania man's lawsuit naming God as a defendant has been thrown out by a court in Syracuse.

Donald Drusky, 63, of East McKeesport, [Pennsylvania,] blames God for not bringing him justice in a 30-year battle against his former employer, the steelmaker now called USX Corp.

The company fired him in 1968, when it was called U.S. Steel.

"Defendant God is the sovereign ruler of the universe and took no corrective action against the leaders of his Church and his Nation for their extremely serious wrongs, which ruined the life of Donald S. Drusky," . . . the lawsuit said.

Drusky wanted God to return his youth and grant him the guitar-playing skills of famous guitarists, along with resurrecting his mother and his pet pigeon. If God failed to appear in court, federal rules of civil procedure say he must lose by default, Drusky argued.

U.S. District Judge Norman Mordue last week found the suit against God, former presidents Ronald Reagan and George Bush, the television networks, all 50 states, every single American, the FCC, all federal judges, and the 100th through 105th congresses to be frivolous.[1]

Reasons to Be Responsible for Your Own Life

It's easy to laugh at such an outrageous abdication of responsibility in another person. But the truth is that all of us have a tendency to blame others for our circumstances and even our choices. We need to overcome that tendency if we want to increase our capacity and live a life with no limits.

Responsibility may not be the most exciting subject, but it is one of the most impacting. And if you're willing to make choices that increase your sense of responsibility, you will see a corresponding increase in your success. Here's why:

1. Responsibility Creates the Foundation for Your Success

Novelist and editor Michael Korda observed, "Success on any major scale *requires* you to accept responsibility.... In the final analysis, the one quality that all successful people have... is the ability to take on responsibility." Winston Churchill, one of the greatest leaders of the twentieth century, expressed that same sentiment this way: "The price of greatness is responsibility." That is as true today as

> "Success on any major scale *requires* you to accept responsibility.... In the final analysis, the one quality that all successful people have... is the ability to take on responsibility."
> —Michael Korda

it was when Churchill led England in resisting Germany's aggression during World War II.

I've understood the positive impact responsibility can have on a person's life for as long as I can remember, even though I was not especially responsible as a kid. I liked to play more than anything else. But my parents worked hard to prepare me for life. My father would often quote Luke 12:48 to me: "To whomsoever much is given, much shall be required." A more modern version says, "Great gifts mean great responsibilities; greater gifts, greater responsibilities."[2] I heard those words echoing in my head as a kid every time I thought about going off track. And eventually, they took hold.

When I was a young man just beginning my career, I was eager to find and seize opportunities. To temper my eagerness and ambition for success, before embarking on an opportunity, I would often ask myself, "Would I be willing to sign my name to this?" In other words, was I willing to be responsible for everything good or bad that accompanied the choice to pursue this opportunity? Asking that question often prompted me to pass on the opportunity or to pursue a different course of action.

Today, after asking myself that question thousands of times over for over fifty years, here is what I know:

- The size of the opportunity requires the same amount of responsibility.
- Opportunity is lost when responsibility is neglected.
- Tomorrow's opportunity is determined by yesterday's responsibility.

One of the reasons successful people are successful is that they see and seize opportunities. Often we see them going through doors of opportunity, making the most of them, and we think to ourselves, *I wish I had that chance.* We see the results, but what we often don't see is the deep level of personal responsibility they had to take to make the most of the opportunity. Without increasing their responsibility capacity, they could not have increased their opportunity capacity.

2. Responsibility Puts You in Control of Your Life

In 2015, I wrote the book *Intentional Living* to help people get control of their lives. Recently I came across a quote by author Roshan D. Bhondekar, and thought, *I wish I could have shared his thought in that book.* Here's what he wrote:

Many people think about their lives as something that just happens to them instead of something that they can control themselves. They drift through life reacting to the actions of others instead of taking steps on their own behalf. Such people are like rudderless boats on the ocean, completely at the mercy of the tides to take them wherever they will. People who don't know where they are going usually end up where they don't want to be.

In the case of a boat on the sea, sooner or later the shifting currents will run it aground or break it upon the rocks. Most people would agree that it would be much better if someone steered the boat past the danger and out into clear waters instead. People are just the same. If we don't take control of the direction our lives will take, we leave ourselves to the mercy of others, often with disastrous consequences.[3]

The way you take control of the direction of your life is to take responsibility for yourself and your everyday actions.

People who embrace responsibility and take control of their lives see dramatic results. Recently at a conference, an attendee approached me and said, "Ten years ago you gave me the greatest advice I have ever received."

Curious, I asked, "What was it?"

"You challenged me to get control of my life, or someone else would," she replied. "I did that. Thanks."

I'd like to give you that same advice right now. Take control of your life. Can you control everything? No, of course not. But you can choose to control the things that *are* within your control. First, acknowledge that you have the ability to choose. Then, identify which parts of your life you can have control of and which you can't. Once you begin taking charge and making choices, your life will begin to change. As former first lady Eleanor Roosevelt said, "In the long run, we shape our lives and we shape ourselves. The process never

> You can choose to control the things that *are* within your control.

ends until we die. And the choices we make are ultimately our own responsibility."

If you've ever had the desire to escape from your life, taking responsibility and starting to shape your life will remove much of the temptation to do that. When you have given yourself permission to live the life you want, you begin to own yourself and no longer need the permission of others to do what you know is right for you. It is at that point that you begin to maximize your capacity.

So take control of what you can control, and don't try to control what you can't control. Greek philosopher Epictetus said, "Make the best use of what is in your power, and take the rest as it happens." It is important to understand the limits of your responsibility. If you don't, you'll create a lot of unnecessary suffering for yourself, waste your energy, and constantly feel overwhelmed.

Years ago I had a staff member on my team who was hyper-responsible. She would often try to be responsible for people and things beyond her control. Every six months she would come to my office, and together we would reestablish what her responsibilities were, and I'd confirm which things she should not be carrying. At the end of these sessions, she would always say, "Thanks, John. I feel lighter." A key to success is carrying the weight for which you're responsible, but dumping the weight of trying to control circumstances or other people.

3. Responsibility Builds Your Self-Esteem

Why do people often have self-esteem problems? It's often because they don't take responsibility for their lives. Novelist Joan Didion asserted, "The willingness to accept responsibility for one's own life is the source from which self-respect springs." People who don't take responsibility for themselves often blame someone else for the bad things that happen, and then they start to adopt a victim mentality. That never leads to success—or to greater capacity.

> "The willingness to accept responsibility for one's own life is the source from which self-respect springs."
> —*Joan Didion*

When you are faced with a difficult choice to do what you know is right, yet you still do it, how does that make you feel? Doesn't it give you a sense of inner satisfaction? Doesn't it make you feel strong? Doesn't it reward you internally with the sense that you did the right thing? I know it does these things for me. Repeated choices to take responsibility give you mental and emotional momentum, which only makes you feel stronger and better about yourself.

When I was in my early thirties, I was offered a great financial opportunity by a friend. At that time, Margaret and I had no money, so my friend also offered to lend me the money to finance my participation in the deal.

This was too good to be true, so I immediately said yes. But after a couple of hours, I began to have reservations. Why? My friend would be doing everything, and taking all the risks, and I would be doing nothing. I thought that wasn't right. So the next day I again thanked him for the opportunity, but said I would only participate in the deal if I could find a way to raise the money I needed myself. I wanted to take responsibility for my part. I had recognized that if it was successful, I would have always felt bad because he had carried me the whole way, and I hadn't carried my own weight.

It took a month of hard work and creativity for me to come up with the money, but I did it. It was my first financial investment, and it was a thrill for me. I loved having the opportunity, but I also felt good because I had taken responsibility. And though the financial return was good, the high return on my self-esteem was even better. My hope is that you experience similar returns as you choose to take responsibility for your life.

4. Responsibility Makes You Ready for Action

Theologian and anti-Nazi dissident Dietrich Bonhoeffer observed, "Action springs not from thought, but from a readiness for responsibility." Taking responsibility helps us to become self-starters, and self-starters do very well in life. Why? Because the fastest person is not always the one who wins the race. Often it's the one who started first. Responsible people don't wait around for someone else to take action. They do. So if you want to set yourself apart from the crowd, be the first to act, whether it's to help, show up, or seize an opportunity.

Engineer, educator, and author Roghu Korrapati, in his book *108 Pearls of Wisdom for Every College Student*, writes,

> It is often said that your thoughts become your actions. But without taking responsibility for your life, those thoughts often just stay on that mental stage and aren't translated into action. Taking responsibility for your life is that extra ingredient that makes taking action more of a natural thing. You don't get stuck in just thinking and wishing so much. You become proactive instead of passive.[4]

Whenever I am faced with a problem, I focus my mind on the issue and remind myself that I am responsible to act. If I lack responsibility, when life calls for action, my response will be ready, aim, aim, aim...but never *fire*. Accepting responsibility makes you take action, not just prepare for it.

5. Responsibility Makes Your Habits Serve You

Are habits good or bad? That, of course, depends on what the habits are and what they do for—or against—us. When we apply responsibility to our habits, it directs them positively and makes them work for us.

Positive habits are decisions that we make once (like "I've decided to exercise regularly"), and then take responsibility to manage daily. When we make a good decision, and then manage that decision day-to-day, we can see positive results through the development of those positive habits. Without management, a good decision dies. With management, the decision lives on. That's why decision managing is at least as important as decision making.

> Without management, a good decision dies. With management, the decision lives on.

Conversely, when we don't take responsibility and neglect to manage our positive habits daily, we often cultivate the negative habits of procrastination, entitlement, and excuses. Before long, those bad habits become our master.

Excuses, for example, are success stoppers. The habit of making excuses creates reasons in our minds for not being responsible for our lives. Every time we make an excuse, we fail to learn from our mistakes. Excuses put the blame on others or on circumstances, which causes you to give up the power to change your life.

Another negative habit is that of feeling entitled, the belief that whether we win or lose, we deserve a trophy. That whether we work or play, we deserve an income. Whether we do good works or act selfishly, we deserve praise. In essence, when we feel entitled, we want someone else to sponsor us in life without our making any effort of our own. Again, this bad habit masters us and distances us from responsibility.

Recently I was privileged to spend some time with Lou Holtz, a good leader, fantastic football coach, and very funny guy. He said, "The man who complains about the way the ball

> "The man who complains about the way the ball bounces is likely the one who dropped it."
> —Lou Holtz

bounces is likely the one who dropped it." It's okay to drop the ball once in a while. We all do. It's not okay to drop it, blame somebody else, and expect them to pick it up!

If we abdicate responsibility, even that is a choice, and we are responsible for making it. Trying to avoid it is like a drunk driver claiming he wasn't responsible for a fatal car accident because he was drunk. The law would argue that he was responsible *before* he started drinking and *chose* to give up that responsibility to alcohol. He remains responsible and accountable for his actions afterward.

Our first responsibility to develop good habits that serve us is to stop the losses (caused by negative habits) that threaten to define us, and start making and managing choices that declare who we are. That all begins when we choose to be responsible, which gives us the power to master our habits, and our lives.

6. Responsibility Earns You Respect and Authority

Respect is gained on difficult ground, and it is not given or granted to us if it is unearned. Often I hear leaders lament their lack of authority. The problem? They rely on titles instead of earning authority through responsible behavior. The late Peter Drucker wrote, "Management has no power. Management has only responsibility." I think that's true.

Too often we hope for respect instead of earning it the hard way. We avoid the difficult conversation we need to have, and hope our problems will just go away. That doesn't happen. Stephen M. R. Covey, author of *The Speed of Trust,* writes about taking responsibility for handling difficult conversations:

> Say what is on your mind. Don't hide your agenda. When we talk straight, we tell the truth and leave the right impression. Most employees don't think their bosses communicate

honestly. This creates a trust tax. This causes speed to go down and costs to go up. We spend entirely too much time trying to decipher truth from spin.[5]

As a young leader who wanted to make people happy, I too often told others what they wanted to hear, not what they needed to hear. I didn't take responsibility for speaking the hard truths that good leaders take responsibility for. I no doubt created a trust tax on myself and others.

Today, I welcome responsibility and desire to earn the respect of others every day. And there are times when that desire is tested. That occurred several years ago at a speaking engagement I did for my friend Todd Duncan at a financial conference. I had spoken for Todd many times before, and I was looking forward to helping the people who would be in attendance. My message was called "Today Matters." But as I was speaking, I could tell something wasn't quite right. It wasn't bad. I could just tell it didn't serve them as well as I wanted it to.

I was scheduled to have dinner with Todd after my session and then fly out later that night. On the way to dinner, I called Linda, because I had a sinking feeling in the pit of my stomach. "Linda, can you look up what I spoke on last year to Todd's group?" I asked.

"Sure. Just a sec." I could hear Linda typing on her computer. "You spoke on 'Today Matters.' "

I was speechless.

At dinner, I apologized to Todd.

"No problem, John," Todd said graciously. "It was nice to hear the message a second time."

Todd was being kind, but I knew I hadn't given him what he needed—or what he'd paid me for. I needed to take responsibility for that. And speaking for him the next day wasn't an option. The schedule was full.

"Todd, I want to come back next year, at my own expense, and speak again for no charge. I owe you that." He tried to protest. "And I want to apologize to your people tomorrow morning before your first session."

"I can do that for you."

"No, I'm the one who made the mistake. I need to apologize to them." And I did. I changed my flight, stayed over an extra night, and apologized to the 2,500 people in the audience, for reteaching a message that many had heard a year before.

As I drove to the airport later that morning, I knew I'd done the right thing. I'd made a mistake, but I'd taken responsibility and done what I could to make it right. And I did return the next year and spoke for Todd. And you'd better believe it wasn't on "Today Matters."

> "At the root of resilience is the willingness to take responsibility for results."
> —*Eric Greitens*

Eric Greitens, in his book *Resilience*, describes the bottom line on responsibility. He says, "The more responsibility people take, the more resilient they are likely to be. The less responsibility people take—for their actions, for their lives, for their happiness—the more likely it is that life will crush them. At the root of resilience is the willingness to take responsibility for results."[6] That willingness is also at the root of capacity.

Responsibility Capacity Questions

1. In the past, have you ever connected the ideas of taking responsibility and increasing your capacity? How specifically do you think becoming more responsible could help you in your personal life and career?

2. On a scale of 1 to 10, how would you rate yourself when it comes to being ready to take action? How might taking greater responsibility increase your readiness?

3. What positive habits would you like to cultivate that could be facilitated by taking greater responsibility? What decision must you make to start the habit, and what actions must you take daily to manage that decision?

11

Character Capacity—Your Choices Based on Good Values

Twice a year the John Maxwell Team hosts an event to certify coaches, teachers, and speakers, and I always speak as part of that process. Over the years, I've taught on a lot of different subjects, depending on what I'm learning at the time. But there's one session that I always teach to every group, and I will continue teaching it no matter what: a session on values. Why do I do that? Because our values determine our character, and our character determines the direction we will go in life. I want the certified coaches who carry my name to demonstrate good character and go in a positive direction.

> Our values determine our character, and our character determines the direction we will go in life.

Values—The Foundation of Character

At nearly seventy years old, I'm finding that my values are probably deeper and stronger than they have ever been in my life. I rely less

186

and less on beliefs, which I seem to have fewer of as I age. What's the difference? Values don't change, but beliefs do—all the time. Every time you learn something new, your beliefs adjust. In my lifetime I've let go of dozens and dozens of beliefs that I once possessed just because I learned more or experienced more.

For example, when I was in my twenties, I strongly believed that environment was the most important factor in the upbringing of a child. I was certain that DNA was less important. Then Margaret and I adopted two children: Elizabeth and then Joel. It didn't take long for us to recognize the strength of genetics. I looked at the children of my brother, Larry, and my sister, Trish, and I could tell exactly what they were doing and why they were doing it. They were Maxwell through and through. But when I watched Elizabeth and Joel, I often couldn't tell why they were doing what they were doing. And I learned that certain traits and behaviors were hardwired into them, and nothing Margaret and I did would alter them.

Both of our children are now in their thirties, married, and successful. They have children of their own. And Margaret and I no longer believe that environment is the main factor in parenting. That's a belief we let go of due to our life experience.

Today I am far less interested in certainty about many things and much more interested in clarity about the few things that matter. And though I am certain about fewer things, I have more clarity than I have ever had before in my life. The things that are crystal clear are my values.

> Today I am far less interested in certainty about many things and much more interested in clarity about the few things that matter.

Why do I put so much emphasis on values? Because values create the foundation of character, and character provides the foundation for success.

Character—The Foundation for Success

In the previous chapter, I talked about how *responsibility* isn't a very exciting or sexy word. Neither is *character*. The idea of building character isn't flashy or exciting. It's not something we regularly add to our list of annual goals. But the results of developing character are life-changing. It's one of only two or three things I can think of that are *most* important in life.

Here's why character is so important, and why you should make the choices needed to develop your character capacity:

1. Good Character Is a Choice You Can Make Every Day

Stephen R. Covey, author of *7 Habits of Highly Effective People*, said, "As you live your values, your sense of identity, integrity, control, and inner-directedness will infuse you with both exhilaration and peace. You will define yourself from within, rather than by people's opinions or by comparisons to others."[1] What Covey's describing is good character being formed by choices based on values.

Every day you either grow your good character or shrink it. When you choose to do the right thing based on a positive value, your character expands. With each right choice, you develop the strength to make other right choices, and more difficult right choices. In contrast, every time you choose to cut corners, compromise on your values, or turn your back on what you know to be right, it shrinks your character. The smaller and weaker it gets, the more difficult it is to make another right choice.

Truett Cathy, the founder of Chick-fil-A, used to say that your commitment to get better needs to be more important than your commitment to get bigger. He was speaking in the context of business, and that's quite a statement, considering that the restaurant chain he created was worth more than $4.5 billion before he died.[2] But his point was accurate: we should always focus more on choices that impact who we are on the inside.

What are you focused on day to day? Making your work more lucrative? Making your company bigger? Rising up in your organization? Or making your character better, deeper, stronger? The choices you make every day make you.

2. Good Character Speaks Louder Than Words

For several years, I had the privilege of being mentored by legendary UCLA basketball coach John Wooden. He once said, "Be more concerned with your character than your reputation, because your character is what you really are, while your reputation is merely what others think you are."

Who we are inside is much more important than how others see us. Abraham Lincoln said, "Character was like a tree and reputation like its shadow. The shadow is what we think of it; the tree was the real thing." Character represents who you really are on the inside: the moral and mental qualities that make you you. And that is what speaks to people. It speaks more loudly than your words or the words others say about you. Your character represents you to the world.

Recently I had dinner with my friend Linda Kaplan Thaler, the advertising executive who invented the AFLAC duck. Linda told me a story about her son, Michael, who is a highly skilled chess player. When he was six years old, he was competing in the finals of a national chess championship, and his opponent made the winning move, but he didn't hit his clock, which was required for the move to count.

Michael looked at his opponent, and said, "You didn't hit your clock." The opponent hit the clock, and Michael lost the match.

Afterward, Linda said, "Michael, if you hadn't told him to hit the clock, you could have won."

Michael looked at her and replied, "Oh, Mom. That's not winning."

Michael might have lost the match that day, but his character is going to win him many more important things in the future.

3. Good Character Is Consistent in All Areas of Life

When a person has good character, he or she has it in every area of life consistently, regardless of the circumstances, regardless of the setting, and regardless of the context.

More than a decade ago, I went to dinner with Laurence J. Kirshbaum in New York City. At that time, he was the chairman and CEO of the Time Warner Book Group. During our conversation, he pitched an idea to me.

"John, I've been wanting one of our authors to write a book on a particular subject, and I think you would be the perfect person to do it. What would you think about writing a book on business ethics?"

"There's no such thing," I answered.

"What?" he asked. I could tell that wasn't the response he expected. "What do you mean?"

I explained, "There's no such thing as business ethics—there's only ethics. People try to use one set of ethics for their professional life, another for their spiritual life, and still another at home with their family. That gets them into trouble. Ethics is ethics. If you desire to be ethical, you live it by one standard across the board."

Good character uses the same standard in every situation. If something is right, it's always right. If it's wrong, it's always wrong. People with good character are consistent. People who try to use multiple standards with different people and in different situations live fragmented lives.

4. Good Character Engenders Trust

When a person lives a fragmented life, people never know what to expect from them. They don't know how the person will act in any given situation. In contract, a person of good character who lives by the same consistent standard invites trust. People know what they're going to get. They know the person's words and actions will line up. They can rely on that person and what he or she says.

Whenever you make a commitment to another person, you create hope. When you *keep* that commitment, you create trust. Good character helps you to follow through on that commitment and develop that trust. Why is that important? As mentioned in the chapter on people capacity, all relationships are built on trust. So by increasing character capacity, you build the trust needed to increase

> Whenever you make a commitment to another person, you create hope. When you *keep* that commitment, you create trust.

people capacity. That not only improves the quality of your life, but it also improves the qualities of your professional relationships, including your ability as a leader. Where trust is absent, leadership falters.

5. Good Character Is Tested in Times of Trouble

I once read a story about two men in their seventies named John and George. They had been friends since their high school days, but they both held strong opinions and were stubborn. As a result, they argued all the time and often went for weeks without speaking to one another.

One day after an especially heated argument over some trivial matter, they exchanged unkind words and went their separate ways. And they didn't speak to each other for months.

But then George became critically ill. He summoned John to his hospital bed, saying that he wanted to heal their relationship before he died. He took John's hand in his and whispered, "John, I forgive you. Will you forgive me?"

John was deeply moved by his friend's final gesture, but before he could reply, George confided, "I have just one more thing: if I get well and don't die after all, this doesn't count!"

> "The weak can never forgive. Forgiveness is the attribute of the strong."
> —*Gandhi*

The story may be silly, but it reveals an important truth. Adversity doesn't build character; it reveals it. It takes a person of good character to forgive and extend grace to another person. As Gandhi said, "The weak can never forgive. Forgiveness is the attribute of the strong."

When you have good character, difficulty only makes you more determined. When your character is weak, difficulty makes you discouraged. What are you doing to build good character every day? Are you making right choices based on your values? Every time you do, it makes you stronger. Work on your character now. When the storm comes, it's too late to prepare.

6. Good Character Always Takes the High Road

Most people want to treat others the way they've been treated. It's human nature. I once heard a well-known businessman say, "When somebody screws you, screw them back in spades" and "Go for the jugular so that people watching will not want to mess with you." That's not the way I want to live. I don't want to treat others worse than they treat me. I want to treat others better than they treat me. I want to always take the high road, and I want to encourage you to do the same.

I learned this from my father, who modeled it every day. When he was the president of Ohio Christian University in the 1960s, I thought the university's board didn't treat him with the respect and consideration he had earned and deserved. But he never retaliated or said anything negative about them.

I remember a time when someone interviewed Dad and asked his opinion about a man who had been particularly nasty to him. When Dad said only nice things about the man, the interviewer proceeded to recount all the terrible things the man had said about Dad. My dad's reply? "You didn't ask me what he thought of me. You asked me what I thought of him."

Taking the low road is easy. It doesn't take any character at all. Low-road people...

- Seek revenge and retaliation when wronged,
- Play the same game that others do,
- Are guided by emotions that constantly go up and down,
- Are reactive, and
- Live no better than anyone else does.

High-road people are totally different. They...

- Extend unconditional love and forgiveness,
- Refuse to play games with people,
- Are guided by good character based on values,
- Are proactive, and
- Live exceptional lives.

I admit that I don't always take the high road with everybody. But I try to. I work at it. When someone treats me poorly, I try to remember that it's a reflection on them, not on me. When someone takes advantage of me, I try to remember that it's the price one has to pay for letting others get close to them. When someone criticizes me, I try to remember that is the price of leadership.

I hope you'll take a similar path. Sometimes you will be hurt. You will be treated unfairly. People will take advantage of you. But wouldn't you rather make the world a better place and help other people?

7. Good Character Delivers on Its Promises

Salesman and author Elmer G. Leterman said, "Personality can open doors, but only character can keep them open." Why is that? Because character delivers. People with good character do what they say they'll do. They follow through. People can depend on them.

When you say you'll do something, do you follow through? Are you known as someone who delivers? Or do others sometimes worry that you may give up or not show up? Booker T. Washington said, "Character is power." Make the most of it.

Scientist Marie Curie observed, "You cannot hope to build a better world without improving the individuals. To that end, each of us must work for his own improvement, and at the same time share a general responsibility for all humanity." If you want to build your character, you need to try to align four things: your values, your thinking, your feelings, and your actions. If your values are good and you make the other three things consistent with them, there's almost nothing you can't improve in your life.

> "You cannot hope to build a better world without improving the individuals. To that end, each of us must work for his own improvement, and at the same time share a general responsibility for all humanity."
> —Marie Curie

I recently learned about a fantastic example of what happens when people embrace good character and make a conscious choice to increase their character capacity. It happened in Guatemala. Back in 2013, my organizations worked together to pilot the roundtable training initiative that I told you about in chapter 9 on leadership capacity. In Guatemala City, we trained facilitators to lead a curriculum of thirty roundtables. Half of the roundtables were about personal growth. The other half were about developing character based on values, such as responsibility, humility, dependability, generosity, ethics, forgiveness, honesty, and hard work. We trained several thousand people in June, and they started leading roundtables immediately across the country. Now I believe more than two hundred thousand people have gone through roundtables.

By the end of 2013, we started hearing about the positive impact that character development was having on the country. For example, we learned that the second largest bank in Guatemala, which had asked about five thousand of their employees to go through the roundtables, was having its best year financially. And guess when the ramp-up began? In June, when their employees began learning about character. Their people's increase in character capacity was having a direct impact on the company's business capacity.

An even bigger story out of Guatemala was about the peaceful protests the people staged against the corruption in government. In September 2015, the people's protests prompted the ousting of president Otto Pérez Molina for corruption. Soon afterward, an outsider candidate named Jimmy Morales, whose slogan was "neither corrupt nor a thief," was elected as president.

Is there direct evidence to connect the peaceful protests to the character development we introduced in Guatemala? Not that I know of. But I can tell you this: Thelma Aldana, the attorney general of Guatemala, who led the corruption investigation that started the removal of the president, vice president, and others, had gone through the roundtables along with other judicial workers before being appointed to her post in 2014. Maybe the actions she took during those thirty weeks helped in some small way to inspire her.

Are you willing to do the mundane work of increasing your character capacity? It probably won't receive any fanfare. You may in fact be the only person who'll ever know what steps you've taken to grow in this area. But I guarantee that you will see positive results and live a better life.

Character Capacity Questions

1. Have you ever identified and defined your values and put them into writing? If not, do so now. If so, review them. Are they the same?

2. On a scale of 1 to 10, how would you rate yourself on consistency when it comes to acting on your values through character choices? If you didn't give yourself a 10 (and who does?), what should you start doing differently to raise your score?

3. When dealing with others, do you most often take the low road, the middle road, or the high road? Why do you respond the way you do? What can you do to become more of a high-road person?

12

Abundance Capacity—Your Choice to Believe There Is More Than Enough

I was not a typical teenager. Like most teens, I resisted going to sleep at night. But where I differed was in how I responded to getting up in the morning. I woke up early every morning, and the moment I woke up, I leaped out of bed, because I didn't want to miss anything. Now really, what was I going to miss? My home was Circleville, Ohio, a sleepy small community. Only corn grew there. Yet I was expecting something wonderful and exciting to happen every day, and I wanted to experience it fully.

I think I was born with an abundance mind-set. My natural inclination causes me to think positively, trust people, feel good about myself and others, and enjoy life. I love options, and I believe nearly anything is possible. My abundance capacity is very high.

I recognize that everyone doesn't think this way. At the other extreme are people who possess a scarcity mind-set. While abundance thinkers believe there is more than enough of everything a person needs in the world, scarcity thinkers believe there is not enough to go around. While abundance people love to say yes, scarcity people feel compelled to say no. These two kinds of people see the world completely differently from one another, and both worlds are equally real to each. What they see, experience, and become is dictated by which world they see.

Over and over, I've observed that people's perspective in this area controls their life today and their potential tomorrow. A belief in scarcity holds people back from reaching their full capacity. A belief in abundance releases them to discover how far they can go. I don't know why this is true, but I know it is. Your perspective will determine what world you live in, and you *can* choose your perspective. You determine whether you are an abundance person or a scarcity person.

How you think in this area determines your choices. That's why you need to focus on changing your thinking about whether or not there's enough to go around. Abundance thinking encourages you to make choices that will expand your possibilities. Scarcity thinking causes you to make choices that will diminish your potential. Abundance calls out to you, "There's more than enough." Scarcity cautions, "Quick, get what you can before it runs out." Abundance says, "Go and you will find the resources." Scarcity says, "Hold on to what you have, because there are no more resources." Abundance says, "Your best days are before you." Scarcity says, "This is as good as it gets." How we respond is determined by the voice we allow to speak to us in our minds.

Tempted by Scarcity Thinking

As I said, I have a naturally strong inclination to think abundance. However, there have been three important times in my life when I was tempted to think scarcity instead of abundance. Each time occurred when I was faced with a major decision about the direction I would take my life. When I looked at the change that would be required of me, I wanted to choose what I knew, the thing that was safe, instead of striking out in a new direction where the potential for greater accomplishment lay.

The first time occurred when I was thirty-three years old. At that time I was leading a fantastic church whose growth and health had been recognized by people in that world. I was doing things I was very comfortable doing, I was working with people I loved who wanted me to stay there. But I was offered a chance to take my ideas about leadership outside of the secure environment where I had developed and used them successfully, and try them out on a larger scale, with dozens of other churches.

I was faced with a decision. Should I stay where it was comfortable? Or strike out into a new world? The people who wanted me to stay made the decision very difficult. For two years I weighed both options, but finally my decision came down on the side of abundance. I left the church to train leaders in a different organization.

The second time occurred when I was forty-eight. I was leading a church again, this time in San Diego. Again, the church had grown tremendously, and I loved the people there. And our work had received recognition. An influential author in the church world had identified the congregation as one of the ten most influential churches in America. The founding pastor of the church had stayed there until he retired, and I could have done the same thing.

However, at that time I had an opportunity to take my writing and speaking to a broader audience, including into the business community, but it was only doable if I resigned my position as leader of the church. This transition had the potential to reach many more people than I ever would if I stayed in the pastorate. But there were also great risks, and it caused me to ask many questions. Did I want to leave the positon and prestige of where I was to start over again at the bottom? Could I be successful with a different audience? Would I be able to learn all I needed to know? How long would it take? Would I actually make *less* of a difference if I made the move?

In the end, I didn't allow the fears driven by scarcity thinking to overpower the possibilities of abundance thinking, and I resigned my position from the church.

The third temptation came when I was sixty-six. I've already hinted at this by telling you the story of the marbles in the jar. Life was good, and I was starting to count down the years to seventy, thinking that at that time I would step away from my organizations. As I told you in the story, Bill Hybels helped to snap me out of that thinking. So did a conversation I had with Mike Hyatt, who told me that I was the face of my organizations. I'm so glad that I "lost my marbles" and chose abundance once again. I can't imagine living a life in which I'm not working to add value to leaders and make a difference in this world.

No or Yes?

Today I think I understand both the scarcity and abundance worlds very clearly. In general, scarcity lives on the other side of "no," meaning people stay where it's safe, while abundance lives on the other side of "yes," meaning they'll try something new. *What does it look like to live on the other side of no?*

- **It's limiting**—because it directs you away from new opportunities.
- **It's easy**—because when you say no, you don't have to do anything or go anywhere.

- **It's comforting**—because it feels familiar. Many people are more fearful of losing the little they do have than they are excited about gaining something they don't have.
- **It's deceiving**—because it appears to be safer, but it's not. As author Steven Pressfield says, "It's one thing to lie to ourselves. It's another thing to believe it."
- **It's crowded**—because that's where average people live.

What does it look like to live on the other side of yes?

- **It's exciting**—because you need creativity to help you figure things out when they're new. It embodies the philosophy of writer and comedienne Tina Fey, who advised, "Say yes, and you'll figure it out afterward."
- **It's enlarging**—because abundance creates more abundance. And the more abundance you experience, the greater your potential for high capacity.
- **It's challenging**—because new paths are not easy to tread.
- **It's rewarding**—because on the other side of yes, you usually find many more yeses.

I realize that no is not always bad and yes is not always good, but most of the time, living a life of no decreases your options, opportunities, and outcomes, while living on the other side of yes increases you and your world. That was true when I changed organizations at thirty-three. I got the opportunity to teach leadership on a wider scale, found out my leadership principles applied to many kinds of leaders in different organizations, and expanded my thinking. It was true when I was forty-eight, because it led to my becoming a best-selling author and expanded my audience ten thousand fold! And it was true at age sixty-six. I would never have gone to Guatemala or Paraguay to help people in those countries, I would not have helped to grow the John Maxwell Team to where it is today. My past yeses are bringing me more options, more opportunities, and more positive outcomes than any other time of my life.

Characteristics of People with Increased Abundance Capacity

At the most recent John Maxwell Team certification event, I noticed that Paul Martinelli's team had set up a station where attendees could ask questions and receive information. Behind the table was a huge sign that said, "The answer is YES!" I loved it. That statement says to everyone, "We will find a way."

That's how people with high abundance capacity think. They believe the answer is yes. There is a way to move forward. It may not be easy to find. It may not be the first choice, but they believe there is a way. And that's how I want you to think. I want to help you adopt an abundance mind-set and increase your capacity in this area. Even if you're a bit of a skeptic, I hope you are willing to give it a try. I hope you'll take a look at these three ways people of abundance think, and make the choice to embrace them:

1. Abundance People Possess High Belief

Why are people who embrace abundance so readily able to say yes? It's because they possess high belief in many areas of life:

They Believe in Themselves—They Say, "There's More to Me Than What People See"

I've always felt that I had more to give than others could see. That was how I felt even when I was young. Others saw my immaturity, my lack of experience, and my frequent fumbles. Many dismissed me. They said I was too young to lead anything. I worked hard to prove them wrong, and I have to admit, when I succeeded it gave me great pleasure. There were plenty of times when I was uncomfortable in what I was doing. But I believed in myself, and that often kept me going when no one else encouraged me. Mark Twain said, "A man cannot be comfortable without his own approval." I was comfortable with who I was. I still am. My personal belief in myself has given me the ability to say yes when others wouldn't affirm me.

Beliefs drive behavior. Lack of belief, which is a characteristic of scarcity, holds us back. We hesitate, not because we are unable to do something, but because we don't have confidence in ourselves. My friend, don't wait for someone else to pick you. Don't wait for someone to give you permission. You don't need anyone else to say you are qualified. Believe in yourself! Believe you can.

They Believe in Others—They Say, "There's More to Others Than I Can See"

I've mentioned to you that I see everyone as a ten. Some people comment on how unrealistic my belief in others often is. I agree that it can be. However, I still want to give everyone the benefit of the doubt. Where does that desire come from? It comes from abundance thinking. Even my desire to write this book on capacity comes from that belief. When I tell you that I believe you have the ability to increase your capacity and improve your life, I mean every word of it.

Henry Ford built his business empire off that type of thinking. He said, "I am looking for a lot of men who have an infinite capacity to not know what can't be done." Now that's belief in other people. It's easy for scarcity people to tell us it can't be done. And they love to do it. But history has shown time after time that people can do what others thought was impossible. Every one of those people who achieved the seemingly impossible had an abundance mind-set. You don't discover new worlds, invent new products, or create new ways of doing things unless you believe there is more!

When people believe in each other, they want the best for each other and expect the best from each other. They bless one another. Professor and author Dallas Willard defines blessing this way: "the projection of good toward someone." I love that. I want to live that. Don't you?

They Believe in Today—They Say, "There's More in Today Than I Can See"

In my book *Make Today Count* I write, "The secret of your success is determined by your daily agenda." What we do every day either makes us or breaks us.

> The secret of your success is determined by your daily agenda.

Abundance people seize the moment because they see potential in it. They believe they can do more than they've done before. They believe they can perform at a higher level than they have before. They believe they can grow more—and keep growing. This belief not only keeps them going, but it also allows them to be the first to take action. And often those who start first are the winners.

They Believe in Tomorrow—They Say, "There's More in My Future Than I Can See"

I'm getting older, but I refuse to become an old person. Have you noticed how old people think their generation is the last great one? They look at younger people and predict doom and gloom. That's happened for a hundred generations. I'm not going to do that! Yes, tomorrow has its challenges. And all youth need to mature. But abundance thinking tells me that tomorrow can be better than today.

I like to think of an abundance mind-set as the Energizer Bunny of our lives. It charges us up with high belief. That high belief gives us high energy. I want to be energized to do worthwhile things and make a difference. Don't you? It's your call.

2. Abundance People Understand the Power of Perspective

Our perspective is not determined by what we see. It's determined by *how* we see, and that comes from who we are. Two people can be in the same situation and see things completely differently. While a scarcity person often looks at a situation and thinks, *There's no way!* an abundance person sees the same things and thinks, *There's got to be a better way!*

> Our perspective is not determined by what we see. It's determined by *how* we see, and that comes from who we are.

The world is a better place as a result of people whose perspective was shaped by abundance thinking. People thought there was no way to get a room warm other than by using a fireplace. Benjamin Franklin thought there was a better way and invented what we call the Franklin stove. People thought there was no way to get anywhere fast on land except by using horses. James Watt thought there had to be a better way and invented the steam engine. People thought there was no way to talk to people miles away from them. Alexander Graham Bell thought there had to be a better way and invented the telephone. People thought there was no way for people to fly under power. The Wright Brothers thought there had to be a better way and invented the first powered, motorized airplane.

Do I need to go on? Change your perspective to one of abundance from one of scarcity, and you open the door to innovation and positive change, not only for yourself, but also for others.

3. Abundance People Are Generous to Others

The final characteristic of abundance people that I want to discuss is generosity. When most people think generosity, we usually think about giving money to charity. While that is truly a mark of generosity, the generosity that comes from abundance goes way beyond that.

There are other kinds of generosity that have nothing to do with money. These include giving people a chance, giving others the benefit of the doubt, and giving others a reason to want to work with you. An abundance person can be generous by giving others opportunities, giving them the resources and information they need to do their jobs well, giving them the credit when they are successful, and giving them grace when they make mistakes. What I'm really talking about here is generosity of spirit.

Generosity is a word that comes out of the Latin word *generosus*, meaning of noble birth. It was associated with members of the aristocracy who, by virtue of their privileges and inherited wealth, were expected to give to others of lesser standing than themselves. All of us are in better places than someone else in life. To those people, we should be generous. And if you're a leader, you need to understand that by virtue of your position and the privileges it brings, you should be generous toward the people you lead. I wish all leaders held themselves to this high standard, though not all do. The leaders who bring an abundance mind-set to their leadership responsibilities can increase the positive impact they make on their teams and organizations.

Some people worry that if they give too much of what they have, they will run short themselves. But I would say the opposite is true. The more you give, the more you get. And that just helps you to become more generous. You can see this in action when you smile at others. What happens when you do that? You usually receive a smile back. And that just makes you want to smile more. The more you help other people, the more they usually want to help others. And that motivates you to help even more. The more you love people, the more love you receive—and want to give others. That's what I call the Abundance Paradox. The more you give, the more you have to give—and want to give.

> The Abundance Paradox: the more you give, the more you have to give—and want to give.

Abundance people don't run out by giving. The opposite is true. They sow into the lives of others and receive a great harvest as a result. Without a question, my greatest return on investment in life has been believing and investing in other people. That's why my daily to-do list is filled with things I want for others. I totally agree with my friend Kevin Myers, who says, "We should want more for people than we want from people." Generous people are always interested in increasing the lives of those around them. And people will always move toward anyone who increases them and away from anyone who makes them feel like less.

I believe you can step out of the scarcity world and become an abundance person, even if you grew up feeling like there's not enough. Why do I say that? Because I've seen people who started out with a scarcity mind-set choose to become people of abundance. One of those people was Kevin Myers, whom I just quoted. I've mentored Kevin for twenty years. He says that one of the most important things I taught him was to change his mind-set to abundance.

> "We should want more for people than we want from people."
> —Kevin Myers

Kevin says, "I used to think that life was like a pie. There were only so many slices, so you had to try to get your piece while you could. John taught me that if you run out of pie, you just go back into the kitchen and bake another one. That was a completely different kind of thinking from what I grew up with. But now I embrace it."

If you're like most people, in your heart you'd like to believe in abundance. My advice to you is follow your heart. It was created for abundance. Talk to yourself. Say aloud, "I believe there is more than enough." That's a small step in the right direc-

> Sometimes the smallest step in the right direction becomes the biggest step in your life.

tion, toward abundance. And sometimes the smallest step in the right direction becomes the biggest step in your life.

Abundance Capacity Questions

1. When faced with an opportunity, are you naturally a yes person or a no person? If abundance usually means saying yes, what can you do to prompt yourself to say yes more often?

2. Belief in abundance begins with a person's belief in him- or herself. How would you rate your self-belief? Is it high, medium, or low? What must you do to raise it and put yourself in a position to embrace a stronger abundance mind-set?

3. What are you currently looking at in your life and saying, "There's no way." Pick something important to you. Tell yourself, "There's got to be a better way." Then start brainstorming ideas for how you can move forward positively.

13

Discipline Capacity—Your Choice to Focus Now and Follow Through

In 2000, I had the privilege of visiting the National Gandhi Museum in New Delhi, India. While I was there I saw a quote from Mahatma Gandhi that said, "The difference between what we do and what we are capable of doing would suffice to solve most of the world's problems." I've thought about that quote often. And I've wondered, *Why is there such a difference between what we do and what we are capable of doing? What would make up the difference and close the gap?*

> "The difference between what we do and what we are capable of doing would suffice to solve most of the world's problems."
> —*Gandhi*

It's not talent. Each of us is very capable, and we can do a great deal with the talent we already have, so that's not the answer. It's not more time. Each of us has the same amount of time allotted to us each day. What is it?

After years of reflection I think I know what would close the gap between what we do and what we are capable of doing. It's discipline.

By discipline, I mean the commitment to do what we should in a consistent way. In this context, discipline would be the difference maker.

You Are the Boss of You

Successful people are highly disciplined in doing their most important work. They are self-disciplined. They guide and encourage themselves to do the work they ought to do, not just the things they want to do. That's what takes them from average to good, and from good to great. And that's why the rewards in this world are usually reserved for those who are willing to do what the majority of people are unwilling to do.

> Discipline is the commitment to do what we should in a consistent way.

I love the way trainer and speaker Mark Tyrrell describes self-discipline. He says,

> Over the years I've come to see self-discipline as an invisible magic. You can't see, taste, or smell it, but its effects are huge. It can transform fat into slim, sag into buff, uninformed into expert, poor into rich, misery into happiness. It's the submerged part of the iceberg others don't see when they see your "genius."[1]

Everyone sees people's success without realizing that 90 percent of what leads to it is unseen, yet that 90 percent is what makes it possible.

That's why top athletes are as good as they are and are able to make their skills look so effortless. Their time playing in the game is only 10 percent—or less—of the time they spend on their sport. That's why brilliant musicians are so fantastic. The two-hour performance you witness is a mere fraction of the time they spend practicing and perfecting their skills. People look at athletes and artists and think, *I wish I had their luck*, when they should be saying, *I wish I had their discipline.*

How to Grow Your Discipline Capacity

Tyrrell says that too many people see life as a waiting room. I think that's true. People sit and wait for for their names to be called. But success does not come looking for us. We won't achieve great things accidentally. Never forget: everything worthwhile is uphill. Achieving what you want takes time, effort, consistency, energy, and commitment. Self-discipline is what makes those things possible and puts success within reach. And here's the good news. Self-discipline is something you can develop. You don't need to be born with it. It's a choice you make and keep on making.

> **Never forget: everything worthwhile is uphill.**

If you'd like to see your capacity for discipline increase, take these ideas to heart and put them into practice.

1. Know What Is Important

I was not a very good student in high school. All I wanted to do was hang out with my friends and play basketball. Students like me made it possible for others to finish in the top half of our class. However, everything changed for me when I went to college. My first semester I became a self-disciplined student who made the dean's list.

What happened? The moment I went to college I knew that I would be preparing myself for what I really wanted to do in my life. I had a purpose, and I knew what was important to achieve it. No more fooling around—I took great notes in class, developed excellent study habits, hung around with good students, and focused on my future. Everything changed, and I started on my self-discipline journey.

Stephen R. Covey made an interesting observation about discipline. He wrote,

Many people simply conclude that they are not disciplined enough. My response to that idea is that it's usually not a discipline problem at all. The problem is more often that the person has not yet sufficiently paid the price to get very clear about what matters most to them. Once you have a burning yes inside you about what's truly important, it's very easy to say no to the unimportant.[2]

> "Once you have a burning yes inside you about what's truly important, it's very easy to say no to the unimportant."
> —*Stephen R. Covey*

That certainly has been true in my life! When my calling became clear, my passion increased. My passion caused me to prioritize and plan my life.

I recently read an article by Brian Tracy that said 97 percent of adult Americans are trying to live their lives without clear, specific, written goals. He likened this to setting off across an unknown country without a road map.[3] That's a good analogy. If we want to get somewhere worthwhile, we need to identify where we're going.

Mark Cole is the CEO of my five companies. When I was sixty-five he asked me to write out my wish list of what I wanted for each company by the time I was seventy. He said, "John, take a few months and give a lot of thought to this request. As your right-hand man, I want to know your head and heart concerning the organizations I am responsible for." I did exactly what he asked. That exercise not only gave Mark clarity, it filled me with determination to see my dreams come true.

Do you know what's important to you? If you haven't thought it through and written it out, it's very likely that any lack of self-discipline you're experiencing is coming from that. The single greatest way to increase your discipline capacity is to know what's important and have that as a touchstone for your life.

2. Get Rid of Excuses

If discipline is the highway that takes us where we want to go in life, then excuses are exits off that highway. And believe me—there are *lots* of exits. Take a look at some of these, and see if you've ever found yourself saying any of them:

- I'll start after the new year.
- I don't want to do it alone.
- My spouse won't do it with me.
- I'll do it when I finish school.
- I'll do it after the kids get out of school.
- I'll do it after the kids go *back* to school.
- I'll do it when I have more energy.
- I'll start it when the weather gets better!
- I'll do it when I'm not as busy.
- I'll do it after my birthday.
- I'll do it tomorrow.
- I'll do it when I retire.
- I'm too heavy—I'll do it after I lose some weight.
- I'm too old. (Are you planning to get younger?)
- I'm too inexperienced.
- I'm too afraid.

- I'm too tired.
- I don't know how to start.

I've used a few of those myself, but I'm not proud of it.

How do you know something is an excuse? Ask yourself, "Would it stop me from doing something I love to do?" If it wouldn't, it's an excuse. Get rid of it.

3. Take Action Before You Feel Like It

If you were to Google "secrets of success," you'd get back 67 million results in less than half a second. People have written extensively about how to be successful for a very long time. So I'd say that knowing the success secrets is no problem. Doing the success secrets? Now that's a problem!

Our culture doesn't help us with this. The message we hear over and over is that we should do what we feel. But what if we don't feel like doing something? Should we wait for inspiration? In the case of writing, every experienced writer will tell you that you have to write when you don't feel like it. Otherwise, you'll never get much done.

Every person has a weak area that is especially hard to discipline. For me, it is eating right and exercising. I can go months without feeling like doing those things. So how do I make myself take action before I feel like it?

I Think About the Consequences of Not Acting

My cardiologist, Dr. Chauncey Crandall, clearly and continually reminds me that the important things I am called to do and love to do will be cut short if I fail to eat right and exercise. He says, "John, when you choose to take care of yourself physically, you increase the years you will live and the people you will help." If I don't make those right choices, there will be consequences. I understand that and remind myself of it. Often.

I Focus on Doing the Right Thing Just for Today

If I think about having to do something I don't want to do every day for the rest of my lift, it threatens to discourage me. So I focus on today. One day at a time works for me. I can handle that.

Recently, Annika Spampinato, a registered dietitian, explained that her main responsibility was to help low-income people learn and apply better dietary practices. To accomplish this objective, she does motivational interviewing. Her questions are directed to help her find common ground with the patient and discover together what they think would be the easiest, most comfortable way to make the needed changes. She says that when they choose what step they will take first and follow through, they increase their odds of success.

I Make Myself Accountable to Someone Else in My Weak Area

Few things are more effective in the area of self-discipline than accountability. Why? Because we need help with our weaknesses! Dr. Laura Balda, my personal physician, weighs me every month and charts my physical progress. Josephine Bunn, my personal trainer, holds me accountable to exercise every week. I tried working on these weak areas in my life without help or accountability, but I wasn't successful. I found that I needed to answer to someone besides myself. When I have only myself to answer to, I don't do nearly as well.

Recently at the gym, I saw a sign that said, "Nothing tastes as good as being fit feels." I try to remember that when I'm at the dinner table or sitting on the couch, and it often prompts me to do the right things when I don't feel like doing them.

What systems do you have in place to prompt you to take the right action when you don't feel like it? Who have you enlisted to hold you accountable? No matter how much self-discipline you have, you could benefit from ways to help you take action when it counts.

4. Don't Let Distractions Distract You

> "Successful men and women are those who work almost all the time on high value tasks."
> —*Brian Tracy*

Brian Tracy observed, "Successful men and women are those who work almost all the time on high value tasks. Unsuccessful men and women are those who waste their time by wasting the minutes and hours of each day on low value activities." What are distractions but low-value activities? And they never stop.

For example, this month it is my goal to finish the writing of this book. That is my major focus. However, in the last three days, I've had to deal with many distractions. People have asked...

"Could you meet with a friend who has a few questions?"

"Would you be able to do a three-minute video for an anniversary?"

"Can you take a few minutes to do one errand with a staff member?"

"There is one call that will move the ball forward for EQUIP; can you make it?"

"A note from you should be written as a follow-up; can you do it?"

"There is an article that you really need to read about transformation. Do you want to see it?"

These are all good things. Some are very important things. But the answer is NO! Not until this book is completed. I have to stay focused.

Stephen R. Covey called this doing first things first. Brian Tracy calls it the Crowding Out Principle. It goes like this: "If you spend all of your time on highly productive tasks, by the end of the day, you will have 'crowded out' all the unproductive activities that might have distracted you from your real work. On the other hand, if you spend your time on low value activities, those low value activities will crowd out the time that you need to complete the tasks that can make all the difference in your life. And the key to this attitude toward time and personal management is always self-discipline."[4]

> The Crowding Out Principle: "If you spend all of your time on highly productive tasks, by the end of the day, you will have 'crowded out' all the unproductive activities that might have distracted you from your real work."
> —*Brian Tracy*

Ask yourself, "What am I crowding out of my life these days?" Are you doing the unimportant or the convenient at the expense of the essential? I hope not, because if you are, you're going to be in trouble. You aren't expending your energy on what really matters.

So ask yourself that question daily as a reminder to feed your focus and diminish your distractions: What am I crowding out today? When you're thinking about and doing those things that bring a high return every day, you won't have time to do the things that have low return. And that increases your capacity.

5. Be Aware of Time

I have never known a person who lacked awareness of time who was self-disciplined. Successful people are time conscious; they know how they spend the time they have, and they understand that every minute matters.

Business coach and author Dan S. Kennedy says,

> If you become aware of the importance of time, you'll have a different concept of time, valuing of time, and how you must exercise control over your use and others' consumption of your time in order to have a reasonable chance of achieving your goals and tapping your full potential. You'll have new awareness of how your time is used or abused, invested or squandered, organized and controlled or let flow about at random.[5]

I've been told before by people who work with me that I have a clock inside of my head. What they mean is that I am always conscious of time and what I must do to maximize my efforts. I'm always very aware that time is slipping past me, my days are numbered, and my time is limited. I think we become more aware of this as we age, but it's true whether you're seventeen or seventy.

If you want to maximize the time you have, then I recommend that you do these two things that I do continually:

Set Upfront Expectations

Have you ever noticed that the completion of tasks often fills whatever time we allot to it? If you have to get an article written and you give yourself a week to do it, the writing takes a week. If you give yourself a day, it takes a day. If you say to yourself, "I have to get this done in two hours," it will take the entire two hours. The same kind of thing happens in meetings—unless you set expectations up front.

Whenever I meet with people, I communicate a time frame that we will be together, and express what I would like to accomplish during that time. This helps make them time conscious, causes them to set their priorities, and allows us to accomplish what is needed in the time allotted.

When you practice the disciplined use of time, you have an edge. Start setting expectations for yourself and others up front. Once you make this a regular practice, you can begin compressing the time you allot and keep compressing it until you figure out how efficient you truly can be with your time. Then you'll know how quickly you can get things done and set aggressive yet realistic time frames for meetings and tasks.

Set External Deadlines

So much of what we do in life has no deadline. As a result, many things get put off and float from day to day on our to-do lists. That's why I give myself external deadlines for nearly everything I want to get done. These visible deadlines create an awareness of time for me.

Every week, I look at my schedule, determine what I need to get done, and give myself deadlines. Right now I have deadlines for writing this book, for developing teaching materials for the volunteer associate trainers at my nonprofit organization EQUIP, and for thinking about what material I will want to teach at the next John Maxwell Team coaching certification event. I also have a deadline for planning the time I need to set aside for rest and recreation.

Every day I keep these deadlines in front of me. I keep a piece of paper on my desk where I can always see it. The deadlines keep me moving mentally.

A friend once told me, "Every moment you stay in dreamland is a moment you lose in working for that dream." How true. Discipline is like a muscle. The more we train it, the better we become in developing it.

> Discipline is like a muscle. The more we train it, the better we become in developing it.

Expectations and deadlines are great friends for any disciplined person. Try using them. I believe you will be amazed at how they increase your discipline capacity and your use of time.

6. Follow Through, Even When It Hurts

In my book *Put Your Dream to the Test* I write, "The dream is free but the journey isn't." People usually don't quit striving for their dream because the dream isn't worthy. They quit because they aren't willing to pay the price. They're not willing to follow through with the daily disciplines needed to achieve the dream. To be successful, we need to do what we should, even when it hurts.

Self-discipline is the fuel that keeps you going. The willingness to hold on in spite of problems, the power to endure—this is a winner's quality. Speaker and author Tony Robbins says, "I believe that life is constantly testing us for our level of commitment, and life's greatest rewards are reserved for those who demonstrate a never-ending commitment to act until they achieve."

Recently I was challenging a group of young leaders to learn how to follow through and finish what they start. I encouraged them to say to themselves each morning, "Today isn't over until I've finished whatever I need to do this day." I challenged them: Don't finish your day until what you set out to do has been done. Respect yourself enough to keep the promises you made in the morning.

When I was in my late twenties, I made it my goal to build a large church, much larger than the average-sized church in America. And I succeeded. What was my secret? Every Sunday afternoon after I'd finished my official duties for the week, I went to my office and got on the phone. My goal was to set up ten outreach appointments for the coming week. I didn't go home until I had accomplished that goal.

Did I like being on the phone to make appointments at the end of a long week? Not really. I would have much preferred being home with Margaret. But I did it. In fact, I did it every week for *seven years*. Over those 350 Sundays of finishing what I started, I gained greater respect for myself, which is the best kind of respect you can have. I also developed the discipline of following through, even when it hurt. Are you willing to do that? If you are, your discipline capacity will increase greatly. And you will achieve the things you desire to do.

The bottom line is that you cannot manage your life if you do not manage yourself. You cannot maximize your capacity if you cannot increase your discipline. Life continually gets busier and more complicated. It doesn't go the other way. If you're older, as I am, you recognize that. Back when I was single and in college, I thought I was busy. Then I got married and started my career, and I could see that those college years were really very simple. Then Margaret and I had kids, and again the pace of life sped up. In my thirties, I started my first business,

> You cannot manage your life if you do not manage yourself.

while working full time and staying engaged with my family. Even now with my children grown and with five grandchildren, I don't have time for all the things I want to do. And if I live to be a hundred, it won't be enough time to accomplish all the dreams I have.

I can't have any more hours in a day. So what can I do? Two things. First, I can expand my discipline capacity, so that I make the most of the time I *do* have. Second, I can partner with others (which I'll talk about in chapter 19). To increase your discipline, you don't have to be rich. You don't have to be a genius. You don't need to come from a great family. You don't need extraordinary talent. You just need to focus and follow through.

Discipline Capacity Questions

1. Self-discipline is where time and priorities meet. What would happen if you looked at your schedule and to-do list every week and allotted specific amounts of time for everything? How much time would that take? And how much time would that save you?

2. What excuses have become a "normal" part of your life? Write a list of the ones you often find yourself using, and write the counterargument to each so that you can be more self-disciplined in the future.

3. What percentage of the time do you follow through? The times when you don't, when do you stop and why? Is there a pattern? What can you do to push through at those times?

14

Intentionality Capacity—Your Choice to Deliberately Pursue Significance

One of my greatest passions is helping people live an intentional life. Why? Because I know that the greatest way for you to upgrade your life is to become intentional with it. When people increase their capacity for intentionality, everything else changes in their lives. When you become more intentional, your life can transform from successful to significant. I'll tell you how you can do that later in this chapter. But first, I want you to know more about intentionality.

The Three Keys to Increased Intentionality

In 2015, I wrote the book *Intentional Living* because I was so passionate about this. After I completed the book, I began teaching extensively on the subject. That was when I developed the idea of uphill dreams and downhill habits, which I discussed in chapter 8. I also distilled intentional living down into three characteristics, which I want to share with you now. If you choose to embrace them, you can live with a much higher capacity for intentionality.

Be Deliberate

Life is not a dress rehearsal. There are no do-overs for days, weeks, or years that we waste. We get only one shot at life, and whatever we fail to do will be left undone. I don't know about you, but I don't want to finish life with a bunch of regrets. I'd like to live in such a way that I create a list of hundreds of failed attempts rather than a list of regrets for things I'd failed to attempt. I am determined to make a difference in the time I have on earth.

How can you make sure you don't end up with a long list of regrets? Be deliberate. Too many people think that good intentions are enough to make a difference. They're not. Good intentions are overrated. The smallest action always surpasses the greatest intention.

When I was a kid, one of my dad's favorite riddles was this: "Five frogs are sitting on a log. Four decide to jump into the water. How many are left?" What do you think the answer is? If you said one, you missed the point. There are still five. Deciding isn't doing. You need to act—deliberately—to accomplish anything.

Be Consistent

The second hallmark of intentional living is consistency. Whatever we continually do in life compounds. If the things we do are negative, life gets worse for us. If we continually avoid work, it compounds. If we continually speak badly of others, it compounds. If we spend more than we earn, it compounds. If we practice instant gratification, it compounds. However, if what we do continually is positive, life gets better. If we practice intentionality, it compounds and life continues to get better.

Consistency is a bit like responsibility, which I pointed out wasn't an exciting word. But its *results* are exciting. And the longer we are consistent, the more the "interest" or benefits compound.

Be Willful

Living a life of intentionality is an act of the will. And it's something you have to be determined to do daily. Most people don't lead their lives; they accept their lives. I would rather make the choice every day to live intentionally. The Greek philosopher Epictetus said, "It's so simple really: If you say you're going to do something, do it. If you start something, finish it." That's what I'm challenging you to do: finish it.

How much do you want to make a difference with your life? You *can* make a difference. Are you willing to fight for it?

From Success to Significance

Do you desire to cross the bridge from success over to significance? I started my journey across that bridge many years ago when my assistant Eileen Beavers gave me a book for Christmas. When I saw the title, "The Greatest Story Ever Told," I opened the book with great excitement, because I wanted to learn what it was about. But all I saw were blank pages. Inside was a note from Eileen that said, "John, your life is before you. Fill these pages with kind acts, good thoughts, and matters of your heart. Write a great story with your life." That day I became intentional about my life and the story it would tell.

I shared that story in *Intentional Living*. When a staff member read it, she suggested that I inspire others as Eileen had inspired me. That prompted me to have a journal created called *The Greatest*

Story Ever Told that people can use to record their own acts of intentionality. Inside the journal I penned the following words:

> Dear Friend,
>
> The Greatest Story Ever Told can only be written by you. I want you to fill these blank pages with intentional acts of kindness that add value to people. Everyday let your words be a record of how you are making a positive difference in the lives of others. Start now & intentionally make a great story with your life.
>
> Your friend
>
> John Maxwell

My hope and desire is for others to live with intentionality and not only make a difference themselves, but also inspire others to strive for a life of significance.

I'm already starting to hear back from people about this. Just this week I received this e-mail:

Hello Mr. Maxwell,

My name is Jared Orth. I am 15 years old and I am a sophomore in high school. My grandfather showed me your books about a year ago and I've been reading them ever since. I absolutely love your books and I can honestly say I wouldn't be the person I am today without them. I just finished *Sometimes You Win, Sometimes You Learn* and I absolutely loved it.

My grandfather always talks to me about you and your speaking. He just recently came back from Fort Lauderdale from one of your meetings and told me everything about it. It really has changed my life.

I went over to see him today and he gave me another book. It was titled *The Greatest Story Ever Told*. When he showed it to me, he began to cry. He told me that he knew I was going to do great things and that he wants me to record all of it in this book. I got so emotional at that time. He also gave me another one titled *Intentional Living*. I plan to start reading it soon.

I want to say thank you for everything your books have taught me. I wish peace to you and your family. Have a great day.

Your Friend, Jared

When I read Jared's words, it made me smile. That's why I write books! But my smile will be even bigger if you become intentional and choose to live for significance.

Everyday Essentials for Intentional Significance

Significance is all about adding value to others. That's an uphill journey. Why? Because we are naturally selfish. We automatically think of ourselves first. If you don't believe that, let me ask you a question. When someone takes a photo of a group that you're in, and then shows it to you, who is the first person you look for? Case dismissed! You look for yourself. That's not an accusation. I look for myself, too. It's proof that we're all selfish. But selfishness is a downhill habit. Significance is an uphill trait. But it is achievable for you and for me.

I want to teach you my five everyday essentials for adding value to people. If you do these things every day, you will make a difference and you will immediately feel the significance of your life.

1. Every Day Add Value to People

In chapter 6 on people capacity, I talked to you about valuing people. This is the foundation for being able to add value to people. People don't add value to others when they don't value them.

So why should you value them? Because they're people. You don't need any other reason. Listen, human beings are human. They make mistakes. They say the wrong things. They hurt our feelings. Many people treat us poorly and are not very lovable. Love them anyway.

If you're wondering what I do to keep valuing people and treat them well no matter what, I can tell you.

I Take a Long, Hard, Realistic Look at Myself

Nothing helps give me greater incentive to extend someone else grace than for me to look at myself. I've said and done a lot of dumb stuff over the years. In the moments when I do something wrong, my greatest desire is for others to overlook my stupidity, extend me grace, and forgive me. Only they can do that for me.

If that's what I long for, it's only fair for me to turn the tables and give that to others. We're all flawed. We all make mistakes. We all hurt one another. We all need grace. It's this simple: I will do for others what I desire for them to do for me.

I Choose to Value People Based on Their Best Moments, Not Their Worst Ones

My worst moments include doing things I should not have done, thinking things I should not have thought, and saying things I should not have said. Is this the same for you? If you can't identify with this, read no further. Instead, stop and book an appointment with a counselor. Because you need help getting a realistic view of yourself.

I have my bad moments, but I also have some great moments. And I do the things I should do, think the things I should think, and say the things I should say. Here's what I know about me—and about you. We are not as good as our best moments and we are not as bad as our worst moments. I'd like to have others give me the benefit of the doubt and see me at my best. So my decision is to value others based on their best moments. When others have done that for me, I've always been grateful. It's the least I can do for somebody else.

I Believe People Have the Capacity to Grow and Get Better

You already know that I believe people have the potential to grow and increase their capacity, because if I didn't, I wouldn't have written this book. Why is this belief so strong in me? Because I know how much *I've* grown. Oh how I wish you could have seen me when I started. You would be greatly encouraged. I wasn't very good. I've had years to learn, change, practice, and grow.

My belief that others can grow moves me not only to value them as they are, but also to see the increased value they can attain. When I see others just starting out and sometimes messing up, I remember where I started, and I smile. I see myself in them. And I keep in mind that they have great potential and need to be valued.

You know how you feel when others devalue you, and how you feel when they value you. Doesn't it make a difference to you? How you're treated impacts how you feel about yourself and how you treat others. Keep that in mind as you interact with people. When you value others, you start creating a cycle of positive interaction that makes life better for everyone.

2. Every Day Think of Ways to Add Value to People

If I said I had a five-minute thinking exercise for you that would give you a huge return in your relationships, would you be interested? Of course you would. What I am about to share with you is exactly that. Doing this has created memories for me and for others that we will never forget, ideas we will continually use, and resources that we will always cherish.

Here's what I want you to do. Spend five minutes every evening thinking about who you will see the next day, and ask yourself, "What can I say to them, give to them, or do for them that will make our time together memorable, be unexpected, and add value to them?"

That sounds too simple, doesn't it? But trust me, this exercise will set you apart from 99 percent of all the other people in the world. And if you'll do this every evening, and then revisit the ideas you come up with the next morning to potentially improve them, you will be amazed by the difference you can make for other people.

I try to do this every day. For example, Margaret and I had dinner last night with Jack and Marsha Countryman. Jack is the founder of J. Countryman Gift Books. For twenty years he has helped me think of ideas for books and also published and distributed many of them. He has been a great asset in my life.

The night before our dinner, I did my five-minute thinking exercise and came up with three things I could do during our dinner time to add value to him and Marsha. That night, the first thing I did was talk about the books we had done together, and how much Jack helped me grow as an author. For example, Jack gave me the title *Talent Is Never Enough*. Why would I go out of my way to talk about that? Because I wanted Jack to know that I remembered it was his idea and I was grateful to him.

Second, I acknowledged and praised a quality that I admired in both of them: their eagerness to learn. Whenever they attended one of my conferences, they would sit in the front row and take notes. I saw their eagerness to learn then and every other time I was with them, despite the fact that they were already highly successful.

Third, I asked Jack if we could do another project together. I wanted Jack to know that I still valued his ability to contribute in my life.

Jack is eighty-two—a beautiful man. As we separated, I gave him a big hug. It was a special night, and it was made more memorable because I thought ahead of ways to add value to him.

People who make a difference think about ways to add value to people ahead of time. Take a look at your day's calendar. Where will you be going? Who will you be meeting? In what ways might you add value to someone else? It only takes five minutes, but the opportunities to make a difference are endless.

3. Every Day Look for Ways to Add Value to People

Last year Greg Brooks became the executive director of my nonprofit organization EQUIP. Before that, he was a staff member. The thing that stood out to me about Greg was that if something needed to be done, he was the first to help. He was always winning the race when it came to adding value to people. I once asked him how he was able to do this on such a consistent basis. I will never forget his reply. "I'm always looking for ways to help people." And guess what. Because he's always *looking* for ways, he's always *finding* them.

Since I spend so much time speaking and writing to help others, I'm always looking for ideas and information I can use to help me help others. It has become part of my mind-set. And when I do find something useful to pass on, I ask myself, "Where can I use this? When can I use this? Who needs to know this?"

As you go through your day, what is your mind-set? Are you intentionally looking for ways to add value to others? If not, you can. It's a capacity choice. If you choose to look for ways, you'll find them.

4. Every Day Do Things That Add Value to People

It's not enough to just look for ways to help people. You have to follow through if you want to make a difference. Intentional living requires intentional doing.

How do I know I've had a good day? When I say yes to the question I ask myself every night: "Did I add value to someone today?"

My ultimate goal in adding value to others is to do something for them that they cannot do for themselves.

Mother Teresa said, "Let no one ever come to you without leaving better and happier. Be a living expression of God's kindness: kindness in your face, kindness in your eyes, kindness in your smile, kindness in your warm greeting." That's something all of us can strive for.

5. Every Day Encourage Others to Add Value to People

I believe nothing is as common as the desire to make our lives count, to make a difference. And there are needs all around us waiting to be met by intentional people. Yet so many never live a significant life. Why? Because doing the right thing is more difficult than knowing the right thing. That's why we need to encourage others to act.

As a young leader, it was my goal to have people follow me. I thought that the more followers I recruited, the more I could get done. The good news was that I was fairly successful. The bad news was that after a while I discovered that the best leaders challenge and encourage people to follow a cause or mission greater than themselves.

Today, as a leader, I don't recruit people to follow me. Instead, I point to significance and challenge people to intentionally add value to others to make a positive difference in the world. I want to do more than be successful by leaving an inheritance *for* others. I want to create a legacy by leaving an inheritance *in* others.

Recently, I was talking with Alan Mulally, the former chairman of the Ford Motor Company. I told him I was writing this book, and I wanted

> "To reach maximum capacity, you have to serve others and add value to them."
> —*Alan Mulally*

to know what capacity meant to him. He said, "To reach maximum capacity, you have to serve others and add value to them." He is so right. Significance begins with you, but it's meant to be shared.

As you make the choice to add value to others and develop the first four habits I outline in the chapter, don't forget the fifth and final step of encouraging others to do the same. You'll be amazed at what can happen when like-minded and like-valued people work together to add value to others and make a difference.

Spreading the Message of Intentionality to a Nation

I want to follow my own advice and encourage you to add value to others by telling you the story of someone who increases her capacity to make a difference by being highly intentional. Her name is Gaby Teasdale, and she is having an impact on an entire country.

Gaby is one of my certified coaches. She's from Paraguay. In 2013, she was one of the coaches who volunteered to go to Guatemala to train facilitators to lead roundtables. She says that she came away from that event feeling certain that what was happening there would also happen someday in Paraguay.

The next year, Gaby was at the John Maxwell Team event to attend the mentoring sessions, and she stood in line while I was signing books to say hello. After she and I talked, she dug in her bag and pulled out her passport. It was the only paper she had with her, and she said, "John, give me a word for the coming year. Write it here." She handed me her passport, and in the back of it on one of the blank pages, I wrote the first word that came to mind: *transformation*, and then I signed it.

Gaby later told me that this prompted her to start being intentional about her desire to bring the coaches to her country to teach values and intentional living.

Her first step was to get me to sign a copy of my book *Intentional Living* for the president of Paraguay. But the problem was that she didn't know the president. She didn't let that stop her. She began talking to people, looking for someone who could get her a meeting, and eventually she found one. She met with the president, gave him the book, and told him about her experience in Guatemala.

A few weeks later, I received a letter from President Horacio Cartes inviting me and my organization to come to Paraguay and teach values in roundtables. The process had begun.

Over the next two years, Gaby, her husband Tim, and a team of people in Paraguay worked tirelessly to build relationships and prepare for the launch that I wrote about in chapter 9 on leadership capacity. And the result was huge. Tens of thousands of people have been helped to live a better life, and they have been encouraged to become intentional in the way they live. As I write this, it's still too early to tell what the results of her efforts will be. But I guarantee a lot of people will have had value added to them.

Gaby could take a lot of the credit for all of this, but she's too humble to do that. She loves the people in her country and simply sees it as a way to help them. She says, "When you're in a better situation, you start asking yourself, 'What can I do to help them, to add value to them, to show them there is a better way?'" I'd say she's done a great job of that.

You can be someone who makes a difference, just as Gaby is. You don't have to try to help a whole country. You just need to try to help someone every day. That's what intentional living is. Every time you think about ways to help others and take action, you're increasing your intentionality capacity, making a difference, and achieving significance with your life.

Intentionality Capacity Questions

1. How do you most enjoy adding value to people? What could you do that you would enjoy but haven't done yet? When can you start doing it?

2. How will you add value to people in the next twenty-four hours? Try anticipating ways you could add value to people on your schedule. You should also look for opportunities in the moment as you go through your day.

3. Who could you encourage to add value to people? What could you do to encourage them?

15

Attitude Capacity—Your Choice to Be Positive Regardless of Circumstances

I'm a great believer in the power of attitude. I guess you could call me an attitude guy. My belief shows up in my relationships, my speaking, my writing—everywhere. I can't remember a single time I was asked to get a better attitude. Of course there are times when I do need to adjust my attitude, but I am always careful to do that quickly and privately.

Although I believe in attitude, I don't believe it is everything. I never have, and I never will. Attitude cannot make up for incompetence. Attitude cannot give you a skill that you don't possess. Attitude doesn't make all your dreams come true. It isn't everything you need in life, but it sets the tone for your life. If all things are equal between two people except for their attitudes, the person with the better attitude will usually be more successful in life—and enjoy life more.

No single change you make in your life will have a greater

positive impact on you and those around you than making a choice to improve your attitude. If your attitude capacity isn't as good as you would like it to be, start the process of improving it by recognizing these truths. You may want to say them aloud:

1. **"I need to change."** Change is personal. Only you can do it for yourself.
2. **"I'm able to change."** Change is possible. Many others have changed.
3. **"I'll be rewarded for change."** Change is profitable. You will see results.

Your attitude is one of the most pliable and resilient parts of you. Regardless of your age or circumstances, you can change it if you're willing to.

Talking to Yourself Is a Good Thing

When I am in need of an attitude adjustment, I practice self-talk. In fact, what I really do is coach myself on my attitude continually throughout the day. Why? Because it's so easy to become discouraged without a good attitude. The greatest separator between successful and unsuccessful people is how they deal with and explain their failures, problems, and difficulties.

Davies Guttmann, the author of *The Power of Positivity*, explains how people can be in the exact same circumstances and react totally differently. He writes,

Imagine two students who receive the same poor grade on an exam. The first student thinks, "I'm such a failure! I always do poorly in this subject. I can't do anything right!"

The second student thinks, "This test was difficult! Oh well, it's just one test in one class. I tend to do well in other subjects." These students are exhibiting two types of what psychologists call "explanatory styles." Explanatory styles reflect three attributions that a person forms about a recent event. Did it happen because of me (internal) or something or someone else (external)? Will this always happen to me (stable) or can I change what caused it (unstable)? Is this something that affects all aspects of my life (pervasive) or was it a solitary occurrence (limited)? Pessimistic people tend to view problems as internal, unchangeable, and pervasive, whereas optimistic people are the opposite.[1]

> "Pessimistic people tend to view problems as internal, unchangeable, and pervasive, whereas optimistic people are the opposite."
> —*Davies Guttmann*

What Guttmann is describing is self-talk. When pessimistic people see their problems as internal, they say to themselves, "This happened because of me." When they believe their problems are unchangeable, they say, "This always happens to me." And when they believe their problems are pervasive, they say, "This affects all aspects of my life."

If this describes you, then I encourage you to self-talk your way to the other explanatory style. When something happens *to* you, recognize that it is external. Identify the source of the problem and say to yourself, "This happened because of that." Remind yourself that it is changeable. You're not trapped. Tell yourself, "I can make changes to prevent this from happening again." And finally, know that just because something negative happened, it won't be that way forever. Tell yourself, "It was a solitary occurrence. It doesn't have to affect the rest of my life."

Positive self-talk is one of the most important tools I have to keep my attitude positive. When something goes wrong, I say something like this: "Wow! That didn't go the way I expected. Okay. That's not what I wanted, but I can get through this. I win more often than I lose, but no one goes undefeated. Now, what can I learn from what I just experienced? What do I need to change? Is there someone who can help me? Because of this, I'll become better, but I won't become bitter. This too shall pass."

My self-talk sometimes continues up to twenty-four hours after a failure or defeat. During that time, I want to process through any negative emotional baggage and put it behind me. That's important, because whatever you can't release possesses you. I also want to articulate what I am learning from it and the changes I need to make to become better. Finally, I identify the behavior I will need to exhibit to bring me out of my problem, because I've learned that I can't *talk* my way out of a problem that I *behaved* myself into.

> I've learned that I can't *talk* my way out of a problem that I *behaved* myself into.

Attitude Behaviors of Choice

Coaching and encouraging yourself is huge when it comes to choosing a positive attitude regardless of circumstances. It is the single best thing you can do to help yourself. That being said, there are some foundational things you can do to put yourself in a positive position most of the time. By doing these three things, you make it easier for yourself to bounce back from difficulties:

1. Become Humble

It is much easier to face life's difficulties and respond positively when you display humility. How do you do that? I love the advice I once heard: "Not all of us can do great things. But we can do small things with great love." Doing small things that may seem unimportant to us but that benefit others helps us cultivate humility. Doing them with love builds on that.

Margaret and I have a vacation cottage in the mountains of North Carolina. We enjoy the coolness of the area during the hot summers, and we love the small-town feel. The pace of life there is different. Everyone is on "mountain time." When we arrive there, my internal engine automatically begins to idle.

Recently my friend Ronnie was building a porch for us, and one day he tentatively asked if I would consider speaking to the local Rotary Club. Ronnie is an active member in the club and enjoys it, but his request came almost in the form of an apology. He shared that the club was small and couldn't pay me. He said he knew that I often spoke to large crowds and made "big money" doing it.

By the time he finished, he was ready to say no for me. But I interrupted him and said, "Yes, I'd be glad to speak to the Rotary Club."

Not knowing what to do with my yes, he again repeated the reasons he felt that I should say no. I assured him that I wanted to come and speak. And I did.

What a wonderful decision. When I got there, we all stood in line with our paper plates to get our food. Once everyone was seated, I got up and walked around from table to table and met each person. I learned more about our little community and the people there. During the proceedings, two high school students were recognized as scholarship recipients from the club. I was pleased to get to encourage them and meet their parents. And then I spoke and received a wonderful response from the club members. At the end of the session, the Rotary chapter chairman presented me with a walking stick as a thank you for my time.

That walking stick sits out on our porch. I often look at it, and sometimes I walk over, pick it up, and hold it in my hands. It reminds me of my early days of speaking. Small crowds, potluck buffets, paper plates, warm handshakes, and down-home folks. Those early days formed me and made what I do today possible. And speaking to my friends was an opportunity for me one more time to practice my calling. That walking stick helps me remember who I am—a guy named John who wants to be people's friend and help them.

2. Become Teachable

I greatly admired South African leader Nelson Mandela. I admire his attitude and his leadership. When he would refer to his twenty-seven years of imprisonment, eighteen of which were on Robben Island, Mandela would often say, "It was a tragedy to lose the best days of your life, but you learned a lot." What a great outlook.

> "It was a tragedy to lose the best days of your life, but you learned a lot."
> —Nelson Mandela

Teachability is an attitude of wanting to learn from every experience and every person. It requires an appreciation for everything we experience, knowing that we can always learn something—if we have the right spirit.

As a young leader, I didn't always display that spirit. I was more interested in looking good than I was in getting better. I wanted to teach others more than be taught. I was not especially teachable. I wish that back when I was young, I had read these words by Kyle Rote Jr.: "There is no doubt in my mind that there are many ways to be a winner, but there is really only one way to be a loser and that is to fail and not look beyond the failure."

> "There is no doubt in my mind that there are many ways to be a winner, but there is really only one way to be a loser and that is to fail and not look beyond the failure."
> —credited to Kyle Rote Jr.

Because I wanted to look good, I covered up my mistakes and didn't look at my failures. As a result, I missed the important lessons I could have learned. The book of Ecclesiastes advises, "In the day of prosperity be joyful, but in the day of adversity, consider."[2] In other words, when trouble comes, be teachable.

As I look back on my youth and early career, and I think about the mistakes I made, I conclude that:

I didn't make enough mistakes, because I wanted to be perfect.
I didn't admit enough of my mistakes, because I wanted to look
     perfect.

Those things are not true of me anymore. My passion to learn has done nothing but grow. And it's still growing. Because I want to learn from everyone and everything, it allows me to learn from everyone and everything. That's a teachable spirit.

What is your attitude toward learning—from your mistakes, from your difficult circumstances, from others who want to help you, from others who oppose you? Are you ready to learn? Teachability not only displays a positive attitude, it also fosters a positive attitude.

3. Become Resilient

To maintain a positive attitude, you need to be resilient and not let anything negative take hold of you. Time spent on being angry about the past means less time moving forward and doing what you desire to do. I keep very short accounts and don't carry any emotional baggage in my life. Why? Because while I'm holding a grudge against someone and nursing my hurt feelings, they're probably out dancing. If you think someone or something other than yourself is responsible for your success or happiness, then you will be neither happy nor successful. You have to learn how to bounce back from rejection.

I think all authors understand rejection. Personally, I've had my share. One of my most embarrassing moments as a writer was when my publisher sent one of my early manuscripts back to me. They didn't even bother tweaking it. They just sent it back and basically said, "Try again."

People outside of the publishing world don't know this, but the submission of even the best manuscript is like a game of Ping-Pong. You send the manuscript in, and they send it back with questions. You send it back with the questions answered, and they send it to you with a request for changes. You send it back with changes made, and they send it back with copyedits. It goes back and forth, back and forth, until everybody is satisfied.

After hundreds of rejections, rewrites, and revisions, I can tell you that I've never gotten used to it. I think it's weird when people say they like setbacks and enjoy disapproval. I don't. I like approval, applause, thumbs up, and standing ovations. But I don't always get what I like. Although I've never gotten used to rejection, I do know how to get through it successfully. How? Practice.

Dean Smith, the great North Carolina basketball coach, had a great perspective on setbacks. He said, "If you make every game a life-or-death proposition, you're going to have problems. For one thing, you'll be dead a lot." I love that, because I recognize that resilient people have a positive outlook. They know that the difficulties they're facing are only temporary. They reflect on the fact that they've overcome problems and setbacks before and survived. And they can do it again. Resilient people don't focus on the negative experience. They focus on what they can learn from the experience.

> Resilient people don't focus on the negative experience. They focus on what they can learn from the experience.

When I played basketball in high school, during the games my coach would always tell us, "Give yourselves a chance to win." What did he mean? He wanted us to battle hard and keep the score close for the first three quarters if we were playing a tough opponent. That way in the fourth quarter, we had a chance to win.

Johnny Majors, a highly successful college football coach, said, "Eighty percent of the college football games are won in the fourth quarter." By his reckoning, four games out of five are close enough to come down to what is done in the last fifteen minutes of play. How do you stay in the game until then? Resilience. Resilience gives us a chance to win.

People say that starting is half the battle. I disagree. Have you ever attended a game where one minute after it started, the buzzer sounded and the players lined up to receive their trophies? Of course not! Anyone can start. Not everyone stays in the game.

Life Is a Long Game

I think it is very easy for us to lose perspective in life and get discouraged. Too often we see a single victory as a finish line, or a single loss as a grave. The reality is that life is a long game. If it were a baseball game, there would be thirty thousand innings. (That's one inning a day for more than eighty years.) If it were a race, it would be more than eighty thousand miles. (That's a 5K every day.) If it were— You get the idea. We need to have the right perspective and remain positive because there are still a lot of at bats or miles ahead of us.

Perspective is especially important if you're a leader. Recently it was my privilege to help consult with a team called Finish Line Leaders. I love that name! While I was with them, I taught a lesson about how to maintain perspective as leaders who want to reach the finish line. Here is a summary of what I taught them:

- **Recruiting:** Entering the race is essential to finishing the race.
- **Qualification:** Qualifying team members on the front end increases the odds of their finishing on the back end.
- **Attitude:** Your attitude as a leader sets the tone for the team as they race.
- **Conditioning:** The finish line is never close to the starting line; you need to train to reach it.
- **Example:** Leaders set the pace for others and demonstrate how to finish the race.
- **Belief:** Leaders inspire others to finish well.
- **Resiliency:** No one crosses the finish line by accident.
- **Teamwork:** Leaders never cross the finish line alone.
- **Celebration:** The more team members who cross the finish line, the greater the celebration.

In the end, as leaders, what we want to do is help the members of our team to cross the finish line with us so we can all celebrate together. It's difficult to start the race, run it with excellence, and make it to the finish line unless we maintain a positive attitude.

I've always felt that people with great attitudes add value to everything they do. That's one of the reasons I've taught leaders about the importance of attitude. Now I have stats to back my belief. I recently read an article in *Fast Company* about the consulting firm DHW. Here's what the article reported:

You probably heard that a happy employee is a productive one who can boost the bottom line. How much? Here are some numbers:

- 33% higher profitability (Gallup)
- 43% more productivity (Hay Group)
- 37% higher sales (Shawn Achor)

- 300% more innovation (HBR)
- 51% lower turnover (Gallup)
- 50% less safety incidents (Babcock Marine Clyde)
- 66% decrease in sick leave (Forbes)
- 125% less burnout (HBR)

It's no surprise that the twenty employees of Delivering Happiness at Work (DHW) compiled this list and toss around the data any chance they get. The startup brainchild of Zappos' Tony Hsieh and business partner Jenn Lim emerged after the publication of *Delivering Happiness*, a book that waxes on the benefits of value-based management and work-life balance.[3]

If you're a leader, you can't afford to ignore the importance of attitude. And if you're not a leader—you can't afford to ignore the importance of attitude. If your attitude is wrong, it's difficult for anything else in your life to be right.

The World Sends Them Garbage

Perhaps the finest example of positive attitudes in the midst of difficult circumstances that I've ever seen is displayed by the Recycled Orchestra of Cateura. They have been called the Paraguay Landfill Harmonic Orchestra. The first time I saw them was when I was in Helsinki, Finland. I was there to speak, and right before I went onstage, they played.

The audience and I could see instantly that they were different from any other orchestra. Most of the musicians were children. Maybe that didn't make them different from all other orchestras, but something else did: their instruments were made out of the trash from their city dump in Asunción, Paraguay. All of us were spellbound as we listened to beautiful music played by beautiful children who have come out of difficult life.

I was proud to have my picture taken with them that day, but I couldn't get the fond memories of them out of my head for weeks afterward. So a few months later when I traveled to Paraguay, I visited their little music school near the dump. I talked with the orchestra's founder and conductor, Favio Chávez. I met the man who makes the instruments out of the trash they collect. And I listened to the families who are being lifted in life by the work of those at their school.

> "Those who know a little train those who know a little less. We work together. The world throws us their trash, and we give back to the world beautiful music."
> —Favio Chávez

Favio started the school to help people. He wasn't even a professional musician. He was an environmental engineer who played guitar. He said of the school, "Those who know a little train those who know a little less. We work together. The world throws us their trash, and we give back to the world beautiful music." They also demonstrate to the world the value of a great attitude.

Most people would say that if you have nothing, you can do nothing. Favio and the children he helps prove that's not true. The members of their little orchestra may have a dump beside them, but they have a great attitude inside of them. As I watched their faces as they played, I thought of the words of American author, philosopher, and civil rights leader Howard Thurman: "Don't ask yourself what the world needs. Ask yourself what makes you come alive and then go do that. Because what the world needs is people who have come alive."

These kids have come alive because their attitude allowed them to overcome adversity. And their ability to overcome adversity is empowering them to add value to others.

Years ago I determined that attitude is a choice. Since that time I haven't felt sorry for anyone who chooses to have a bad attitude. I just try to help the ones I can by encouraging them to increase their attitude capacity. And as for the ones who won't change, I just try to avoid them.

> "Don't ask yourself what the world needs. Ask yourself what makes you come alive and then go do that. Because what the world needs is people who have come alive."
> —*Howard Thurman*

If your attitude gets better because your circumstances improve, then that says nothing about your attitude. It's only a sign that your situation has changed. How can you tell that your attitude has gotten better? You know that your attitude capacity has increased when your attitude is remaining positive even as your difficulties rise. When that happens, you know you can weather almost any storm and come out of it better than ever.

Attitude Capacity Questions

1. What kind of self-talk do you engage in? Have you ever paid attention to it? If not, take some time to observe it. What could you do to make what you say to yourself more positive?

2. How would you score yourself in the three areas discussed in the chapter: humility, teachability, and resilience? Which of the three could you most readily improve? What can you do immediately to improve it?

3. If there is so much evidence that having a good attitude makes people happier and more productive, why do you believe people still choose to have negative attitudes? What could you do to encourage others to choose to have more positive attitudes?

16

Risk Capacity—Your Choice to Get Out of Your Comfort Zone

It is impossible to write a book about the subject of capacity and avoid the topic of risk. Poet T. S. Eliot said, "Only those who will risk going too far can possibly find out how far one can go." How far are you willing to go? Are you prepared to test your limits?

Not everyone is a natural risk taker. But I have to admit, I'm pretty comfortable taking risks and pushing to see how far I can go. I like taking new territory. Right now at almost seventy I'm living at the highest risk level in my entire life. Many people tell me I've lost my mind. At times, I'm tempted to agree with them!

The Next Big Step

You may wonder why I say I'm living at a time of high risk. I'll tell you. For twenty years, my nonprofit organization EQUIP has been training leaders around the world. In those years, we've trained over five million leaders. As we crossed into the millions of leaders, we also made it our goal to train leaders from every nation in the world. That's 196 countries. And on June 26, 2015, we reached that milestone in Fiji, when several EQUIP team members and I trained a group of leaders from the small island nation of Kiribati. Twenty-five hundred people were there celebrating that significant event with us, and let me tell you, it was a joyful occasion.

That day could have been the crowning moment of my leadership life. As far as I know, no nonprofit organization in history had ever accomplished that task before. EQUIP was the first. I could have ridden off into the sunset after that. I could have—but I really couldn't. As much as I enjoyed what we had accomplished, I knew that our celebration that day was not going to be our final accomplishment. I felt compelled to push farther, to risk more, and to see what we could achieve. I wanted these trained leaders around the world to take on a new challenge: to become intentional agents of transformation in their countries.

As I contemplated this new effort, I wondered, *What would happen if we could actually do this? Should we dare even think about it? Was this too big of a dream? What are the chances we could actually pull this off?* I had to face reality. The odds of helping leaders to be transformed so they could be catalysts for transformation in entire countries were very low. On the other hand, I had led high-risk ventures before. What I concluded was this: For me to lead this charge, I had to feel called. A work this big would be beyond me and my abilities. And it would not be *for* me. I would have to believe that God wanted me to do this for others. In the end, I had that sense of confidence in the calling.

Next, I had to be sure I wanted others to follow me. I was. I also concluded that I was comfortable with the possibility of setbacks, disappointments, bad surprises, failures, and even losses. These would not define me, nor would they detour me. I know who I am, and I would rather come up short attempting something big than to be successful at something small that wouldn't make a difference.

The decision was made. My small army of transformational leaders and I would take on the high-risk mission of trying to help bring transformation into entire countries. And we would either do something significant, or fail trying. (If you want to get an idea about how we're doing, go to http://iEQUIP.org.)

What You Must Know to Increase Your Risk Capacity

Perhaps you're facing a risky challenge right now. Or you are considering taking on a high-risk project. Or maybe you desire to do something significant, and you sense that something big but risky is on the horizon. If so, I know how you are feeling, because I've been in your shoes.

On the other hand, maybe you've been risk averse your whole life, and you recognize how much it has held you back and limited your capacity. No matter what your circumstances are, the rest of this chapter can help you to make good decisions concerning risks. Here are some things you need to know that will help you to take more risks:

1. Reality Is Your Friend During High-Risk Times

Businessman and author Max De Pree said that the first responsibility of a leader is to define reality. That's also true for anyone striking out to take a big risk. When taking big risks, you can't depend on hype or wishful thinking, because those things cannot withstand the heat of risk. You need to understand what you're dealing with, look at the worst-case scenarios, and look reality dead in the eye.

That's what I did after I decided I wanted to launch an international transformation initiative. Then I began to gather an army of people who were intrigued with the idea of being a part of a potential transformational movement. I knew that my first responsibility to them was to define the reality of this cause. As I said, I shared with them that the odds for success were very low. The journey would be uphill all the way. I felt certain it would cost more than we wanted to pay, take longer than we wanted to stay, and it would be harder to accomplish than any of us could imagine. But we would make the attempt anyway.

Perhaps I'm more prone to taking risks than some others because I have had a near-death experience. Nothing makes life more real than to almost lose it. In the words of Steve Jobs, "Remembering that you are going to die is the best way I know to avoid the trap of thinking you have something to lose. You are already naked. There is no reason not to follow your heart."

Death can come at any moment for any of us. We don't have forever. The time we have to be all that we are meant to be and to do all that we have the potential to do is limited. How limited, we don't know. That's why we owe it to ourselves and those we love to be truly alive and authentic in each moment. That means facing reality and taking the risk anyway. That is the only legacy we can be proud to leave behind.

How do you look reality in the face when evaluating a risk? Ask yourself some questions:

- Who else has done it?
- How bad can it get?
- How good can it get?

- Can I try it on for size?
- Is there room for error?
- Does the past say "yes"?
- Is there enough momentum to make it?
- Do I believe in myself?
- Do I believe in my team?

The more questions you ask and answer, the better prepared you are to weigh the risk and gauge whether the risk is smart or foolish.

2. You Must Learn to Become Comfortable Outside of Your Comfort Zone

Risk is rarely comfortable. It requires us to get out of our comfort zone. Yet that's where we need to live when we're risking big. How do you deal with that? For me, anything worthwhile that I've ever done initially scared me to death. First speech? Frightened beyond belief. First board meeting? Scared stiff. Conducting my first wedding? I almost fainted! I was never good the first time, and I was always scared on top of that. Maybe that's why I wasn't good.

After many times of being overcome by fear and worry, I knew I needed to develop a process to deal with fear, so I did. It didn't cure my fear, but it tamed it enough for me to keep taking risks. It goes like this:

- **Identification:** Who am I? I am a person of worth attempting to do something worthwhile.
- **Action:** What will I do? Take action and do the right thing regardless of feelings.
- **Emotion:** How will I proceed? I will allow my actions to shape my feelings.

My discovery? Each time I acted with courage and did what was right rather than giving in to what I felt, my will overcame my fears. My fears have never completely left me, but they no longer control me.

> "The amateur believes he must first overcome his fear; then he can do his work. The professional knows that fear can never be overcome."
> —Steven Pressfield

I love the way author and writing guru Steven Pressfield says this: "The amateur believes he must first overcome his fear; then he can do his work. The professional knows that fear can never be overcome." Since you can't defeat fear, you have to learn to deal with it. I call this becoming comfortable outside of your comfort zone.

To take the steps forward in the face of risk, you have to deal with your emotions and doubts. For me to continually succeed in high-risk environments and to model the right behavior to my team, I have to be continually comfortable being uncomfortable. How do I do this?

I Don't Look in the Mirror

I begin by taking the focus off myself. I need always to keep in mind that life is not about me. I can't worry about how I look to others. That was hard for me for many years. When I first started speaking publicly, I wore glasses to try to look more intelligent. I only looked stupid wearing them, because I didn't need them. Hall of Fame baseball player Lou Brock said, "Show me a guy who's afraid to look bad, and I'll show you a guy you can beat every time!" I can't be afraid of looking bad.

> "Show me a guy who's afraid to look bad, and I'll show you a guy you can beat every time!"
> —Lou Brock

I Don't Count Losses—Instead I Count Lessons

I'm naturally a very competitive person. I love winning and hate losing. And I used to keep score for everything. I avoided losses and focused heavily on increasing my wins. Not anymore. Instead of avoiding losses, I now learn from them. I ask, "What did I learn?" Why? Because we *always* learn more from our losses than from our wins—if we're willing to look for the lesson. When you seek lessons more than you avoid losses, you become more comfortable with risk.

I Focus Less on My Fear and More on My Dreams

One of my heroes was Robert Schuller, the founder of the Crystal Cathedral. In his book *Success Is Never Ending, Failure Is Never Final*, he wrote, "You'll start moving from 'out' to back 'in' when you start to dream again."[1] In other words, when you focus on your dreams, your heart is 100 percent in.

3. Good Leadership Gives You a Greater Chance for Success

The statement I'm probably known for more than any other is this: everything rises and falls on leadership. That is never more true than during times of risk. The size of the leadership must be equal to the size of the risk. If you're going to attempt something difficult, you need good leadership. You need to either provide it yourself or find a partner who can help you lead. And if you're going to try something huge, you'll need lots of leaders. Any great attempt without great leadership is destined to fizzle out.

There are times when I long to go back to my early leadership years. Back then, nobody knew me. Nobody cared what I was doing. There were few to no expectations of me. The small projects I was leading in the beginning allowed me to make my leadership mistakes anonymously. But today people are watching. More important, more people are depending on me to lead well. I don't want to let them down.

If you are preparing to take a big risk, it may require every leadership skill you possess to accomplish it. Don't take that lightly. Keep growing as a leader. The more you increase your leadership capacity, the more you increase your potential for risk capacity.

And if you're already a leader, you also need to provide others with a pro-risk environment so that they're willing to deal with their fears and take steps forward outside of their comfort zones. Dan Denison of IMD Business School says, "There is always a premium on being able to deal with the unknown. People will venture there if they feel they'll be secure in doing it. It is a leader's job to create that sense of security."

4. The Bigger the Risk, the More Help You'll Need from Others

While it's fun to dream about the potential upside of any risky venture, the reality of it can make us want to yell "HELP" at the top of our lungs. The greater and more risky the venture, the more our need for help. And to be successful, you don't just need help; you need the right kind of help.

When I started out in my career, I tended to do everything myself. As I grew in leadership, I started to recruit people onto my team, but I wanted to include everybody. And I wanted everybody to be happy. I was more of a poll taker than a risk taker. My problem wasn't fear of failure; it was fear of what others might think about me. Being obsessed with being liked, I avoided taking risks for fear of looking bad if I failed.

My first step in correcting this problem came after a friend said to me, "Quit worrying about what other people are thinking. They're not even looking at you!" I had to get over myself. And I had to value the vision more than I valued people's opinions. When I made that change, it was a major step in my development. And it increased my capacity to risk and to achieve. It also made me more discerning when it came to the kind of people I recruited to help me.

Mass movements don't begin with the masses. They always begin with a few. But if those few are the right people, there is the potential for a mass movement. What are the characteristics of the right people?

They Like a Challenge

For years I've maintained that winners stretch to a challenge and whiners shrink from a challenge. When you cast vision for something big, it is both a uniter and divider. People of high capacity who like a challenge rally to you. Small people leave. The size of the vision determines the size of the person who signs up. Do you want to attract bigger people? Challenge them with this:

> Wanted: Persons with high tolerance for pressure and a desire to make a difference. Reward: An exciting adventure that requires 100 percent effort and fulfillment at life's end. Applications now being accepted.

If a person you want to recruit doesn't get fired up by that, then you don't want him or her on your team.

They Play Big

Nelson Mandela said, "There is no passion to be found playing small—in settling for a life that's less than the one you are capable

> "There is no passion to be found playing small—in settling for a life that's less than the one you are capable of living."
> —Nelson Mandela

of living." I know there are people who believe that playing big is dangerous, but do you want to know what's more dangerous? Never taking a risk. When you're doing nothing, nothing good happens.

Years ago I came across a little poem that describes people who don't want to take risks and as a result, play small their whole lives. It went like this:

There once was a man who never risked.
He never tried,
He never laughed,
He never cried,
Then one day, when he passed away,
His insurance was denied.
They said since he never really lived,
Then he never really died!

Wow. How sad. People who play big are totally different. If at first they do succeed, they try something harder. Though all high-impact players may not necessarily have a lot of things in common, they do have one thing: they are willing to take risks. My friend Bill Purvis once said at a conference my team hosted, "If you want some things you've never had before, you must be willing to do some things you've never done before."

> "If you want some things you've never had before, you must be willing to do some things you've never done before."
> —Bill Purvis

As you look for people to join you in taking a big risk, you want people willing to do that, to try something new, even if it's difficult.

They Are Honest with Themselves

When you're taking big risks and attempting something difficult, you want people on your team who know themselves and are honest with themselves. They have to know what they're capable of and know what the stakes are. And as a leader, you need to help make sure they know those things.

Recently I spoke on transformation to a large group of my certified coaches. It was right before we planned to leave for Paraguay. And I wanted to do something that would make them take a look at themselves and assess where they stood. So I talked about the differences between Moment Leaders and Movement Leaders. Take a look at the differences:

Moment Leaders ask, "How long will this take?"
Movement Leaders ask, "How far can I go?"

Moment Leaders think *Great things can happen easily and quickly.*
Movement Leaders think *Everything worthwhile is uphill.*

Moment Leaders lead with emotion and let it control them.
Movement Leaders lead with character and let it strengthen them.

Moment Leaders are bigger on the outside than on the inside.
Movement Leaders are bigger on the inside than on the outside.

Because so many of these coaches are people who want to accomplish big things, they connected with the vision of movement leadership, and by the time I was done speaking, they were on their feet cheering. They were ready to go! That's why I love them. They want to make a difference. And they know that every great endeavor on the outside begins first on the inside. You cannot travel without until you have first traveled within.

Even if you're not someone who owns a company, holds a leadership position, or leads some kind of team, you may still need help when you tackle a risk. Look for like-minded people who are willing to face challenges to assist you. It will greatly increase your risk capacity.

5. Taking Risks Always Requires Personal Courage

Writer Anaïs Nin said, "Life shrinks or expands in proportion to one's courage." If you want to expand your capacity, and therefore your life, you need to be willing to take greater risks. You need to be willing to stand alone. You need to gather the courage to do what others might not do—not just for the sake of doing something bold and risky, but because you can see the potential reward.

What's great about taking smart risks is that it not only expands your possibilities, but it also inspires other people to want to join you in your efforts. People follow courage. When someone is willing to stand alone in the beginning and face opposition, they can earn respect and credibility. Eventually, others see their courage and rally around them.

> If you're not living on the edge, you are taking up too much room.

It's been said that if you're not living on the edge, you are taking up too much room. Risk is an important part of life. Publishing executive Walter Anderson asserts, "Our lives improve only when we take chances."

So what are you going to do? Bruce Barton said, "Nothing splendid has ever been achieved except by those who dared believe that something inside them was superior to circumstances." Are you willing to increase your risk capacity? Are you willing to fail doing something big? Are you willing to count lessons more than losses? Are you willing to model the way by becoming comfortable outside of your comfort zone?

These are no small things. But if you're not willing to do them, you better become comfortable with only small things. Because you'll accomplish big things only if you're willing to take big risks. I hope you are.

Risk Capacity Questions

1. How good are you at facing reality and assessing the odds when you prepare to take a risk? If you're not especially good at it, who can you enlist to help you count the cost?

2. When you prepare to take a big risk, how much consideration do you normally give to leadership and the formation of a team to help you? Explain. How must you change to improve in this area?

3. Have you learned how to deal with the discomfort of being out of your comfort zone? Have you learned how to function in spite of your fear? Or does being in risky territory stop you? What must you do to grow in this area?

17

Spiritual Capacity—Your Choice to Strengthen Your Faith

This is a chapter that I *had* to write. But you don't have to read it. I'm writing about my relationship with God. I cannot omit spiritual capacity, because my faith choice has been instrumental to increasing my capacity in every area of my life. My choice to strengthen my faith has done more to enable me to grow than any of the other choices in this book.

However, if this subject offends you, as I said, you can stop reading and skip this chapter. I won't value you less. Many of my friends are not Christians. I don't judge others. I share my faith because I love people, but everyone makes his or her own choice in this area.

Let me start by saying that every year in December, I pray and ask God to give me a word or phrase for the coming year. It becomes a point of focus for me. In 2016, I sensed that my phrase for the year was "God Room." Those two words led me to Ephesians 3:14–20. Throughout the year I prayed using the words of that passage as my guide while praying for myself and others. The result? I've had a year like no other. At nearly seventy, my capacity has enlarged and my ROI from speaking, writing, leading my companies, and partnering with others has been incredible. It's been my greatest year ever.

My Capacity Prayer for You

I want the same for you. I want your capacity to increase. I want your return to be high on the investment you make in your work. I want your relationships to flourish. I want you to have your greatest years ahead of you. So I'm praying for you, too. Specifically, here is my prayer for an increase in your spiritual capacity, based on the passage in Ephesians:

1. I Pray That You Will Know God

Ephesians 3:14–17 says,

My response is to get down on my knees before the Father, this magnificent Father who parcels out all heaven and earth. I ask him to strengthen you by his Spirit—not a brute strength but a glorious inner strength—that Christ will live in you as you open the door and invite him in.[1]

It's amazing and humbling to me that Christ wants to live in me. I know me, and sometimes I don't even want to live with myself. But God does. What a beautiful picture of God that paints.

> If you are 1,000 steps from God, He will take 999 steps in your direction.

If you are 1,000 steps from God, He will take 999 steps in your direction. And then He will wait for you to open your heart and ask Him into your life. God wants you to want a relationship with Him.

I took that step. For fifty-three years I have known God in this personal way. My relationship with Him has been the catalyst for all the good things that have happened to me.

One of my favorite Scriptures is Jeremiah 9:23: "Don't let the wise brag of their wisdom. Don't let heroes brag of their exploits. Don't let the rich brag of their riches. If you brag, brag of this and this only: that you understand and know me."[2]

I'm smiling as I read these words. People often come to me and ask for advice. It's true that I've experienced a few leadership exploits that were outstanding. Financial blessings have come my way. I've sold millions of books. But none of these things comes anywhere close to knowing God and having a daily relationship with Him. God is my greatest gift and my greatest friend. That's why when people ask me who I know that they should know, my answer is "You should know God. He's my best friend."

2. I Pray That You Will Experience God's Love

The passage in Ephesians continues:

And I ask him that with both feet planted firmly on love, you'll be able to take in with all followers of Jesus the extravagant dimensions of Christ's love. Reach out and experience the breadth! Test its length! Plumb the depths! Rise to the heights! Live full lives, full in the fullness of God.[3]

God wants us to live a full life with full capacity. He truly wants the best for us. Jesus said, "I have come that they might have life, and have it abundantly!"[4] As you read that statement, did you notice the comma? Which side of the comma do you live on? Are you living the life of abundance you desire? That's what Jesus offers. He offers extravagant love and life at its fullest.

Mother Teresa is quoted as saying, "The most terrible poverty is loneliness and the feeling of being unloved." I'd like to add that the most wonderful joy is to have a relationship with God and experience His amazing love. How amazing is it? Think about the words from Ephesians and understand that you can do these things:

Experience the Breadth of God's Love

When Scripture says that God's love has breadth, it means that God's love includes everyone. God loves everyone—of every faith, of every race, of every nationality, and of any age or stage of life. Scripture says, "This is how much God loved the world: He gave his Son, his one and only Son. And this is why: so that no one need be destroyed; by believing in Him, anyone can have a whole and lasting life."[5]

> "The most terrible poverty is loneliness and the feeling of being unloved."
> —*Mother Teresa*

Sometimes when I'm communicating and speak about God's unconditional love, I will ask people in the audience to repeat aloud after me these words:

"God loves me." Everyone likes saying that.

"God loves you." They like saying that.

"God loves people I don't know." They like this, too.

"God loves people I don't like." There is always a hesitation when I ask them to say this. People aren't sure they like that. But it's true. My friend, God's love is broad; it includes people we have a hard time liking. You may be thinking of some of the difficult people in your life and wondering, *How can God love them?*

> "God loves us, not because we are lovable but because He is love."
> —*C. S. Lewis*

Here's how. In the words of author and professor C. S. Lewis, "God loves us, not because we are lovable but because He is love." Stop reading for a moment and say to yourself, "God loves me." Whether or not you've ever thought of it, know this: it's true.

Experience the Length of God's Love

God asks us to test the length of his love. What is its length? Forever! God's love is never-ending. And the best part of that is that His love doesn't depend on me or on you. God loves you as you are, not as you would like to be, or as you appear to be, but just as you are. And nothing you can do can make Him love you more!

The people who choose to connect with God know Him and are known by Him. Jesus said, "My sheep recognize my voice. I know them and they follow me. I give them real and eternal life. They are protected from the Destroyer for good. No one can steal them from out of my hand. The Father who put them under my care is so much greater than the Destroyer and Thief. No one could ever get them away from him."[6] I don't know about you, but I know that makes me feel secure. If I could write country music, I'd pen a song about it called "God's Grip Don't Slip."

Experience the Depth of God's Love

What does it mean to plumb God's depths? The implication is that no matter how low you go, God's love is deeper. God is forgiving. For many of us, the bad news is that our capacity to sin has taken us lower than we ever felt we would go. The good news is that God's capacity to forgive us is greater. In fact, God not only forgives our sins, but He also forgets our sins. He said, "I will be merciful to them in their wrongdoings, and I will remember their sins no more."[7] Wow!

In our relationship with God, we are somewhat like the young son who played hide-and-seek with his father. The lad would hide behind a tree while his dad shouted, "Where's Christopher? I can't find Christopher!" Then the child would burst out, "Here Daddy. Look for me here behind this tree." Most of us are torn like that, aren't we? We alternately hide from God, yet long desperately to connect with him.

Experience the Height of God's Love

Rising to the height of God's love means being lifted up by him. There is no one more uplifting than God. I began to experience this at the age of seventeen when I asked God into my life. Three days later I experienced what I would call a redemption lift within me. It occurred when I read these words in 2 Corinthians 5:17: "Therefore, if anyone is in Christ, the new creation has come: The old has gone, the new is here!"[8] That day as I went to school I felt lifted by God's love. That is the experience of every Christ follower. There is a lifting of our life that is the result of experiencing the extravagant dimensions of God's love.

Jesus, not Norman Vincent Peale, first said, "Anything is possible if a person believes."[9] Jesus, not Robert Schuller, first said, "Everything is possible with God."[10] Jesus, not Tony Robbins, said, "If you had a mere kernel of faith...there is nothing you wouldn't be able to tackle."[11] God wants you to reach your full capacity. He created you with a plan and gave you gifts to help you accomplish that plan. He will be the greatest lifter in your life if you let Him.

For all the negative things we think about ourselves, God has a positive answer for us.

You say, "I'm too tired."
God says, I will give you rest. (Matthew 11:28–30)
You say, "It's impossible."
God says, All things are possible. (Luke 18:27)

You say, "Nobody really loves me."

God says, I love you. (John 3:16 and John 13:34)

You say, "I can't go on."

God says, My grace is sufficient. (2 Corinthians 12:9 and Psalm 91:15)

You say, "I'm not able."

God says, I am able. (2 Corinthians 9:8)

You say, "I can't forgive myself."

God says, I forgive you. (1 John 1:9 and Romans 8:1)

You say, "I can't manage."

God says, I will supply all your needs. (Philippians 4:19)

You say, "I'm afraid."

God says, I have not given you a spirit of fear. (2 Timothy 1:7)

You say, "I'm not smart enough."

God says, I give you wisdom. (1 Corinthians 1:30)

You say, "I feel alone."

God says, I will never leave you or forsake you. (Hebrews 13:5)

You say, "I can't figure things out."

God says, I will direct your steps. (Proverbs 3:5–6)

You say, "I'm always worried and frustrated."

God says, Cast all your cares on me. (1 Peter 5:7)

God has an answer for every question, and an assurance for every doubt we possess.

In his book *A Gentle Thunder: Hearing God Through the Storm,* my friend Max Lucado writes a wonderful description of how God feels about you and me:

If God had a refrigerator, your picture would be on it. If he had a wallet, your photo would be in it. He sends you flowers every spring and a sunrise every morning. Whenever you want to talk, he'll listen. He can live anywhere in the universe, and he chose your heart. And the Christmas gift he sent you in Bethlehem? Face it, friend. He's crazy about you.[12]

I don't know that there's a better way to say it.

3. I Pray That You Allow God to Do Great Things in Your Life

Hang on my friend! You are about to read the greatest capacity statement ever written. It completes the passage from Ephesians I've been praying for you. As you read the words, embrace them because they are for you.

God can do anything, you know—far more than you could ever imagine or guess or request in your wildest dreams! He does it not by pushing us around but by working within us, his Spirit deeply and gently within us.[13]

These words apply to you, but they must be activated by your faith. Jesus said, "According to your faith will it be done to you."[14] I call this the faith factor. There are many factors that influence your capacity over which you have no control: your background, nationality, age, giftedness. These were determined by the sovereignty of God. But there is one important factor you do have control over: how much you choose to believe in God. God puts no limitation on faith; faith puts no limitation on God.

> "According to your faith will it be done to you." I call this the faith factor.

As I mentioned at the beginning of the chapter, in 2016, the phrase that impressed itself on me was *God Room*. Today, those are the words I use to express my faith. What do I mean by God Room? Let me explain by quoting again from the passage in Ephesians:

God Room Is All about God

God can do anything.

That statement is certainly not about me. It's not about us. It is about God. These words should set the bar of our expectations about God at a very high level. We need to be aware of how great a space there is between what we can do and what He can do. That's God Room—room for God to do what only He can do. We do the possible. God does the impossible. That shows us who He is.

God Room Is Bigger Than I Am

God can do anything, you know—far more than you could ever imagine or guess or request in your wildest dreams!

How much is far more? It's not a *little* more or *some* more. It's *far* more. It's so much more that I don't think we can comprehend it. The writer of Hebrews tried to use words to give us some kind of idea about how much more far more is: "far more than you could ever imagine or guess or request in your wildest dreams!" But even then, we don't really get it.

Don't even try to understand how much bigger God is than us. We can't. No words can ever come close. God is God and we are not. That is both simple and humbling.

As I try to grasp this fact, it's as if God is saying to me, "John, don't ask me to cram my plan into your puny little mind, because then I will be limited to your understanding. And I'm God." If we can explain our life and believe we can solve everything in it, then we're not giving God room to live in it.

God Room Is a Place within Me Where I Choose to Let God Do What Only He Can Do

He does it not by pushing us around but by working within us, his Spirit deeply and gently within us.

God doesn't force anything on us, not even his love. He offers it to us gently. And He works within us only because we choose to let Him do that. Now that is a huge capacity choice. The question we all have to answer is simply "How much room will we give God?" It's like His love; we can experience as much as we desire.

God Room Is Unexplainable and Undeniable

Perhaps the most amazing thing about God Room is that God allows average people like you and me to have access to it. And as a result, God can do amazing things with and through us. One of the best descriptions of this can be found in 1 Corinthians 1:26–31. It says,

Take a good look, friends, at who you were when you got called into this life. I don't see many of "the brightest and the best" among you, not many influential, not many from high-society families. Isn't it obvious that God deliberately chose men and women that the culture overlooks and exploits and abuses, chose these "nobodies" to expose the hollow pretensions of the "somebodies"? That makes it quite clear that none of you can get by with blowing your own horn before God. Everything that we have—right thinking and right living, a clean slate and a fresh start—comes from God by way of Jesus Christ. That's why we have the saying "If you're going to blow a horn, blow a trumpet for God."[15]

We don't have much to offer God except ourselves. God wants our willingness, not our strengths. If you think you can do everything on your own and you're searching for some secret reservoir of strength, then stop. Because

> Perhaps the most amazing thing about God Room is that God allows average people like you and me to have access to it.

there isn't one. Focus on God's endless resources. He can do what we cannot do. And He's willing to do it if you're willing to give him credit for it.

Well, that's my prayer for you. And I will continue to pray for you.

I'm glad you decided to read this chapter. God's invitation is extended to you. He loves you. I hope you will accept that love, if you haven't already. Not only will it blow the cap off your capacity, it will change every aspect of your life. If you don't yet know God, you have no idea what He can and will do for you.

Spiritual Capacity Questions

1. Up until now, how did you think of God? Is what you read in the chapter consistent with your beliefs, or did you learn something new?

2. When you read that God loves you no matter what and that you can do nothing to make Him love you more than He already does, how did that make you feel?

3. What action do you intend to take in response to God's invitation to you?

18

Growth Capacity—Your Choice to Focus on How Far You Can Go

Personal growth is a subject that I am very passionate about, and I've written about it pretty extensively. So I'm going to take an approach to it here that's somewhat different from what I've done in the past. But before I do, I want to lay some groundwork.

One of the books that has influenced my thinking on the subject of growth is *Mindset: The New Psychology of Success* by Carol Dweck. It affirms a lot of what I believed and experienced before I saw her research. What Dweck discovered is that people naturally possess one of two mind-sets. Some have a fixed mind-set. That's a belief that their personal qualities, such as intelligence, character, creativity, people skills, and so on, cannot change. They are basically set for life. Others possess a growth mind-set. These people believe that their personal qualities can be developed.

Dweck found that people who possess a fixed mind-set are forever trying to prove their worth. She writes, "I've seen so many people with this one consuming goal of proving themselves—in the classroom, in their careers, and in their relationships. Every situation calls for a confirmation of their intelligence, personality, or character. Every situation is evaluated: *Will I succeed or fail? Will I look smart or dumb? Will I be accepted or rejected? Will I feel like a winner or a loser?*[1]

In contrast, Dweck describes the growth mind-set as one in which people explore and develop. She writes,

> This growth mindset is based on the belief that your basic qualities are things you can cultivate through your efforts. Although people may differ in every which way—in their initial talents and aptitudes, interests, or temperaments—everyone can change and grow through application and experience.
>
> Do people with this mindset believe that anyone can be anything, that anyone with proper motivation or education can become Einstein or Beethoven? No, but they believe that a person's true potential is unknown (and unknowable), that it's impossible to foresee what can be accomplished with years of passion, toil, and training.[2]

In other words, a person's capacity is limitless. And our desire should be to explore how far we can stretch it.

Even though Dweck's research indicates that people naturally fall into one of these two camps, I believe that even a person born with a set mind-set can adopt the thinking and habits of a growth mind-set and become more open to growth. Dweck confirms this. She says we have a choice:

> When you enter a mindset, you enter a new world. In one world—the world of fixed traits—success is about proving you're smart or talented. Validating yourself. In the other—the world of changing qualities—it's about stretching yourself to learn something new. Developing yourself.

In one world, failure is about having a setback. Getting a bad grade. Losing a tournament. Getting fired. Getting rejected. It means you're not smart or talented. In the other world, failure is about not growing. Not reaching for the things you value. It means you're not fulfilling your potential.

In one world, effort is a bad thing. It, like failure, means you're not smart or talented. If you were, you wouldn't need effort. In the other world, effort is what makes you smart or talented.[3]

Which world do you live in? Do you want to change? You can!

In my formative years, most of the people I knew had a fixed mind-set. I never bought into that world and realized I needed to find people and places that had a growth mind-set. What I began looking for was a growth environment. In this chapter, I want to share with you what that looks like. If you possess a fixed mind-set, then putting yourself in a growth environment will help you to change, grow, and adapt. If you already have a growth mind-set, then a growth environment will accelerate your development and increase your capacity at a higher rate. And if you happen to be a leader, you can study the characteristics of a growth environment and begin to *create* one within your department or organization that will help develop your team members. I shared these ideas with ATB Financial in Canada several years ago, and it inspired them to become committed to providing a growth environment for their people.

A Growth Environment Is a Place Where...

I've studied different environments and created a few as a leader. In my forty-plus years of experience, I've identified ten characteristics of a positive growth environment:

1. Others Are ahead of You

Are you at the head of your class? If so, then you're in the wrong class. You need to find people who are ahead of you so that you can learn from them.

All my life I have been very intentional about finding people who are faster, better, smarter, bigger, and older than I am to learn from. I always stretch better when someone is ahead of me. So will you.

Recently when I spoke for the Beachbody fitness organization, I decided to go to an exercise class. Out of the 123 people there, I'm pretty sure I ranked 123rd. Boy, did it make me want to work harder! A couple of years ago, Margaret and I went on a dream trip to Italy. The people on that trip were financially way ahead of us, and I learned a lot during our conversations over dinner. The last few years, I've gotten to play in the AT&T Pro-Am golf tournament. Trust me, none of the pro golfers ever asked me to read a putt for them, but I've continually watched their play and picked up things from them. And when I host a conference, and I bring in someone like Alan Mulally, the former chairman of Ford Motor Company, you'd better believe I'm in the front row taking notes.

As much as I love communicating, I would still rather learn than teach. I prefer asking questions to giving answers. I guess you could say that I like the deep end of the pool more than the wading pool. I use the power of proximity to get next to the people who can help me get to the next level. When I do, I try not to think about how far ahead of me they are. Making the comparison would just discourage me. Instead I look at their success journey and use it as inspiration for mine. They've gotten far; maybe I can, too. I just need to go through what they've gone through. It always makes me better when I hang around with better people. If I tried to race them, maybe I wouldn't win. That's okay. Winning is overrated. Growing is underrated.

In your environment, are there people who are ahead of you? If not, you need to find some.

2. You Are Continually Challenged

Most people wake up and yawn. I prefer to wake up with a gulp. I want to know that I'm facing something big ahead of me every day.

That's certainly true for me this week. I will challenge 150 volunteer associate trainers who have worked with my nonprofit organization EQUIP and ask them to help me start roundtables in countries around the world. Our goal is to have one million people in roundtables next year. That's a goal that's bigger than I am. I will challenge that same group to help the leaders we've already trained around the world to become transformational. That's also bigger than I am.

Later this week, I'll talk to eight hundred Wall Street executives and ask them to make an impact on society that's greater spiritually than financially. That's bigger than I am. And my week will conclude with an address to the graduating class of Florida Southern University, where I'll tell them how they can be a person of significance right now—and not wait until they are fifty, sixty, or seventy. That's bigger than I am. In fact, just writing all that is making me gulp right now!

Some of the most significant things in life take great time and effort. The joy of the journey toward them comes from the new discoveries we make along the way. Our new knowledge and discoveries become the motivation for us to continue the journey. It is only after we go a long distance that we can look back and realize what we didn't know. Soon we begin to realize that it is not the destination we're seeking. Rather, we desire the growth that we experience, and we find ourselves embracing the journey with full knowledge that there is no finish line. At that time, we stop asking, "How long will it take?" and begin to wonder, *How far can I go?*

Author Robert Anthony said, "Some people drink from the fountain of knowledge—others just gargle." What's your capacity? What is mine? I don't know. But I do know that it can expand. At one time Johnny Weissmuller was called the greatest swimmer in the world. He held over fifty world records. Doctors and coaches said, "No one will ever break his records." Do you know who breaks his records now? Thirteen-year-olds! A challenge can always make you better.

3. Your Focus Is Forward

In a positive growth environment, your focus is on moving forward. Tony Robbins says, "Where focus goes, energy flows." My advice to you when you are distracted is to feed your focus and diminish your distractions. Say no to the good so you can say yes to the best.

During a very busy time in my life, when I was trying to focus on moving forward but I was being bombarded with distractions, I penned the following letter. I never sent it but it was great therapy for me.

John Maxwell thanks you for your letter but regrets that he is unable to accept your kind invitation to: send an autograph / help you with your project / provide a photograph / read your manuscript / give you counseling / deliver a lecture / be interviewed / attend a conference / talk on the radio / act as chairman / appear on TV / become an editor / speak after dinner / write a book / give a testimonial / give an endorsement / accept an honorary degree.

I'm almost seventy, but I'm looking forward, not backward. And I'm staying focused on getting better. Old people talk a lot about yesterday. They reminisce about the "good ole days." Well, let me tell you, the good ole days weren't that good. Old people just think they were because they're old and can't remember. I don't want to look back. And neither should you.

4. The Atmosphere Is Affirming

When I started my career, my dad said, "Value people, believe in them, and unconditionally love them." What he was really saying was to create an environment that's affirming. And that's what I've tried to do for more than forty years. He knew then and I know now that people do best when they are encouraged.

Do you live and work in an environment where you are affirmed for being who you are? Do people encourage you to grow and cheer you on when you make choices that make you better? If so, you know how much that helps. If not, you need to find a place where people build each other up, not pull them down.

5. You Are out of Your Comfort Zone

You've read an entire chapter on risk and getting out of your comfort zone, so I don't need to say too much here. But I do want to tell you this: there is no growth in your comfort zone and no comfort in your growth zone.

> There is no growth in your comfort zone and no comfort in your growth zone.

My friend Paul Martinelli, the president of the John Maxwell Team, says, "Everything you want in life is outside your comfort zone." I believe that's true. Here's how this works when it comes to growth:

When you're out of your gift zone and out of your comfort zone, it's a catastrophe.

When you're in your gift zone and in your comfort zone, you're coasting.

When you're in your gift zone and out of your comfort zone, you're creating a new you.

One of the ways I get out of my comfort zone is by facing and embracing new experiences. This year I have gone paragliding in Peru, gone snowshoeing in Colorado, ridden a campaign bus in Iowa during the primaries with a presidential candidate, written a children's book, and conducted an orchestra. But I'm not done. I also hope this year to learn how to paddle board, rescue a malnourished baby in Guatemala with my family, and maybe parachute from a plane. (That would *really* be out of my comfort zone!) I want to live until I die and not get the two confused. How about you? Are you getting out of your comfort zone on a regular basis?

6. You Wake Up Excited

One of the great mysteries in life to me is the number of bored people in this world. They yawn when they wake up and keep yawning all day. I can't live that way. Every day I wake up with a feeling of excitement. Why?

I Get to Help People

Is there anything better than that? The people I help love it and so do I.

I'm Good at What I Do

I'm not good at a lot of things. Trust me. Highly talented people amaze me. That's not me. I do only a couple of things well, but I do them really well. And that's fun! To be able to do something well and then to do it continually is a beautiful thing.

I'm Getting Better at What I'm Doing

I'm still growing and improving. I'm not sure how long this ride will last, but I'm sure enjoying it right now.

I Love the People I Work with

I have a great team. A couple of people have worked with me for more than twenty years. They are trusted friends and very competent in their work. They give me security and they understand me. Newer members of the team are full of energy and creativity and are truly giving me some of my best days. I'm smiling as I write these words. I love the people on my team.

I'm Called to Make a Difference

What I do is a calling for me, not a career. A career you can change or leave. A calling is not an option. It's an opportunity to fulfill your destiny.

> A career you can change or leave. A calling is not an option. It's an opportunity to fulfill your destiny.

Do you wake up excited every morning? Every day we have a choice to explore and make the most of our opportunities for growth, or ignore them. What choice are you making?

7. Failure Is Not Your Enemy

Another characteristic of a growth environment is that you are allowed—or even encouraged—to fail. Once at a leadership conference I mentioned that my passion for trying is greater than my fear of failing. Later in a Q & A, I was asked many questions about failure.

One of the questions was "When do you know that failure is not your enemy?" Here is what I said:

- **When you value the lessons failure has taught you.** Failure is inevitable; learning is optional.
- **When it helps you to develop resilience.** Eric Greitens called *resilience* endurance with direction.
- **When you use your failures to teach others.** You have lost your fear of failure when you are not afraid to share those failures with other people.

I love teaching about my failures and what I've learned from them. At this stage of my life, people see me at the top of my game, but I want them to know where I started from. Why? I don't want people's seeing me at the end of my journey to discourage them at the beginning of their journeys. If the gap looks wide, that can happen. Believe me, if they could have seen me then, they'd be greatly encouraged. They'd be saying, "If that boy made it, so can I!"

8. Others Are Growing

Speaker Jim Rohn said, "You can't achieve beyond your level of development. You don't achieve goals. You grow into them." That's well said. If you want to grow into your goals, you'll benefit greatly by being surrounded by others who are growing. If you do not see other people around you growing, then you know you're not in a growth environment.

> "You can't achieve beyond your level of development. You don't achieve goals. You grow into them."
> —*Jim Rohn*

A place where I'm growing and others are growing—that's the kind of environment I want to live in. And as a leader, I have some responsibility for creating such an environment. That's not always easy. Over the years I have learned to never underestimate the power I have to grow personally, and to never overestimate the power I have to help others grow. Early in my career, I thought helping others grow would always be easy. But I discovered that not everyone wants to grow. After several failed attempts to help others develop, I started asking myself three questions before investing in someone:

Do they want to grow?
Will they do it?
Can they do it?

The answers need to be yes, or else why waste the time and effort trying to invest in them? And by the way: I don't answer those three questions. I ask the people I would like to develop to answer them—before I start helping them. Their answers determine my effort.

9. People Desire Change

My friend Gerald Brooks says, "Every level of growth requires a new level of change." How true. We can change and not necessarily grow, but if we grow we will change.

Early in my career I felt that I would find something I did well and then do that the rest of my life. Initially, I thought that meant being a pastor. However, my reality is that I have changed career roles at least ten times. Here are some of my past and current roles: preacher, pastor, speaker, trainer, resource provider, consultant, author, mentor, company founder, leader, entrepreneur, and father figure. That is a lot of changes. Each fit my giftedness, but how I apply it has changed and grown. Growth is our only guarantee that tomorrow is going to get better.

There are many doors of opportunity that lie before you. You must open and walk through those doors in order to go to the next level of your life. Many of those doors will not be what they seemed in the beginning. There will be times when you'll need to turn around, close that door, and go in a different direction. That's okay. This is all a part of change. When a door doesn't lead somewhere worthwhile, make a U-turn. I have done this often. Over the years, I've closed a lot of doors. I've even developed a set of questions for when to close doors. Ask yourself these questions. Every yes is a sign that it's time to turn around and close the door behind you:

1. Is this door less promising today than the day I opened it?
2. Did this door have surprises behind it that are not beneficial to my development?
3. Have I failed to discover anything of value or to do everything that is behind this door?
4. Am I missing other doors of opportunity because this door is so time-consuming?
5. Would I avoid going through this door again, knowing what I now know?

By the way, if you're not sure if you're answering those questions honestly, then ask yourself one more: Would the people who know me best agree with my answers to the previous five questions?

While you are thinking about your answers to those questions, keep these ideas in mind:

1. Don't be afraid of backtracking. When you do it correctly, you haven't lost ground; you've just found your footing.
2. Don't close a door until you know the lesson you have learned from that experience.
3. Don't close a door to quit. Go to another door. When you leave something, have something to go to.

4. If you keep opening and closing the same doors, the problem is not lack of opportunities. The problem is you. Ask the people who know you best and love you most to speak honestly into your life.

Change can be difficult to master, yet change is always required for growth. I hope you find these insights about doors of opportunity helpful as you navigate through uncharted waters.

10. Growth Is Modeled and Expected

In my book *The 15 Invaluable Laws of Growth*, I teach the Law of Modeling, which says it's hard to improve when you have no one but yourself to follow. That's why good modeling and an expectation of growth are so important in a positive growth environment. Ideally, that modeling should occur from the very top, all the way down into every area of the organization. Nobody is too high or too low to grow.

You can determine if you're in an environment where growth is modeled and expected by asking these two questions:

1. Who brings the best out of me in this organization?
2. Who do I bring the best out of in this organization?

If you can readily list the names of people who are bringing the best out in you, and others could write your name as a model of growth, then you are in a growth environment.

Don't Just Go with the Flow

I hope you will make growth a priority for yourself and the people in your life today. It is one of the most important and profitable choices you can make. Sadly, too many people don't. Instead of the journey of growth, they go on what I call the Niagara Journey. They jump into the river of life, like someone going tubing, and float their way down. They don't become proactive. They don't choose their destination. They just let the river take them. They let the current choose their course and their speed. They are led by their environment instead of by their values.

Then one day as they're floating along, they hear the sound of raging waters. Finally, they're awakened to their situation. But by then, it's too late. The current has them. They're going to take a fall. Sometimes it's an emotional fall. Sometimes it's a physical fall. Sometimes it's a financial fall.

The time to save yourself from a fall is now, not when you're already downstream. Choosing to increase your growth capacity does exactly that. It's directing your own course. It's like building your own vehicle, getting out on the open road, and choosing your own destination. It's being as active as you can be in your own destiny. I hope you choose that course.

Growth Capacity Questions

1. How many of the ten characteristics described in the chapter does your current environment possess? What does that say about that environment? Do you need to make any changes? If so, what are they?

2. Who have you actively chosen to mentor you in your life? Do you currently have a mentor? If not, who should you approach to help you become better?

3. What direction would you like to go in your life? How do you need to grow to get there? What steps can you take today to start you off in that direction?

19

Partnership Capacity—Your Choice to Collaborate with Others

There's one more critical choice you can make in blowing the cap off your capacity. I've saved it for last because it may be the choice that will most quickly multiply the impact of all the other choices. The essence of it is contained in a quote often attributed to Mother Teresa: "I can do things you cannot, you can do things I cannot; together we can do great things." Whether or not she said it, what's being described is partnership—your choice to collaborate with others.

> "I can do things you cannot, you can do things I cannot; together we can do great things."

I learned this lesson when I hit a wall in my personal productivity. I literally could not work harder, faster, or longer. I was maxed out. Yet I still wasn't where I wanted to be. There was only one other choice available to me: partnering with others.

At that stage of my life, I was reminded of a quote by the great Andrew Carnegie: "It marks a big step in your development when you come to realize that other people can help you do a better job than you could do alone." Since then, I've had hundreds of partnership experiences, and I can assure you that if you want to multiply your effectiveness, you need to work with others.

It Takes Great Partners

An example of partnership can be seen in the creation of this book. I've been thinking about the idea of capacity for about two years. For a year, I've been actively working on it, seeking ideas to help me understand and teach capacity. Some days I find great stuff, each thing a seed that has growth potential. Other days, I'm just turning soil.

I live with these seed ideas for months, and eventually they sprout. Some I use as quotes. Some grow into principles. Some become major points or chapter titles. It's like a garden of ideas.

Remember the chapter on thinking capacity where I taught you how I think until I think through? That's how I work on an idea. It lives in me for a long time. I have to be convinced of its worth before I try to convince a reader like you of its worth.

Once convinced, I develop a thesis for the book and an initial outline. That's when the partnership process begins. I bring together a group of highly gifted people to brainstorm on the subject. I don't bring them together in hopes of getting an idea. I want them to help me improve and expand the one I've already developed. Sometimes we spend a few hours. Sometimes half a day. I give them my outline ahead of time, and they come prepared. I want them to improve what was good, help me get rid of anything that's bad, and create new ideas that I hadn't thought of. Every time I have one of these meetings, I walk out happy.

After that, I write for several more months, and then I engage in the partnership with Charlie Wetzel. I described that in the chapter on Thinking Capacity. And then when the publisher receives it, other partnerships begin. Their editorial team gets the text into its final form, creates the cover and design, and prints it. Then their sales team gets it out into the marketplace. And I could go on about other partnerships with booksellers, and others who helped before getting the book into your hands. None of this would be possible without the help of other people.

The Partnership Mind-set

Do you believe in partnerships? Do you develop them? If you don't recognize how powerful they are, then do this. Work hard on something for a long time by yourself. When you have maxed yourself out and can do no better, bring in a few qualified people and ask for their help. You will be both humbled and blessed. Humbled by how *quickly* they can improve what you were doing, and blessed by how *much* they can improve what you were doing.

If you are not partnering with good people right now, you are not even close to reaching your capacity. Ask yourself these questions:

When was the last time you asked someone to make you better?

When was the last time you realized someone *could* make you better?

When was the last time you craved a fresh perspective from others?

When was the last time you tapped into the thinking of someone else?

When was the last time you asked for others' advice and opinions?

When was the last time you got better because someone made you better?

When was the last time you gave credit to others?

Having partners is like adding one plus one and coming up with three. I'm nearly seventy, and my best days are right now. Why? Because my efforts are being multiplied by partnerships. My companies are gearing up, not winding down. I'm giving my best to others and receiving their best in return, which is much greater than mine.

How to Be a Great Partner

To enjoy great partnerships, you need to be a great partner. Recently the John Maxwell Company signed a partnership agreement with the Hendrick Automotive Group. On the official start day, hundreds of leaders from Hendrick joined me and my team to launch this exciting interaction. On behalf of the John Maxwell Company, I extended my hand of partnership to the Hendrick people, and I spoke to both companies on "the Potential of Partnership." What I shared with them, I now want to share with you.

To be a great partner...

1. Place Their Agenda at the Top of Your Agenda

If you want to partner up with others, then be the first to meet them where they are. Find common ground, and place their agenda at the top of your agenda. In essence, become a servant leader, and measure each day by the seeds you sow more than by the harvest you reap.

The person in my world who models this best is Mark Cole, the CEO of all my companies. Mark is held in high regard by hundreds of leaders of other organizations, as well as the leaders in my companies. At my age, I am blessed. Mark is the best right-hand man I have ever had, because he always places my agenda ahead of his own agenda.

While I was working on this chapter, I asked Mark to write about how he does this so that you could benefit from his perspective. In his own words, here is what Mark had to say:

> I don't place John's agenda above mine. His agenda is *my* agenda! This is not natural for me or any strong leader. Doing this is a result of discipline, years of doing the right thing regardless of what I wanted, and the development of learning to trust the person I serve.
>
> Here's how that plays out:
>
> **I Am Available to John**
>
> As I said, John's agenda is mine. Whatever I am doing can change in a moment when John needs me. And I always figure out how to fit what he wants to accomplish into what I want to accomplish.
>
> **I Remain Close to Him Daily**
>
> Proximity is the only way I can maintain his agenda as mine. Every day I do the double E with him. He is either within eyesight or earshot on the phone.
>
> **I Ask Questions to Understand What He Wants**
>
> John has taught me to not lead by assumption. Our conversations are filled with my questions. Since I often speak on behalf of John, my communication with others must reflect his. When people see me, I want them to see John. When they hear me, I want them to hear John.
>
> **I Allow John to Be John**
>
> John is very creative in seizing business opportunities and wants options to ensure the success of his ventures. I let him change, dream, and grow without making sacred cows of his past agendas. Flexibility is essential for me to partner with John correctly.
>
> **I Make Sure My Direct Reports Know John and I Are on the Same Page**

I want everyone to know that I always represent John and his vision. This enables my team to adjust and adapt in light of John's leadership. To lose that is to lose our way. Too many subcultures are created when the team's accomplishments do not link back to John's vision.

I Take Responsibility for Solving Problems That Could Jeopardize John's Agenda

Anytime the leaders of John's organizations are doing things that add value to his agenda, I bless them. Anytime there are challenges to John's vision, I share them with John, along with solutions.

I Love My Leader and His Agenda

Because I know John's heart, I can keep the heart of his agenda. Years of working together have enabled us to think as one. This is the fruit of a great partnership, not the seed. The seed was making John's agenda mine. The fruit is living it out.

If you desire to engage in great partnerships, you need to make your partner's agenda your agenda. Only when you are on the same page trying to accomplish the same goals is there the kind of synergy that partnerships can provide.

2. Add Value to Them on a Daily Basis

Adding value is the only way a partnership will work. Partnerships begin to disintegrate when one person starts receiving more than they are giving. A Chinese proverb says, "One may be a leader for a time, but by helping others succeed, one will be a leader forever."

My companies focus on adding value to others. The John Maxwell Team certifies coaches and speakers. Every day they add value to hundreds of thousands of people. EQUIP has trained five million leaders in every country of the world, and is now teaching those leaders how to intentionally add value to the people on a daily basis. The John Maxwell Leadership Foundation is committed to helping people in many countries by training them in values, intentional living, and transformational leadership in roundtable settings. The John Maxwell Company provides resources and training to organizations and companies who want their leaders to grow and improve.

Here is what I and the team members in my companies know: The only way that we will be given an opportunity to partner with others tomorrow is to add value to them today. If you want to be a good partner and benefit by increasing your partnership capacity, you need to add value to your partners.

3. Give Them Influence, Ideas, and Tools as Resources

One of my great joys in life is providing resources to people. In the early days when I first began training leaders, I realized that teaching wasn't enough. If I provided people with resources, they were able to go to whole new levels in their leadership. Today, I try to help people by sharing three things with them.

Influence—Who Do I Know That They Should Know?

I have benefitted greatly from introductions from people with influence. Jeff Brown introduced me to John Wooden, who became a mentor. Scott Fay introduced me to Paul Martinelli, who now leads the John Maxwell Team. Rick Goad introduced me to Ron Puryear, founder of World Wide Dream Builders.

Who do you know that your partners should know? How can you connect people who would otherwise never meet? This is a fantastic way to add value to others. It's one of the reasons that every good partnership increases potential relationships.

Ideas—What Do I Know That They Should Know?

My friend Ken Blanchard says, "Some of my best thinking has been done by others." That's also been true for me. But I'd also add that some of my best thinking has been done *with* others, as I explained earlier in this chapter.

> "Some of my best thinking has been done by others."
> —*Ken Blanchard*

How can you help others by sharing ideas? What can you give that they can't provide for themselves? Every time you share an idea, you take nothing away from yourself, but you add tremendously to your partners.

Tools—What Do I Use That They Could Use?

Tools are systems and practices that are proven to be successful. I have found that systems are the best pathway to achieve desired results. I believe practices are the best behaviors that give desired results. What systems and practices can you share with your partners to help them become better?

I'm a naturally competitive person, and for many years in my life, I wanted to keep a competitive edge on others, even when we were on the same side. I had to learn to share what I knew. When I did, not only was I able to help others, I experienced a deep satisfaction knowing that I was making a difference.

4. Tailor Your Service to Meet Their Needs

My first responsibility as a partner is to know you, know your organization, know your needs, and know how I can add value to you. How can I do that? By asking you questions. Questions are the great connectors.

For example, this week I will go to Las Vegas and speak to Commvault, a fantastic technology company. I've spent time over a dinner and a lunch with Bob Hammer, their CEO, getting to know their company. I followed that up with a phone call with four of their leaders to talk about their Las Vegas conference. Ninety percent of these conversations have consisted of my questions. Their answers have prepared me to add value to them when I speak. Their theme this year is "Going Beyond," so that will be my topic, and I have placed illustrations, ideas, principles, and application in my speech that will meet their needs. That is my partnership responsibility and privilege.

I also work to serve the leaders of my own companies. Every year I ask them, "What can I do this year to provide a growth environment for you?" Each of them has different needs and expectations, which I would not know if I hadn't asked. And I try to give them what they need. Leadership by assumption is ineffective.

> **Leadership by assumption is ineffective.**

Are you tailoring what you give according to what your partners need? If you're not, you won't be partners for very long.

5. Never Violate the Trust They Have in You

Trust is the foundation of any solid relationship. Trust can't be established quickly; it must be earned, proven, and tested over time. Once it has been established, your partnerships benefit from a trust advantage, which makes them function more smoothly.

When the John Maxwell Company began to partner with the Hendrick Automotive Group, I quickly discovered that they had built tremendous trust within their organization. After I spoke to their leaders, one of them, Jim Perkins, came up to me to talk about Rick Hendrick, the company's founder. Jim said, "I would rather have a handshake deal with Rick Hendrick than a contract with someone else." Wow! That's trust! Perhaps the highest compliment you can receive from another partner is, "I can count on you."

I wanted the John Maxwell Company to earn their team's trust, so one of the things I did was introduce all of Hendrick's leaders to the president of the John Maxwell Company. And we did something else. We gave them his personal cell phone number, and I said, "Anytime you feel that we are failing in our partnership to you, call him, and he will immediately rectify the situation." To be a good partner, we need to be dedicated to adding value to others and being faithful to the trust they have put in us.

6. Exceed Their Expectations in Everything You Do

In recent years, I've received recognition for my contribution in the area of leadership. At first I was surprised to receive these wonderful honors. But then I thought about how I have tried to exceed the expectations of the people I've partnered with for forty-five years. So I guess slow but steady can win a race.

When I began my career, no one had high expectations of me. So I set high expectations for myself, and worked hard to meet them. I committed myself to daily personal development, and I worked hard at that, too. As my friend Karen Ford, Mary Kay independent national sales

> "To do more, you must become more."
> —*Karen Ford*

director, says, "To do more, you must become more." And I started to exceed those expectations.

As I grew and improved, I began the practice of setting the bar of expectations for myself higher. Once I did that, I discovered something beautiful. That practice set me apart from many others. Most people don't fight to consistently meet expectations, much less to exceed them. And others started to notice. This opened doors for me, but I knew that an open door can close quickly if you don't continue trying to exceed expectations, so I made it a continual goal, and it has become a lifestyle within me.

Do you want to develop great partnerships and continue to thrive in them? It's very simple. Consistently exceed the expectations of your partners, and your partnerships will expand. Everyone will want to be a part of whatever you are doing.

7. Respect the Relationship and Grow in It

Too often people gain a partnership, and then take it for granted. When that happens, the partnership begins to deteriorate. It becomes strained. And it's only a matter of time before it falls apart. For that reason, I practice gratitude for the partnerships I have, and I also work hard to earn the respect of others. Partnership cannot thrive today on respect that was earned yesterday. It must be continually re-earned. What do I do to recultivate respect?

I care more than I have to.
I serve more I have to.
I work harder than I have to.
I produce more than I have to.
I grow more than I have to.

> Partnership cannot thrive today on respect that was earned yesterday. It must be continually re-earned.

When I do those things, I not only feel good about myself, but I earn the respect of others.

Do you respect the partnerships you have, whether you earned them yourself or gained them from the work of others? Are you doing the hard work to keep re-earning respect? Don't take for granted the people who work with you, or what they bring to the table.

If you want to take your capacity to the highest possible level and achieve more than you ever dreamed possible, then choose to collaborate with others and increase your partnership capacity. There's no greater way to increase your potential. And no more enjoyable way.

Howard Schultz, the former chairman and CEO of Starbucks, says, "Victory is much more meaningful when it comes not just from the efforts of one person, but from the joint achievements of many." I have certainly found that to be true.

> "Victory is much more meaningful when it comes not just from the efforts of one person, but from the joint achievements of many."
> —*Howard Schultz*

Partnership Capacity Questions

1. Are you naturally a soloist or someone who wants to be part of an ensemble? Do you think of ways to work with others, or do you plan to work alone? How can you change your thinking to develop more partnerships?

2. What work are you currently doing that would benefit from partnership with someone else? Who could you ask to partner with you today?

3. If you are a leader and have people who report to you, do you think of them as partners you serve? Or as employees who serve you? How would your capacity increase if you thought of them as partners?

20

Conclusion—Your Life with No Limits

Several years ago, I came across a story attributed to Robert Schuller, the author of *Tough Times Never Last, But Tough People Do.* Here's what it said,

> When I was in London, I visited a hall where a man named Mallory was honored with a banquet years ago. In the 1920s, Mallory led an expedition to try to conquer Mount Everest. The first expedition failed, as did the second. Then, with a team of the best quality and ability, Mallory made a third assault. But in spite of careful planning and extensive safety precautions, disaster struck. An avalanche hit and Mallory and most of his party were killed.
>
> When the few who did survive returned to England, they held a glorious banquet saluting the people of Mallory's final expedition. As the leader of the survivors stood to acknowledge the applause, he looked around the hall at the framed pictures of Mallory and his comrades who had died, and he addressed the mountain on behalf of Mallory and his dead friends. "I speak to you, Mount Everest, in the name of all

brave men living and those yet unborn," he began. "Mount
Everest, you defeated us once; you defeated us twice; you
defeated us three times. But Mount Everest, we shall someday
defeat you, because you can't grow any bigger and we can!"[1]

That's true of all of us. We can grow. And we can conquer
the highest mountains. A few decades after the time of this story,
Edmund Hillary and Tenzing Norgay made it to the summit of Everest. And since then, more than seven thousand people have successfully made it to the top.[2]

You Can Make It

Recently I had a revealing conversation while talking with a very
well-known radio personality. We were talking about adding value to
people, and he said, "John, you've built your reputation on the foundation of being passionate about adding value to people. How have
you kept your passion hot and your energy up for forty-five years?"

I couldn't wait to answer his question because we were talking
about my passion, my life. The reasons I stay excited about it are
simple:

I value people.
I believe people can improve their lives.
I am improving mine so I can give more.
I know how to help people improve their lives.
I see results in the many people I have helped.

"Do you add value to everyone?" he asked.
"Of course not," I replied, "but I believe that I can."
Why do I have great faith in people's ability to make their lives

better, to make positive changes, to increase their capacity? Because I've experienced all these things myself, and I know that if I can experience them, others can, too. That includes you!

As you finish reading this book, I want you to know that I believe in you, and I believe in your ability to reach your capacity. All you have to do is follow the formula:

AWARENESS + ABILITY + CHOICES = CAPACITY

If you are aware of yourself and your ability to improve, if you develop the abilities you already possess, and if you make the everyday choices that help you improve, you will reach your capacity.

I hope that you now realize that your life need not have limits. As long as you're breathing, you have places to go and ways to grow. You can improve. You can do more. You can make a greater difference. It's all within your reach. My hope and prayer is that you'll seize it.

Notes

Chapter 1: Do You Know What's Limiting You?

1. Roberto Verzola, "10 Hypotheses about Abundance and the Commons," *Daily Good*, June 15, 2013, http://www.dailygood.org/story/149/10-hypotheses-about-abundance-and-the-commons-roberto-verzola/, accessed January 19, 2016.
2. Robert J. Kriegel and Louis Patler, *If It Ain't Broke...Break It!* (New York: Warner Books, 1991), 44.
3. Jesse Itzler, *Living with a SEAL: 31 Days Training with the Toughest Man on the Planet* (New York: Center Street, 2015), 108.
4. Ibid., 91.
5. Ibid., 229.
6. Ibid., 52–53.
7. Ibid., 245.

Chapter 2: Blow Off the Caps That Limit Your Life

1. Nick Vujicic, *Life Without Limits* (Colorado Springs: Waterbook, 2010), 200.
2. Bob Brown, "Life Without Limbs: It's All in the Attitude," ABC News, May 9, 2008, http://abcnews.go.com/m/story?id=4531209&sid=26&p=7, accessed September 9, 2016.
3. Stoyan Zaimov, "Nick Vujicic Talks 'Unstoppable,' Overcoming Suicide and Joy of Married Life," *Christian Post*, September 13, 2012, http://www.christianpost.com/news/nick-vujicic-talks-unstoppable-over coming-suicide-and-joy-of-married-life-81531/, accessed September 9, 2016.
4. Michele Rosenthal, "7 Ways to Change Negative Beliefs About Yourself," *Spirituality & Health*, http://spiritualityhealth.com/articles/7-ways -change-negative-beliefs-about-yourself, accessed April 19, 2016.
5. Nick Vujicic, *Limitless: Devotions for a Ridiculously Good Life* (Colorado Springs, CO: WaterBrook, 2013), 32.

Chapter 3: Energy Capacity—Your Ability to Push On Physically

1. Jim Loehr and Tony Schwartz, *The Power of Full Engagement: Managing Energy, Not Time, Is the Key to High Performance and Personal Renewal* (New York: The Free Press, 2003), 4–5.
2. Tom Rath, *Are You Fully Charged? The 3 Keys to Energizing Your Work and Life* (New York: Silicon Guild, 2015), 3.
3. Ibid., 7.
4. Michael Howard, "The New Science of Happiness and What It Means for Parents," *Fatherly*, June 27, 2015, https://www.fatherly.com/kids-health -and-development/the-new-science-of-happiness-and-what-it-means-for -parents/, accessed May 10, 2016.
5. Tony Schwartz and Catherine McCarthy, "Manage Your Energy, Not Your Time," *Harvard Business Review*, October 2007, https://hbr.org/2007/10/ manage-your-energy-not-your-time, accessed May 10, 2016.
6. Quoted in Stephen R. Covey, *Everyday Greatness* (Nashville: Thomas Nelson, 2009), 219.

Chapter 4: Emotional Capacity—Your Ability to Manage Your Emotions

1. Og Mandino, *The Greatest Salesman in the World* (New York: Bantam, 1985), 80.
2. Eric Greitens, *Resilience: Hard-Won Wisdom for Living a Better Life* (New York: Houghton Mifflin Harcourt, 2015), 168.
3. Henry Cloud, "How to Add Climate Control to Your Life," MariaShriver .com, February 6, 2014, http://mariashriver.com/blog/2014/02/how -to-add-climate-control-to-your-life-dr-henry-cloud/, accessed May 16, 2016.
4. Proverbs 16:32.
5. Lolly Daskal, "How to Be More Resilient When Things Get Tough," *Inc.*, April 9, 2015, http://www.inc.com/lolly-daskal/how-to-be-more-resilient -when-things-get-tough.html, accessed May 16, 2016.
6. Greitens, *Resilience*, 46.

Chapter 6: People Capacity—Your Ability to Build Relationships

1. Greitens, *Resilience*, 210.
2. Brian Bethune, "The True Measure of Nelson Mandela," *Maclean's*, February 10, 2015, http://www.macleans.ca/politics/the-true-measure-of -nelson-mandela/, accessed June 2, 2016.

Chapter 7: Creative Capacity—Your Ability to See Options and Find Answers

1. Paul Farhi, "Jeffrey Bezos, Washington Post's Next Owner, Aims for a New 'Golden Era' at the Newspaper," *Washington Post*, September 3, 2013, https://www.washingtonpost.com/lifestyle/style/jeffrey-bezos-washington -posts-next-owner-aims-for-a-new-golden-era-at-the-newspaper/2013/09/02/ 30c00b60-13f6-11e3-b182-1b3bb2eb474c_story.html, accessed June 2, 2016.
2. Susan Robertson, "Why You Should Have a Child-Like Imagination (and the Research That Proves It)," Ideas to Go, March 2013, http://www.ideas togo.com/the-science-of-imagination, accessed June 2, 2016.

Chapter 10: Responsibility Capacity—Your Choice to Take Charge of Your Life

1. Associated Press, "Pennsylvania Man Loses Lawsuit Naming God as a Defendant," *Beaver County Times*, March 14, 1999, available at http://news.google .com/newspapers?nid=2002&dat=19990314&id=7cMiAAAAIBAJ&sjid=hr YFAAAAIBAJ&pg=4271,3392209&hl=en, accessed August 8, 2016.
2. Luke 12:48 (The Message).
3. Roshan D. Bhondekar, *Love—The Key to Optimism: Path Toward Happiness* (Chennai, India: Notion Press, 2015), 311.
4. Raghu Korrapati, *108 Pearls of Wisdom for Every College Student* (New Delhi: Diamond Pocket Books, 2014), Kindle edition, location 1497.
5. Stephen M. R. Covey, "The 13 Behaviors of High Trust Leaders," Move Me Quotes and More, http://www.movemequotes.com/13-behaviors -high-trust-leaders/#more-18223, accessed June 8, 2016.
6. Greitens, *Resilience*, 106.

Chapter 11: Character Capacity—Your Choices Based on Good Values

1. Stephen R. Covey, *The 7 Habits of Highly Effective People* (New York: Simon and Schuster, 2008), 69.
2. Brendan Coffey, "Hidden Chick-fil-A Billionaires Hatched as Value Soars," *Bloomberg*, July 31, 2012, http://www.bloomberg.com/news/articles/2012-07 -31/hidden-chick-fil-a-billionaires-hatched-as-value-soars, accessed June 9, 2015.

Chapter 13: Discipline Capacity—Your Choice to Focus Now and Follow Through

1. Mark Tyrrell, "7 Self-Discipline Techniques," UncommonHelp.com, http://www.uncommonhelp.me/articles/self-discipline-techniques/, accessed June 11, 2016.

2. Stephen R. Covey, "Work-Life Balance: A Different Cut," *Forbes*, March 21, 2007, http://www.forbes.com/2007/03/19/covey-work-life-lead-careers -worklife07-cz_sc_0319covey.html, accessed June 11, 2016.
3. Brian Tracy, "Successful People Are Self Disciplined," Brian Tracy International, http://www.briantracy.com/blog/time-management/successful -people-are-self-discipline-high-value-personal-management/, accessed June 11, 2016.
4. Ibid.
5. Dan S. Kennedy, "Why Self-Discipline Will Make You Unstoppable," *Entrepreneur*, December 20, 2013, https://www.entrepreneur.com/article/ 230268, accessed June 13, 2016.

Chapter 15: Attitude Capacity—Your Choice to Be Positive Regardless of Circumstances

1. Davies Guttmann, *The Power of Positivity: Reaching Your Potential By Changing Your Outlook* (Stoughton, WI: Books on Demand, 2014), 114.
2. Ecclesiastes 7:14 (King James Version).
3. Lydia Dishman, "Happiness Secrets from the Staff of Delivering Happiness at Work," *Fast Company*, May 22, 2013, http://www.fastcompany .com/3009940/dialed/happiness-secrets-from-the-staff-of-delivering -happiness-at-work, accessed June 14, 2016.

Chapter 16: Risk Capacity—Your Choice to Get Out of Your Comfort Zone

1. Robert Schuller, *Success Is Never Ending, Failure Is Never Final* (New York: Bantam, 1990), 212.

Chapter 17: Spiritual Capacity—Your Choice to Strengthen Your Faith

1. Ephesians 3:14–17 (The Message).
2. Jeremiah 9:23 (The Message).
3. Ephesians 3:18–19 (The Message).
4. John 10:10 (Tree of Life Version).
5. John 3:16 (The Message).
6. John 10:27–30 (The Message).
7. Hebrews 8:12 (The Living Bible).
8. 2 Corinthians 5:17 (New International Version).
9. Mark 9:23 (New Living Translation).
10. Mark 10:27 (New Living Translation).
11. Matthew 17:20 (The Message).

12. Max Lucado, *A Gentle Thunder: Hearing God Through the Storm* (Nashville: Thomas Nelson, 2009), 122.
13. Ephesians 3:20 (The Message).
14. Matthew 9:29 (Berean Study Bible).
15. 1 Corinthians 1:26–31 (The Message).

Chapter 18: Growth Capacity—Your Choice to Focus on How Far You Can Go

1. Carol S. Dweck, *Mindset: The New Psychology of Success* (New York: Ballantine, 2006), 6.
2. Ibid., 7.
3. Ibid, 15–16.

Chapter 20: Conclusion—Your Life with No Limits

1. Original source unknown.
2. "How Much Does It Cost to Climb Mount Everest?" AlanArnette.com, http://www.alanarnette.com/blog/2015/12/21/everest-2016-how-much-does-cost-to-climb-mount-everest/, accessed June 17, 2016.

Look for John C. Maxwell's other bestselling books

THE 5 LEVELS OF LEADERSHIP

Learn the stages of influence and grow to reach the pinnacle—where your influence extends beyond your immediate reach for the benefit of others.

THE 15 INVALUABLE LAWS OF GROWTH

The fifteen laws that will help you become a lifelong learner whose potential keeps increasing and never gets "used up."

SOMETIMES YOU WIN—SOMETIMES YOU LEARN

A road map for winning that examines the eleven elements that constitute the DNA of learners who succeed in the face of problems, failures, and losses.

GOOD LEADERS ASK GREAT QUESTIONS

John Maxwell answers the toughest questions he's ever received and shows you how to use questions to improve your ability to connect with others and become a better leader.

INTENTIONAL LIVING

You don't need to have money, power, or fame to achieve a life of purpose and significance. You just need to live an intentional life. This book shows you how.

Available now from Center Street wherever books are sold.

Also available in Spanish and from ⊡ hachette AUDIO and ⊡ hachette DIGITAL

CENTER
STREET

John C. Maxwell's Bestselling Successful People Series
Perfect compact reads for today's
fast-paced world

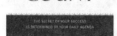

MAKE
TODAY
COUNT

HOW
SUCCESSFUL
PEOPLE
THINK

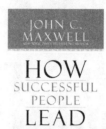

HOW
SUCCESSFUL
PEOPLE
LEAD

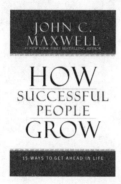

HOW
SUCCESSFUL
PEOPLE
GROW

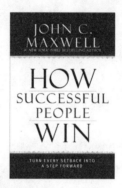

HOW
SUCCESSFUL
PEOPLE
WIN

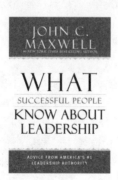

WHAT
SUCCESSFUL PEOPLE
KNOW ABOUT
LEADERSHIP

Also available in Spanish and from ⎣⎦hachette AUDIO and ⎣⎦hachette DIGITAL

Available now from Center Street wherever books are sold.

CENTER
STREET

GET YOUR FREE
MENTORING CALL
WITH
JOHN C. MAXWELL

Start setting goals to blow past your capacity today with a FREE mentoring call with John C. Maxwell. He'll equip you with the tools and practical thinking that will kick-start your journey to bigger goals, a better plan and an intentional life.

LEAD. GROW. INSPIRE. EXCEL. SERVE. SUCCEED.

MINUTE
WITH MAXWELL

Join me each and every day for "A Minute with Maxwell" as I inspire, challenge, and equip you with leadership teachings to apply to your life and career. I am excited to share my short, powerful, FREE video messages with YOU.

Words are vital to communication and leadership. "A Minute with Maxwell" will grow YOUR library of leadership words! Words like... teamwork, potential, strive, connection, clarity—to name a few!

SO, WHAT ARE YOU WAITING FOR?
www.JohnMaxwellTeam.com